THE
COMPLETE
CAGE
AND
AVIARY
BIRD
HANDBOOK

THE
COMPLETE
CAGE
AND
AVIARY
BIRD
HANDBOOK

David Alderton

PHOTOGRAPHY
BY
Tony
Tilford

Published by T.F.H. Publications, Inc.
211 West Sylvania Avenue,
PO Box 427, Neptune, NJ 07753.

First impression 1986
Text © 1986 David Alderton
Photographs © Tony Tilford

© 1986 The Paul Press Limited

ISBN 0-86622-113-1

Typeset by Peter MacDonald, Twickenham
Origination in Singapore through Print Buyers' Database Ltd
Printed in Italy by Poligrafici Calderara

This book was edited, designed and produced by
The Paul Press Ltd, 22 Bruton Street, London W1X 7DA

Art Editor	Antony Johnson
Project Editor	Sally MacEachern
Editorial	Margaret Daykin
Designers	Tony Paine
	David Ayres
Art Assistants	Sarah McDonald
	John Graves
Illustrations	Malwyn Toothill
	Kevin Richardson
	of Garden Studios
	Alan Suttie
	Anthony Maynard
Index	Margaret Cooter
Art Director	Stephen McCurdy
Editorial Director	Jeremy Harwood
Publishing Director	Nigel Perryman

CONTENTS

INTRODUCTION

Part of the fascination of birdkeeping, or aviculture as it is often known, stems from the constant acquisition of knowledge. No matter how long one has been keeping birds, there is always something to be learnt. Birds are individuals, and only by close observation can their requirements be fully appreciated. **The Complete Cage and Aviary Bird Handbook** should provide a sound basis for anyone who is planning to embark on this hobby, as well as providing an up-to-date source of reference for the established aviculturist. Everyone devises their own management system, but I trust that the ideas expressed in the following pages will provide a useful basis in this regard.

The last decade has been one of change, as far as aviculture is concerned. There have been many significant advances, which have been pioneered largely through the efforts of dedicated individuals. Methods of sexing species where the sexes cannot be distinguished visually have contributed towards more successful breeding results. This is particularly true of the larger parrots. Artificial incubation, initially used for poultry and for birds which similarly hatch in an advanced state of development, has been adopted as a routine means of regularly rearing other species, by hand from the egg. The most recent developments are in the field of artificial insemination, for parrots especially, and in a few years this may have become a regular practice.

Such techniques are not only of significance for the hobbyist whose enthusiasm helped to spawn their development, but have a much wider application. And yet it is a sad fact that this progress has yet to be fully appreciated, most notably in the conservation sphere. Here, the philosophical viewpoint that birds (and indeed other creatures) are "better dead than bred" in captivity is still too prevalent. The techniques which have been pioneered in avicultural circles may yet prove to be vital in supporting, and even saving, various species which are endangered in the wild. This need not even entail the capture of breeding birds themselves. Eggs obtained from a nest can be transferred to an incubator, with the resulting young subsequently being hand-reared. The adult birds will invariably lay again, if their eggs are taken shortly after being laid, and this will immediately double their reproductive potential. There is a vital need for much closer co-operation between fieldworkers and aviculturists if maximum benefit is to be derived in this area.

Millions of people enjoy keeping birds as companions. The bond between owner and parrot, for example, is truly unique and quite unlike that with any other pet, if only because of the powers of mimicry of such birds. By this means, people who may otherwise have no contact with exotic wildlife are afforded a unique insight into the natural world, and its intrinsic value. It is no longer a remote, celluloid image, but part of the individual's experience. In short, they are more likely to care, not only about the bird, but also its environment.

Once having kept a bird as a pet, you may want to expand your area of interest and construct an aviary. The breeding of birds under controlled conditions affords a different insight into the lifestyles and habits of the species concerned. Indeed, it is largely because of the activities of aviculturists that so much data has been collected about the breeding habits of many species. This information, including development of the chicks, has only rarely been acquired directly by field ornithologists, and thus can help to fill a vital gap in our knowledge.

Each year, aviculturists add to the existing literature through publishing their notes in avicultural journals. For this reason, it is always worth keeping records of breeding attempts by birds in your collection, even if they prove unsuccessful, as your experiences could be vital to someone else in the future. It is also useful from your own point of view to have some means of comparison available. Is the parrot chick growing normally? What should its weight be at this stage in the hand-rearing cycle? Such assessments can only be made by careful compilation of data.

Similarly, when breeding birds for colour, a clear indication of their parentage will be required. A number of mutant forms are well-established in bird-keeping circles, and provide another facet of the hobby. While traditionally the Budgerigar is best-known for its attractive colours, similar mutational forms of other species are popular. In the case of some, such as the Bengalese or Society Finch, these are often developed for exhibition purposes, being bred to conform as closely as possible to prescribed standards for the variety concerned.

Whatever branch of aviculture appeals to you however, it is likely to prove a long-lasting attraction. Many aviculturists are lifelong devotees, being fervently committed to their chosen hobby. Just a brief glance at Tony Tilford's strikingly natural photographs of the birds themselves will show why they attract such a strong following. Clearly, problems will arise at some point, but I hope that with the assistance of this book, they can be minimized from the outset, enabling you to enjoy your birds to the full, whether you have just a single pet, or a large collection comprised of various species.

David Alderton

AVIAN ORIGINS
AND
FEATURES

No other group of vertebrates has ever achieved such mastery of the air as birds. Their evolution can be traced back to the Upper Jurassic Period, approximately 150,000,000 years ago. They have changed almost out of all recognition from their reptilian ancestors. Internal skeletal changes accompanied the development of wings, and it is believed that the reptilian scales evolved into feathers, some of which became highly specialized for effective flight. However, traces of their evolutionary origins remain. Birds' legs are still covered in scales, and their bills still possess a horny covering, although both bills and feet display an enormous range of adaptations for particular functions.

RESPIRATION

The whole of the bird's body has undergone modifications to adapt it to its aerial mode of existence. Flight imposes a high oxygen demand on the wing muscles, and simultaneously generates body heat. Bird's lungs are relatively inelastic, unlike those of mammals, but they are linked to a series of air-sacs, which in turn, depending in part on the species, can connect with hollow bones, notably the humerus, (all allowing for a considerable increase in the volume of air). There are normally four pairs of air-sacs, with an additional unpaired sac. The blood circulation has also adapted to meet the oxygen demand of the musculature; the heart is a relatively large

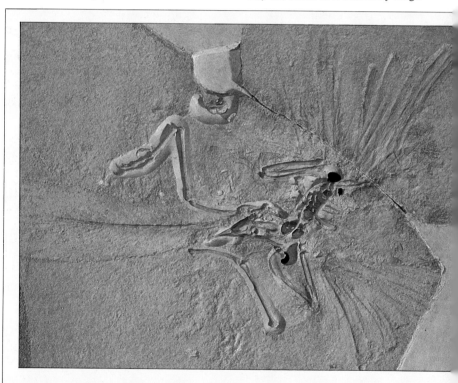

The fossil of archaeopteryx was discovered in 1861 and proved that birds have descended from reptiles. It had a brain that was more reptilian than bird-like, its jaws had sockets to hold teeth, it had a long bony tail and no keel on its breastbone for the attachment of flight muscles. Yet it is regarded as the first bird because it had feathers, and was warmblooded. Its legs and feet, too, resembled those of modern birds.

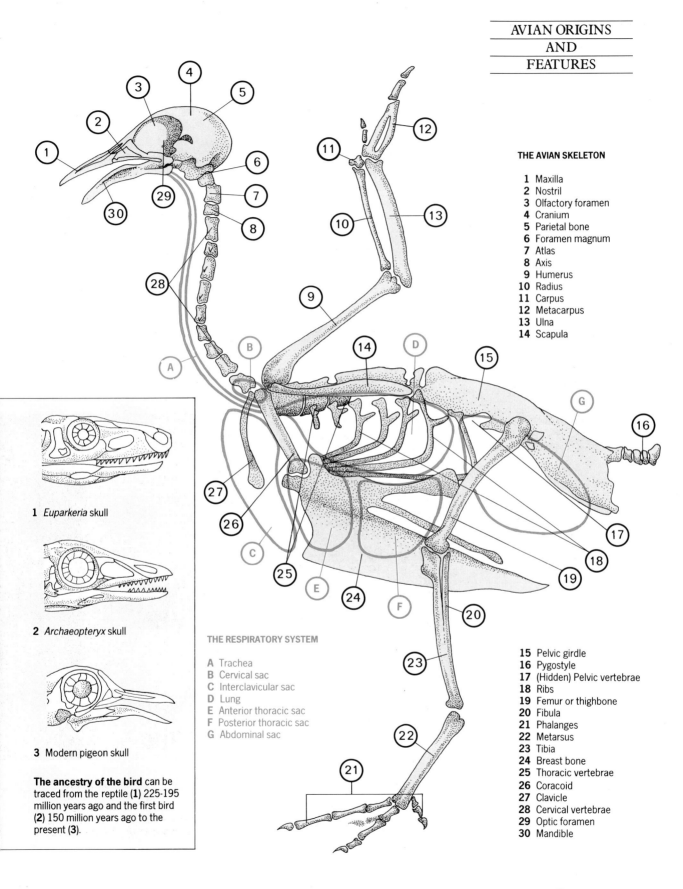

THE AVIAN SKELETON

1 Maxilla
2 Nostril
3 Olfactory foramen
4 Cranium
5 Parietal bone
6 Foramen magnum
7 Atlas
8 Axis
9 Humerus
10 Radius
11 Carpus
12 Metacarpus
13 Ulna
14 Scapula

1 *Euparkeria* skull

2 *Archaeopteryx* skull

3 Modern pigeon skull

The ancestry of the bird can be traced from the reptile (**1**) 225-195 million years ago and the first bird (**2**) 150 million years ago to the present (**3**).

THE RESPIRATORY SYSTEM

A Trachea
B Cervical sac
C Interclavicular sac
D Lung
E Anterior thoracic sac
F Posterior thoracic sac
G Abdominal sac

15 Pelvic girdle
16 Pygostyle
17 (Hidden) Pelvic vertebrae
18 Ribs
19 Femur or thighbone
20 Fibula
21 Phalanges
22 Metarsus
23 Tibia
24 Breast bone
25 Thoracic vertebrae
26 Coracoid
27 Clavicle
28 Cervical vertebrae
29 Optic foramen
30 Mandible

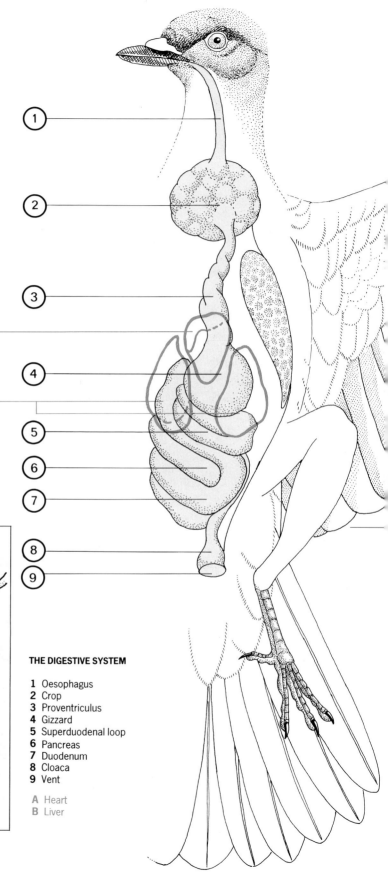

organ, and its beat is faster than in mammals. The red blood cells, which transport oxygen around the body, are also enlarged, having lost their nuclei at some stage in the evolutionary process.

SKELETON AND DIGESTION

Birds have also undergone changes to lighten their body weight relative to their size, making flight more efficient. Apart from a hollow skeletal structure in most species, teeth and the corresponding development of the jaw bones and muscles have been lost. In their place, birds have evolved a unique digestive system. Food is swallowed without any mastication, and passes either to the crop, where it is stored, or directly into the gizzard. In the gizzard, foodstuffs are effectively macerated, usually by particles of grit in the case of seedeaters. This process exposes the maximum surface area for the later stages of digestion which commence in the proventriculus – the equivalent of the mammalian stomach. Waste products of body metabolism are concentrated in the form of uric acid, rather than as dilute urine stored in a bladder.

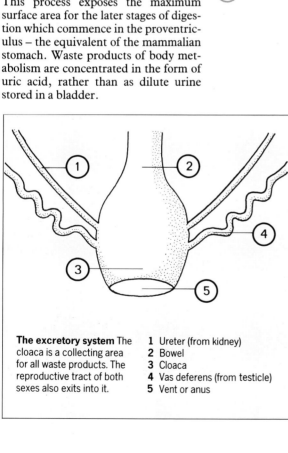

The excretory system The cloaca is a collecting area for all waste products. The reproductive tract of both sexes also exits into it.

1 Ureter (from kidney)
2 Bowel
3 Cloaca
4 Vas deferens (from testicle)
5 Vent or anus

THE DIGESTIVE SYSTEM

1 Oesophagus
2 Crop
3 Proventriculus
4 Gizzard
5 Superduodenal loop
6 Pancreas
7 Duodenum
8 Cloaca
9 Vent

A Heart
B Liver

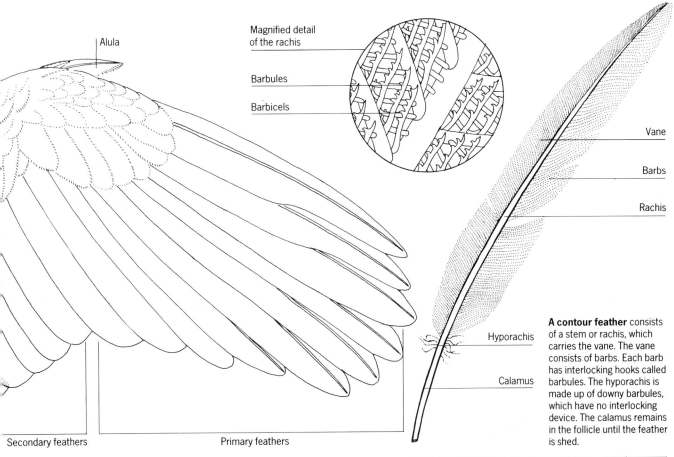

Alula

Magnified detail
of the rachis

Barbules

Barbicels

Vane

Barbs

Rachis

Hyporachis

Calamus

Secondary feathers

Primary feathers

A contour feather consists of a stem or rachis, which carries the vane. The vane consists of barbs. Each barb has interlocking hooks called barbules. The hyporachis is made up of downy barbules, which have no interlocking device. The calamus remains in the follicle until the feather is shed.

WINGS AND FLIGHT

A bird's wings are controlled by powerful flight muscles. These muscles generate large amounts of heat, which is regulated by the respiratory system.

However, it is the feather which is responsible for the fact that birds can fly. During forward flight the bird is propelled by the large primary feathers at the ends of the wings. On the downstroke the feathers are closed flat against one another, so that they encounter maximum air resistance, while the primaries bend back, biting into the air and propelling the bird forward. On the upstroke the primaries separate to allow easy passage of air, the wing tips move backwards and upwards, providing slight propulsion, while the secondary feathers and the inner part of the wing give lift. Then the cycle begins again.

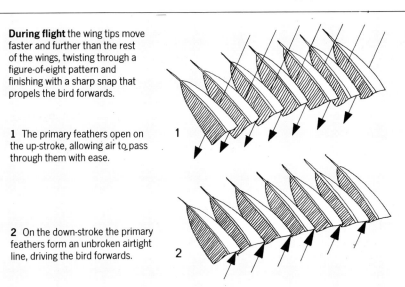

During flight the wing tips move faster and further than the rest of the wings, twisting through a figure-of-eight pattern and finishing with a sharp snap that propels the bird forwards.

1 The primary feathers open on the up-stroke, allowing air to pass through them with ease.

2 On the down-stroke the primary feathers form an unbroken airtight line, driving the bird forwards.

1

2

EYES

The eyes of birds are highly developed, both for navigating and hunting purposes – especially in the case of raptors (birds of prey) – and birds are capable of distinguishing between colours. Avian powers of hearing are less sensitive than in mammals, with some exceptions, notably in nocturnal species such as owls. Birds do have taste buds, but these are few in number, compared with mammals. The significance of both the sense of smell and touch is also reduced, with a few notable exceptions, such as waders probing in mud in search of food.

The eyesight of a bird is adapted to suit its particular needs.

THE POINTS OF THE EYE

1 Cornea
2 Iris
3 Lens
4 Choroid
5 Scelera
6 Optic nerve
7 Sclerotic
8 Ciliary body (incorporating Crampton's muscle)
9 Aqueous humour
10 Vitreous body

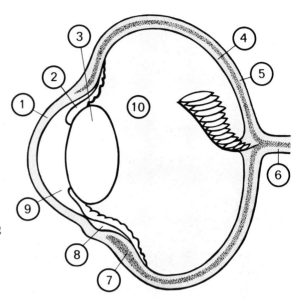

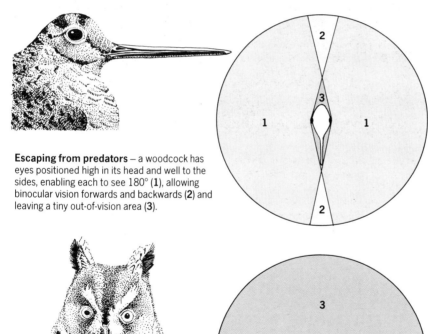

Escaping from predators – a woodcock has eyes positioned high in its head and well to the sides, enabling each to see 180° (**1**), allowing binocular vision forwards and backwards (**2**) and leaving a tiny out-of-vision area (**3**).

Predator – an owl has eyes facing forwards in a relatively flat face, giving it better binocular vision than any other bird. To see to the side or rear, they have to turn their heads.

WHY KEEP BIRDS?

Birds were initially domesticated either as a source of food, as in the instance of the fowl, or as a means of procuring food, in the case of certain birds of prey, which were trained to hunt for the benefit of their owners. The keeping of aviary birds for pleasure dates back to ancient Egypt, and remained popular throughout classical times. The Renaissance and the discovery of the New World then focussed attention on parrots, and their powers of mimicry. These birds were popular pets of the rich, and were frequently associated with royalty. A talented talking Grey Parrot was kept at Henry VIII's palace at Hampton Court, near London, while another bird of this species, owned by a mistress of Charles II, was passed to a taxidermist when it died in the 17th century, and is thought to be the earliest remaining avian example of this craft.

The 19th century witnessed the development of the canary fancy which was essentially an artisans' movement. Then, extending into the early years of the present century, came the rise of the budgerigar. More recently, improvements in air travel from the 1950s onwards have meant that species could be transported from country to country rapidly, and this led in turn to a growth of interest in foreign birds. At first, they

were often kept solely for decorative purposes but now, with much greater understanding of their requirements, many species are reproducing quite freely in aviaries, adding a fascinating dimension to this pastime, and providing overall a vast amount of new information about the biology and habits of such birds.

International trade in birds and other creatures is strictly regulated under the terms of the CITES (Convention on International Trade in Endangered Species of Fauna and Flora) agreement, while prescribed transport standards are set down in the International Air Transport Association's regulations, which are reviewed at regular intervals. Most exporting countries impose quotas and set levies, only permitting restricted numbers of birds to be sent overseas. This ensures that such trade will not deplete the overall population. Wildlife

management of this type can also help to protect the environment directly by raising revenue, which in turn can be used to fund conservation programmes. And instead of having to spend precious resources on destroying pest species in agricultural areas, farmers can obtain some measure of compensation for crop damage by the sale of such birds.

Throughout the world, from the backwaters of the River Amazon to the fashionable apartments of New York and suburban gardens of Britain, millions of people derive immense pleasure from keeping and breeding birds. Few pets can be considered so adaptable, being housed in such a wide range of surroundings. In the case of the large parrots especially, one can almost be assured of a companion for life. Yet only now, after centuries, are sociological studies beginning to reveal the real, positive health benefits that can result

Bird shows became increasingly popular in the mid-19th century. This 1865 exhibition was held at the Crystal Palace, London. Canaries were the most numerous of the exhibits on display, but there were also a variety of British song birds, talking parrots, cockatoos, parakeets, pheasants, and even a pair of emus, which proved to be a star attraction.

from caring for birds kept in the domestic environment.

Companion birds can be a great source of pleasure to young and old alike, while an attractive aviary can provide hours of relaxation in a garden. Various studies have shown how ownership of a pet budgerigar can lead to a significant improvement in the physical and mental well-being of the person directly involved in the bird's care. This is almost certainly true in other cases, whether birds are being kept indoors or in a garden aviary.

THE PET BIRD

For most people seeking a pet bird, the obvious choice will be a member of the parrot family, which includes a wide variety of species, ranging from the budgerigar to the macaw. Many psittacines, as the various parrots are collectively described, will become very tame and responsive towards members of their immediate circle. They will also learn to mimic speech and other sounds. These unique combined qualities have ensured the popularity of parrots as pets throughout the world over the course of centuries.

Many members of the starling family can also mimic sounds, but even the Greater Hill Mynah, which is considered the most responsive in this regard, does not usually relish physical contact with its owner, unlike parrots which often enjoy being touched and handled by their owners. Nevertheless, mynahs will become tame, while retaining a brash, lively personality, if obtained when young.

There are other features which appeal to the pet-seeker however, such as the singing prowess of the bird. It is essentially for this reason that canaries have been domesticated and become so widely kept in the home. Variations in the colour of their plumage have further contributed to the popularity of the canary as a pet bird.

Other birds are more suited to being kept in groups, as they will not become tame as a general rule. This includes the majority of finches as well as some softbills. These birds are more suited to an aviary existence, where their lively natures can be fully appreciated. They can be kept indoors however, in a suitably large enclosure which also affords some seclusion.

THE CHOICE OF A PARROT

Virtually all psittacines will become tame, if they are obtained at an early age. And now that increasing numbers are being bred and reared by hand, it is becoming much easier to obtain a suitable bird direct from the breeder. Bear in mind that the vocal repertoire and powers of mimicry in some species are vastly superior to others. In this respect, the Grey Parrot is generally accepted as being the most talented psittacine, although these birds can be shy with strangers. Their natural calls are quieter than those of other large parrots, which is an important consideration for people with close neighbours. Amazon parrots as a group have powerful voices, and are given to regular periods of screeching morning and evening. They can be unbearably noisy at these times, but it is very difficult to deter such behaviour, even in a domestically-raised bird. Nevertheless, they can become very tame and affectionate. Also, they speak with a clear intonation and will master a good vocabulary.

Cockatoos, also, have extremely raucous calls; moluccans are often regarded as the worst offenders in this regard. Individuals can become temperamentally unreliable when they are in breeding condition and even tame birds may bite anyone who attempts to touch them. Cockatoos can be highly-strung birds, and are not very proficient talkers, but they are highly responsive to training. Both in the United States and Britain, there are performing cockatoos, which will ride small bicycles and carry out other tricks in front of audiences.

The problem of satisfactorily accommodating the larger macaws in the home can be a deterrent to keeping them, as a suitable cage may have to be purpose-built and is likely to be expensive. Also, these birds have very powerful beaks, and in a confined area their loud calls can be a further drawback. The smaller dwarf macaws are less of a problem in these respects, although their coloration is not so striking. Young birds will become devoted to their owners, even if they master only a few words.

Among the lesser known neo-tropical psittacines, the *Pionus* parrots have much in their favour as pet birds. They are relatively small, and quieter than amazons. Also, their coloration, although not vivid is attractive, and they should learn to talk well.

As a group, conures are less expensive than the *Pionus* parrots, and they can become equally tame. Their smaller size makes them much more satisfactory as pets for children than most of the species already mentioned, and the majority will learn to say a few words. The *Brotogeris* parakeets are equally suitable, if they are obtained when young but, at present, relatively few are bred under aviary conditions.

The colourful Australian parakeets will not settle as pets, and can only be kept adequately in aviary surroundings. The Budgerigar is the noted exception, and remains the most popular pet psittacine. Millions are kept in homes throughout the world. Their lively chatter and talking powers, coupled with their gentle and confiding ways have a universal appeal, and the enormous choice of colours has also helped the budgerigar to retain its popularity among bird owners.

The Cockatiel is becoming increasingly appreciated as a pet, particularly the lutino mutation which is very similar to a cockatoo in appearance. Cockatiels will tame readily, and have an attractive warbling song, which should not prove disturbing in domestic surroundings. In Australia, where few large parrots are available because of importation restrictions, peach-faced lovebirds are widely kept as pets, and considerable numbers are being bred in aviaries each year. Currently, they are not valued so highly elsewhere, yet they have much in their favour, becoming extremely tame, although they develop only a limited vocabulary. Various attractive colour forms now being bred have fallen considerably in price over the last few years.

The other major genus of parrots from mainland Africa includes the popular Senegal and Meyer's parrots. The adult birds are extremely wild and will not settle satisfactorily as pets, but domestically-raised chicks reared by hand can be delightful companions. Their natural calls are not harsh, being comprised of a series of whistling notes.

The long-tailed Asiatic parakeets can

Lesser Sulphur-crested Cockatoo

Cockatiel

Blue and Yellow Macaw

Budgerigar

Yellow-shouldered amazon

make good pets in certain circumstances, with alexandrines probably being the most suitable. They do have loud voices, but these are not used frequently. Smaller members of this genus *Psittacula*, such as the Plum-headed Parakeet, are generally more nervous. Other Asiatic psittacines which can make delightful companions, are the lories and lorikeets, but their feeding habits indoors may present difficulties. Their liquid droppings are extremely messy, and their cage may have to be cleaned twice a day. Also, the cage will have to be screened, to prevent soiling of nearby furniture.

SELECTING CAGES

The pet bird in the home is totally dependent on its owner to provide an environment which will meet its needs. To begin with, as big a cage as possible should be chosen. A variety of designs is available, and rectangular ones are preferable. The traditional square parrot cage allows very little opportunity for the bird to exercise, and merely getting a larger version is not enough, because if a small parakeet or cockatiel is kept in a larger design, the spacing of the bars may prove dangerous. Too wide a gap will encourage the bird to put its head through, and it may get stuck. As a general rule, the more ornate the cage, the less suitable it will be. The tall, circular cages marketed for finches, for example, would be much better if they were laid horizontally, as this would allow considerably more flying space.

However, it is possible to acquire attractive yet functional cages for the home, and for ease of mobility they can be mounted on castors. Flexible designs, comprised of individual components that clip together to form a large area, are to be recommended. Without doubt, it is preferable to keep a pet parrot of any species in a small flight (*see p.26*) rather than a cage. Birds housed in spacious aviaries much more rarely succumb to the vice of feather plucking than do pet birds living in cramped surroundings on their own.

SUITABLE PERCHES

Perches of the appropriate diameter are vital; they must allow the bird to exercise its feet. Being kept on perches of a standard diameter is likely to lead to pressure points becoming evident as swellings on the underside of the feet. These are relatively common in budgerigars, particularly in the heavier, exhibition-type bird kept as a pet. The sore areas can become infected, giving rise to the condition known as bumble-foot (*see Chapter 6*). Apart from dowelling, plastic is used increasingly· for perches. While they can be washed very easily, these rigid perches appear to be most uncomfortable for all birds. They often become reluctant to perch, and spend most of their time hanging on to the cage bars, or on the floor of the cage.

Natural branches are the best option for furnishing a cage, because they provide exercise for the beak, as well as the feet. Also, fresh cut wood is safer than dowelling, being much less likely to splinter. Macaws especially can suffer from splinters becoming stuck in their fleshy cheeks. Parrots generally are destructive, and a regular supply of fresh wood for gnawing will prevent their beaks from becoming overgrown. It will also lessen the risk of boredom, and associated problems such as feather plucking. Even budgerigars derive considerable benefit from stripping the

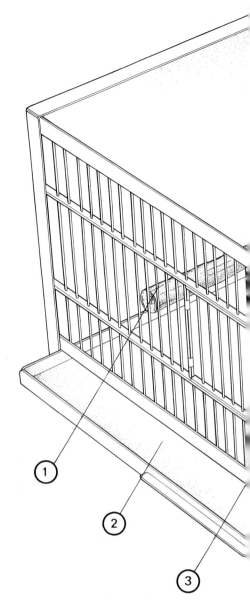

HOUSING YOUR BIRD		
TYPE OF CAGE	**SUITABILITY**	**ADVANTAGES**
BUYING A CAGE		
Wire bird cage	Budgerigars/canaries	Permits good visibility
As above, with plastic base	As above	Easy to clean thoroughly
Parrot cage	Parrots	Usually secure
Mynah cage	Greater Hill Mynah	Box sides prevent food being scattered
Box-type cage	Finches	Provides cover for these rather nervous birds
BUILDING A FLIGHT CAGE		
Wire mesh flight	All species	Can design a spacious enclosure.
Box cage	Budgerigars, canaries and other finches	Standard cage fronts can be purchased separately to be fitted at the front

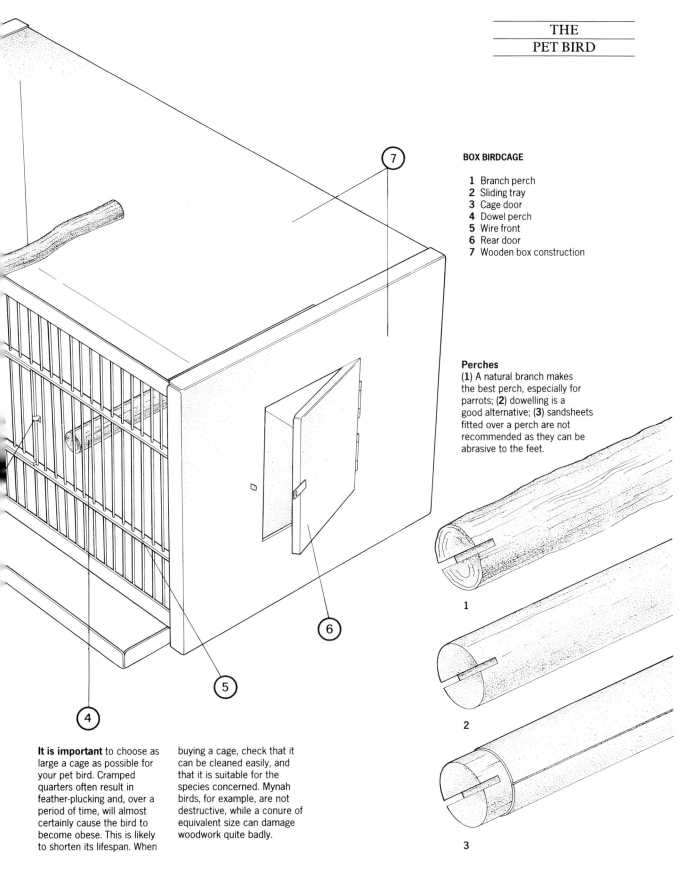

BOX BIRDCAGE

1 Branch perch
2 Sliding tray
3 Cage door
4 Dowel perch
5 Wire front
6 Rear door
7 Wooden box construction

Perches
(**1**) A natural branch makes the best perch, especially for parrots; (**2**) dowelling is a good alternative; (**3**) sandsheets fitted over a perch are not recommended as they can be abrasive to the feet.

It is important to choose as large a cage as possible for your pet bird. Cramped quarters often result in feather-plucking and, over a period of time, will almost certainly cause the bird to become obese. This is likely to shorten its lifespan. When buying a cage, check that it can be cleaned easily, and that it is suitable for the species concerned. Mynah birds, for example, are not destructive, while a conure of equivalent size can damage woodwork quite badly.

bark off a suitable branch. The circumference of the wood selected for perches should not be so small as to cause the bird's feet to curl round so far that the front claws could dig into the back of the foot. Alternatively, the perches must not be so broad that they prevent the toes from gripping on the wood.

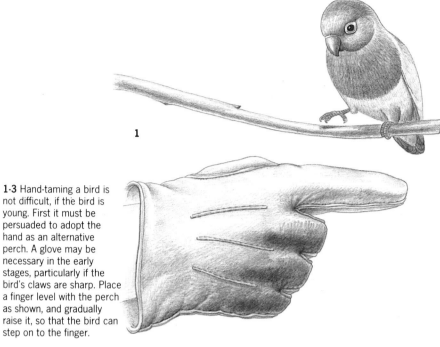

1-3 Hand-taming a bird is not difficult, if the bird is young. First it must be persuaded to adopt the hand as an alternative perch. A glove may be necessary in the early stages, particularly if the bird's claws are sharp. Place a finger level with the perch as shown, and gradually raise it, so that the bird can step on to the finger.

OBTAINING A YOUNG PARROT

To obtain a young, hand-reared parrot, it may be necessary to study the specialist magazines, where breeders advertise. However, it is often easier to acquire budgerigars and canaries from a local pet store or through a newspaper advertisement. Adult tame parrots are also offered for sale on occasion, but these can be more costly than a youngster. Also, they could have acquired bad traits, such as a dislike for people of one or other sex. They may also prove less receptive to a new owner, and show little inclination to expand their vocabularies.

As a general rule, young parrots can be recognized by their completely dark eyes. For example, grey parrots lack the straw coloured irides (irises) which characterize an adult of this species.

There may be other indications, depending upon the particular species concerned. Young budgerigars for example are known as barheads, because at the fledgling stage in most varieties, the bars on the head extend right down to the base of the beak – the bare patch at the base of the upper part of the beak. Only when the bird starts to moult out, at an age of around 12 weeks, will the clear forehead become apparent, while the spots in the mask become bigger and the eyes gain their characteristic irides. More specific details can be found under the relevant species headings in Chapter 8.

SETTLING IN

The bird will take at least a week or so to settle in its new home. And those first few days can be a crucial period, particularly for young birds which may prove unwilling to eat on their own. Therefore, the food must be clearly visible. Unfortunately some cages, especially those intended for budgerigars and canaries, have hoods over the feeding pots. Most birds – if they are not used to such containers – are reluctant to eat from them at first, so some seed should be sprinkled on the floor of the cage close to the main source. The bird will be attracted here and should then start feeding of its own accord.

The presence of seed husks in the cage, and the droppings, provide a useful guide to the state of the bird's appetite. Thin, predominantly greenish droppings suggest that it has not been eating properly and its plumage may hang loosely, giving a fluffed up rather than a sleek appearance. With hand-reared parrots in particular, any sudden dietary changes should be avoided at this stage as these could precipitate digestive disorders which have similar symptoms (that is, greenish droppings and fluffed plumage) and require urgent veterinary treatment.

TRAINING TECHNIQUES

To a large extent, the training process will be influenced by the character of the individual bird. Parrots of the same species can differ significantly in personalities, some birds being much bolder and more responsive than others. A docile bird that is already an established pet should settle in quite quickly, but it will still take time to win the bird's confidence. A young hand-reared parrot is likely to be most adaptable, and will tend to regard humans as suppliers of food. Even when able to eat independently, hand-reared parrots tend to beg for food if an opportunity presents itself. Such birds should take pieces of fruit readily from the hand, and are much easier to tame as a result, since their natural fear of humans is almost absent.

FIRST STAGE

Training an adult parrot can prove much more protracted, and sometimes even futile. Nevertheless, the basic technique is the same in all cases. At every opportunity, the bird should be encouraged to take food directly from its new owner. At first, food can be offered from outside the cage if the bird is nervous. Patience will be required but, ultimately, the parrot should approach and extend its head to seize whatever is on offer, before withdrawing to the far side of the cage.

The parrot is unlikely to attempt to bite the fingers, but it is important that

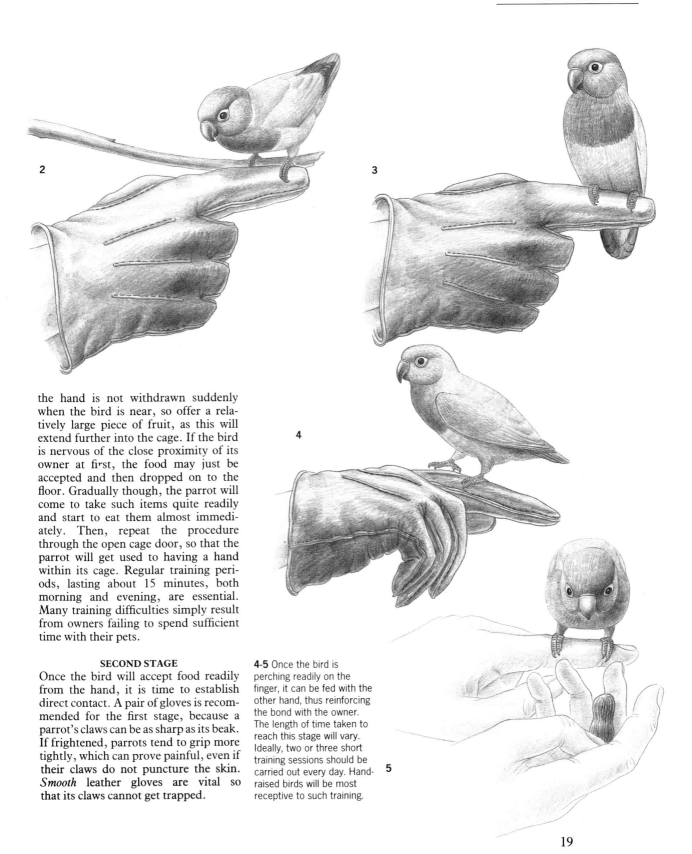

2

3

4

the hand is not withdrawn suddenly when the bird is near, so offer a relatively large piece of fruit, as this will extend further into the cage. If the bird is nervous of the close proximity of its owner at first, the food may just be accepted and then dropped on to the floor. Gradually though, the parrot will come to take such items quite readily and start to eat them almost immediately. Then, repeat the procedure through the open cage door, so that the parrot will get used to having a hand within its cage. Regular training periods, lasting about 15 minutes, both morning and evening, are essential. Many training difficulties simply result from owners failing to spend sufficient time with their pets.

SECOND STAGE
Once the bird will accept food readily from the hand, it is time to establish direct contact. A pair of gloves is recommended for the first stage, because a parrot's claws can be as sharp as its beak. If frightened, parrots tend to grip more tightly, which can prove painful, even if their claws do not puncture the skin. *Smooth* leather gloves are vital so that its claws cannot get trapped.

4-5 Once the bird is perching readily on the finger, it can be fed with the other hand, thus reinforcing the bond with the owner. The length of time taken to reach this stage will vary. Ideally, two or three short training sessions should be carried out every day. Hand-raised birds will be most receptive to such training.

5

Parrots possess considerable powers of memory, not just confined to the simple repetition of words or tunes, and the appearance of a glove used for catching purposes is likely to cause an immediate outbreak of panic and screeching. So it is important to use clearly differentiated gloves for training purposes. It can prove to be a slow process, but birds should never be hit if they fail to respond to a command, as this will destroy their confidence in their trainer. They will be unable to comprehend the reason for such treatment and may actively turn against the person concerned. Tame parrots are sometimes advertised as disliking either men or women; although birds occasionally do show an active preference for an owner of one particular sex, it is more likely in such cases that they have been mistreated by a previous owner and have remained hostile as a result.

Hand-reared parrots generally do not resent being picked up, having become used to this sensation from an early age. They may not be so confident about perching on a hand or arm however, depending on the amount of attention that they received at the nestling stage.

The initial step is to persuade the parrot to sit confidently on the hand. With a bird in a cage, the hand should be moved slowly towards the perch, until contact is made. At first, the parrot may step on to the sides of the cage, but ultimately, it will be possible to touch its feet with the gloved hand. The bird can be coaxed on to the hand if this is slowly raised directly over the top of the perch. The next stage is to move the hand, with the parrot remaining in place. It may be possible to lift the parrot out of the cage on the hand, but this is likely to prove difficult. The bird will probably sit on the gloved hand until it gets to the door, but will then climb off on to the side of the cage again.

With encouragement however, this trait can be overcome. If a parrot will sit readily on the hand in its cage, but refuses to come out, the only alternative is to tempt it out with a suitable titbit.

Once out of their cages, most parrots are happy to remain on the roof, and should it be necessary as a last resort to lift the bird out, this will serve as a suitable initial perching site. Once the parrot is relatively tame, it is possible to start stroking the neck region. This area is a common site for mutual preening between a pair of parrots, and the action reinforces the bond between them.

THE NEED FOR EXERCISE
It is very easy for parrots kept in cages to become obese, and this is likely to shorten their lifespan. In addition, should surgery be required at any stage, the risk of complications arising is greatly increased in a bird that is overweight. Unfortunately, the diet offered to many parrots tends to encourage obesity. Oil-based seeds such as sunflower, hemp and peanuts are likely to contribute to the development of excessive fatty tissue, particularly in birds that are kept in a relatively warm environment where little energy will be used to maintain a constant body temperature and there is little opportunity for exercise.

There is no reason why the diet cannot be altered to decrease this depen-

Although wing-clipping may seem distasteful, it can, in fact, help to save a bird from serious injury in the home, until it is used to its surroundings. Cut carefully across the feathers of one wing using sharp scissors, as shown. Make sure that there is no blood supply evident. Never cut right down to the base of the quill (rachis), but leave a short distance before the shaft (calamus).

Secondary feathers   Primary flight feathers

dence on oil seeds and, at the same time, to stimulate the bird's interest in a variety of other foods. Fruit and greenstuff may not be taken at first – by newly-imported parrots in particular – but if offered regularly, they will be sampled, especially if they are placed near the food pot. Chapter 4 deals with this question of diet in detail.

In addition, every psittacine should be encouraged to exercise its wing muscles outside the confines of its cage. Perches attached to walls around the room by means of rubber suckers can be a useful way of stimulating flying activity in budgerigars. However, letting any psittacine out of its cage to exercise in the room may cause problems, because of the various hazards that may be present. Poisonous plants, live electrical flex, uncovered fish tanks and windows are just some of the possible threats. Windows in particular must be screened with net curtains, because the parrot is otherwise likely to attempt to fly through the glass, with possibly fatal consequences. Indeed, someone should be present in the room whenever a parrot is out of its cage, to reduce the

likelihood of accidents, and the damage to furniture that the bird's beak may inflict.

It will be much easier to persuade a young home-bred parrot to exercise safely within the home than would be the case with an imported adult bird, which is likely to fly off wildly around the room. An established bird is likely to spend much of its time sitting on top of its cage, and it can be encouraged to use a T-shaped stand, with a dirt tray beneath. Leg chains should not be used however, as they are likely to prove dangerous, particularly if the parrot has clipped wings. If startled, it may fall off the perch and be kept dangling helplessly from the end of the chain.

WING-CLIPPING

Clipping a bird's flight feathers will handicap its power of flight, and thus reduce its ability to exercise. Nevertheless, it will sit on its cage and flap its wings vigorously, still using its wing muscles. Newly-imported parrots often have their flight feathers cut, and it may be safer to adopt this approach when allowing a parrot out of its cage – until it

Wing-clipping will prevent the bird from flying with full force, until the next moult, when the clipped feathers will be replaced. If in any doubt, seek expert advice before starting.

is used to its environment – to decrease the risk of injury. To a great extent, the decision must depend on the individual bird. A domestically-raised, hand-tame youngster is far less likely to be nervous than an imported bird.

There are various ways of clipping the flight feathers, but generally this should be restricted to one wing only, so the bird will retain a limited power of flight. New plumage will replace the clipped feathers during the next moult, so it is only a temporary method of restraint, and providing the bird can exercise its wings, no problems are likely to arise. However, cutting should never be undertaken when the bird is moulting because, at this time, the feathers receive a blood supply. This is evident in their shafts as a pinkish colour. Severe haemorrhage will result if the feathers are cut at this stage.

MENTAL STIMULATION

Exercise for a pet bird should not be thought of as being just a physical need; parrots are intelligent birds, and require mental stimulation if they are not to become bored. Various toys can be purchased or devised for this purpose. They do not need to be elaborate. For example, a small piece of wood with a hole bored through it, fixed on to a stout piece of wire so that it can be slid up and down, will provide hours of entertainment. It can be mounted on the side of the cage, and easily replaced at negligible cost when the wood becomes badly chewed. Wool and string must never be used for attaching toys and similar items in cages, since the bird may become caught up and strangle itself, or even swallow the material with equally disastrous consequences.

As far as toys that are manufactured for birds are concerned, sturdy, easy to clean designs are essential. The type of toy that is appropriate depends on the bird in question. For example, the plastic toys produced for budgerigars are unsuitable for larger parrots, because the latter have more powerful beaks. The cage should not be cluttered with toys; a mirror that clips on to the cage framework, and a ping-pong ball on the floor will suffice for a budgerigar. A ladder can be included if space permits, as long as the bird cannot get itself caught between the rungs. Some owners prefer not to include a mirror, for cock budgerigars in particular, believing that it encourages them to regurgitate seed in an attempt to "feed" their reflection constantly. If this does appear to be the case, simply remove the mirror. There is no truth in the story that having a mirror in the cage prevents a bird from talking. Mirrors are appreciated by larger parrots, but are best located outside the cage, where they cannot be damaged.

Swings still feature in cages, but they are not favoured by many birds, including psittacines – with the possible exception of the budgerigar. Bells are also most popular with budgerigars. Various chews are more appealing for parrots.

The safety aspect should never be overlooked when buying a toy. For example, metal bells may have sharp edges which could lacerate a toe or tongue severely, while the beak may become caught up in a chain used for attaching the toy to the side of the cage. Toys for parrots outside a cage, such as miniature skateboards or roller skates, are only likely to be used by very tame birds.

The best form of exercise for a pet parrot is the type that stimulates natural behaviour. Spraying, for example, will encourage a bird to preen, and thus keep its plumage in good condition. Though many parrots are frightened of a mist sprayer when it is first used, they rapidly learn to appreciate their bath, which also helps to minimize feather dust in the room where they are kept. This is important, because people can become allergic to feather dust, and develop respiratory symptoms. Cockatoos, particularly, produce relatively large amounts of dust, especially when moulting. A daily spray with tepid water should ensure that the bird's plumage will not become dry and brittle, as is likely if it does not bathe.

A selection of the toys which can be obtained for smaller birds such as budgerigars. Toys for parrots should be more robust and can be home-made.

Mental stimulation is
important for all caged birds
and toys will provide hours
of entertainment. Do not
overcrowd the cage with toys
– it is better to start with one
or two and then change them.
Always check that the toys
are safe and that they are
suitable for the bird in
question.

COMPANIONSHIP

Adult, nervous birds may appear most likely to become feather-pluckers but, in fact, hand-tame psittacines deprived of company are equally susceptible to this habit. Once the problem starts, it can be very difficult to remedy, even if the underlying trigger(s) are rapidly identified and rectified. The parrot housed on its own depends entirely on humans for companionship. Bearing in mind that these birds are essentially gregarious in the wild, forming life-long pair bonds in some cases, probably the most significant exercise for a pet parrot is its physical and mental interaction with its owner. Set periods of time should be devoted to the bird each and every day.

Parrots can become extremely devoted to one member of the family, and may actively resent apparent interference by others, not hesitating to bite if the opportunity presents itself. Jealousy can also be directed towards other pets, such as dogs, and is often manifested by periods of screeching when the unfortunate animal is nearby. Such situations are best prevented from an early stage, by involving the whole family in the bird's care and exercise routine, and never neglecting it in favour of other pets.

Problems are most likely to arise if the parrot is left on its own for long periods in the day, with little mental stimulus during this time. Leaving a radio on will help to alleviate boredom until the owner returns. It must be appreciated right from the outset that a pet parrot is among the most demanding of companion animals. Some of the onus will be shifted off the owner if two birds of the same ,species are acquired simultaneously. They will engage in mutual preening and exercise together, so that the boredom threshold will be dramatically increased, even if the owner is not present for much of the day. It is easier to introduce both birds to the home simultaneously, rather than acquire a second bird later, since rivalry and jealousy then arise. Generally, however, when given the opportunity to exercise their personalities to the full, parrots can be the most rewarding of all pets.

TALKING

The ability of certain birds to mimic human speech has fascinated their owners for centuries. There has been considerable debate as to whether birds are capable of comprehending the meaning of words, and thus can truly communicate with their owners. Recent American research carried out in the United States at Purdue University, Indiana, suggests that the African Grey Parrot is capable of logical reasoning with its owner. The bird used in the study, christened Alex, was able to use the word "No" in a meaningful manner, and could distinguish between different items in response to a request. The means by which birds can speak clearly is also engaging medical scientists, because birds do not possess a larynx, necessary for normal vocalization in humans.

TEACHING SPEECH

The procedure for teaching a bird to talk is straightforward, and should be carried out at the same time as the basic taming process. Although specifically-designed tapes can assist, there is no substitute for human involvement to concentrate the bird's attention. Words or short phrases should be repeated regularly, as often as possible, and gradually, as these are mastered, the vocabulary can be increased. Some birds will prove more talented than others. The most talkative budgerigar on record, christened Sparkie, mastered 558 individual words during his eight years of life, and was even capable of reciting eight nursery rhymes from start to finish.

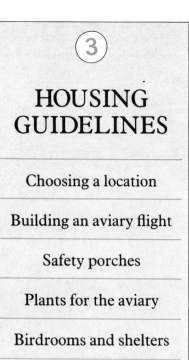

The basic unit for housing birds out-of-doors is the aviary, comprised of a flight and connecting shelter. The design of the shelter can be expanded to form a larger structure known as a birdroom. Here breeding cages can be kept, as well as seed. Indoor flights can also be incorporated, to hold young stock, for example. The addition of a birdroom thus makes the overall structure more versatile.

The type of accommodation required will depend greatly on the birds that are to be kept. For example, parrots generally are destructive and thus require more substantial and expensive aviaries than finches. Adequate thought must be given to winter accommodation, particularly in temperate areas, and a birdroom may be necessary for this purpose. Serious exhibition breeders will also need a structure of this type, where their stock can be bred under closely supervised conditions, and trained in readiness for competition. The provision of electricity in the birdroom, for heating and lighting purposes, is likely to be essential, and a water supply may also be desirable.

CHOOSING A LOCATION
The factors mentioned above need to be considered when siting the structure, and a location close to the house, where the birds can be seen from indoors, will add to the enjoyment of keeping them. This may not be practicable however, if there are close neighbours who might object to the birds' calls. Parrot-like species usually prove the worst offenders. The chosen site needs to be in a sheltered and slightly-shaded location, away from overhanging trees. Also, the aviary should not be visible from the road, or it might attract vandals or thieves, while car lights at night can disturb sitting birds, causing them to desert their nests or chicks.

Various regulations may affect the building of an aviary, such as zoning restrictions in the United States, and local planning laws. Before work starts therefore, consult the appropriate authorities to check whether or not official permission will be needed for the structure. A rough sketch of the site, and the proposed dimensions will provide a useful starting point. It is always worth planning for possible expansion from the outset!

DIMENSIONS
The dimensions of the aviary will depend on the size and numbers of the birds you intend to keep. In most cases, the flight component will need to be at least 2.7 m (9 ft) in length, but for larger softbills and Australian parakeets for example, a minimum length of 3.6 m (12 ft) is recommended. The width of the aviary is less crucial than its length, except with long-tailed birds. But it should not be under 90 cm (3 ft), if only to allow cleaning to be undertaken without difficulty. The height of the aviary should be sufficient to allow easy access, because catching birds in cramped surroundings can prove difficult.

If the aviary is constructed at home, the dimensions should take into account the width of the mesh that will be used to clad the flight panels. This will make construction easier and prevent unnecessary wastage of materials. In most cases, mesh of 90 cm (3 ft) or 1.2 m (4 ft) is preferable. Wider mesh of 1.8 m (6 ft) will tend to sag on the framework and look unsightly.

SITING AND FOUNDATIONS
The site will need to be made as level as possible to facilitate building work. The aviary should be mounted on brickwork, to exclude vermin such as rats and to prevent it from rotting prematurely. In addition, some birds such as motmots may start tunnelling into the aviary floor if it is grass, and so could escape.

Therefore, the bricks or blocks will need to extend to a depth of about 30 cm (12 in) below ground level and, irrespective of the flight floor, the shelter should have a solid concrete base. With the birds being fed inside, this is where the majority of cleaning will be re-

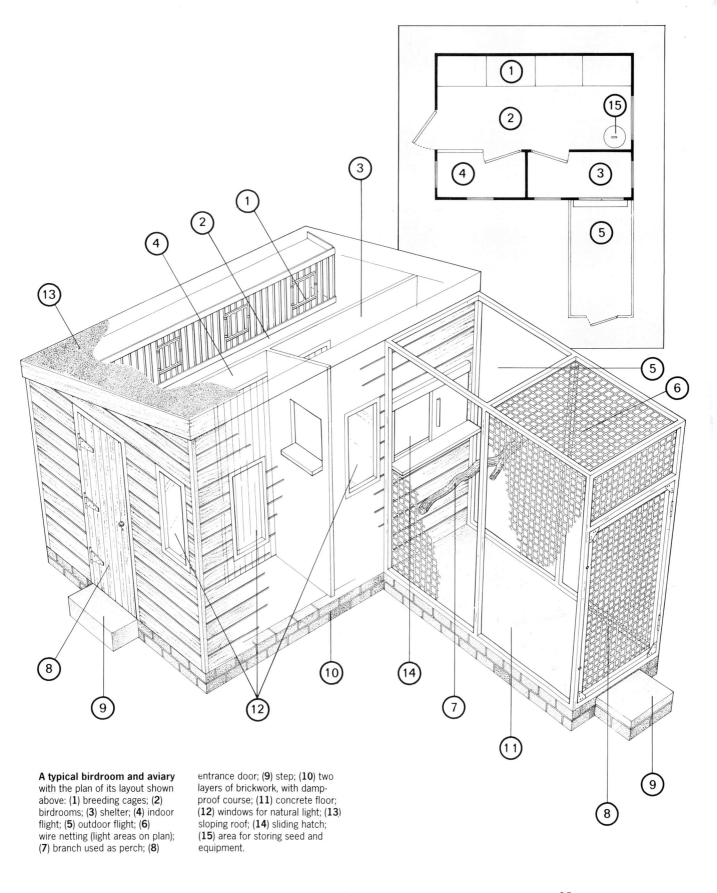

A typical birdroom and aviary with the plan of its layout shown above: (**1**) breeding cages; (**2**) birdrooms; (**3**) shelter; (**4**) indoor flight; (**5**) outdoor flight; (**6**) wire netting (light areas on plan); (**7**) branch used as perch; (**8**) entrance door; (**9**) step; (**10**) two layers of brickwork, with damp-proof course; (**11**) concrete floor; (**12**) windows for natural light; (**13**) sloping roof; (**14**) sliding hatch; (**15**) area for storing seed and equipment.

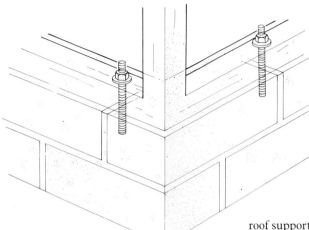

To fix the wooden frame to the brick base, first sink evenly-spaced bolts into the masonry and then lower the frames, with pre-drilled holes, into position. A simpler method is to use frame fixers, which are inserted into holes which have been pre-drilled through the frame and masonry.

obtain the wood from demolition contractors or a similar source. However, all timber should be free from woodworm and flaking paintwork. Lead-based paints are likely to prove toxic if ingested in small amounts over a period of time.

THE FLIGHT FLOOR

The floor covering will vary according to the birds concerned as well as the size of the aviary. Those which generally destroy vegetation, such as the vast majority of parrots, are not suitable for a planted flight. In contrast, finches and even most large softbills, will appreciate access to grass and bushes, which provide essential breeding cover for many of these species.

The major problem associated with this more natural environment is ensuring that the aviary can be kept clean and the soil will remain fresh under such conditions. This can be achieved in part by having concrete areas under the main perches, where most droppings accumulate, and cleaning these off regularly. Another alternative is to have a concrete floor, and

quired, and concrete can either be swept or washed off without difficulty. A damp-proof course of thick, undamaged plastic sheeting needs to be set in this base, which will be built on top of suitable hard core such as blocks, bricks and flints.

THE AVIARY FLIGHT

The construction of an aviary flight unit is quite standard, and it is possible to purchase wired panels for rapid assembly. These are advertised in most avicultural publications, alongside ready-made sectional aviaries. It is vital, however, to select panels covered with mesh of the appropriate size and gauge (that is, individual "hole" size) for the species concerned. Nevertheless, you can make considerable savings by building the aviary yourself.

Wood usually forms the basis of the framework for the structure, because it is relatively cheap when compared with materials such as metal tubing, and is quite durable when treated with a suitable preservative. A further advantage is that it is an easy material to fix the aviary mesh on to, leaving no gaps through which it would be possible for a small finch to escape. However, other options, such as flights made of stonework pillars with horizontal wooden

roof supports can look very decorative.

Assuming that wood is chosen, then timber 37 mm (1½ in) will suffice for the majority of species, but parrots especially are best kept in flights with a framework 50 mm (2 in) square. This will enable the wire to be attached over a larger area, and the strain on the netting staples will be correspondingly less when a bird flies on and off the wire. Otherwise, over a period of time, this friction will begin to pull the staples out of the woodwork, and parrots, unlike other birds, will climb readily over the mesh.

The timber need not be planed smooth, but avoid badly-warped lengths. The cost of building the structure can be halved if it is possible to

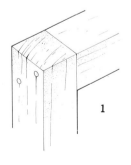

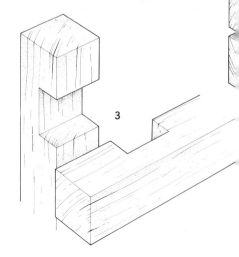

Three methods of jointing the woodwork: (**1**) halving joint; (**2**) butt joint; (**3**) cross-halving joint.

provide "natural" vegetation in the form of shrubs and plants growing in pots. To make it easier to move these as necessary, to allow thorough washing of the birds' quarters, stand the heavier pots on small, platform "trolleys".

In a small aviary, a grass floor rapidly becomes waterlogged and moss takes over. Also, the ground may become a reservoir for potential infections, which can include various parasitic worms. It is possible to scrape off the top layer at regular intervals, but obviously then no grass will become established. Commercially-acquired turves should be regarded with caution, because they are often treated with weedkillers, and grass seed is also frequently dressed with toxic chemicals. If a concrete floor is decided upon, it should be sloped away from the flight to allow rainwater to run off and down into a suitable drainage hole. As a less permanent feature, paving slabs can be used in a similar way, the gaps between the slabs being filled with mortar.

PREPARING THE WOOD
The lengths of timber must be treated several times before being assembled into flight panels. This is most conveniently undertaken once they have been cut to the required size and the joints have been prepared. The whole surface area can then be thoroughly coated with a preservative, using a paintbrush. Jointing the wood will make the finished aviary more stable, and the structure will be stronger and easier to

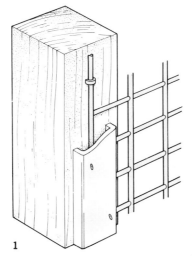

Mesh edges must be covered to protect birds from sharp edges. (**1**) Thin battening is suitable for most birds. (**2**) Parrot aviaries require a more robust finish.

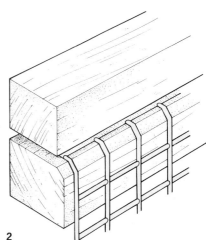

handle if it has to be dismantled later and moved to a new site. Following the final coat of preservative, the timber should be left to dry out thoroughly for several weeks before the birds come into contact with it. This is because most weather-proofing agents are potentially poisonous.

CONSTRUCTING THE PANELS
Use glue and screws to assemble the individual panels, having first numbered each face to show its intended position in the completed flight. The glue should be waterproof and non-toxic. Rectangular or square mesh is preferable for covering the panels, since these are easier than wire netting (chicken wire) to cut without loose ends becoming a problem. For the smaller seedeaters, 12 mm (½ in) 19 gauge (G) mesh will suffice. Thicker, 25 mm (1 in) square 16G mesh is suitable for larger softbills, which will probably consume any mice that enter the aviary. In areas where rodenticide poisons may be used however, it is safer to opt for 25 x 12 mm (1 x ½ in) netting, as this excludes most rodents. Mesh of these dimensions is also most suitable for parrots, with 16G being adequate for most species, apart from the larger macaws and cockatoos, which may require 12G. Under no circumstances should there be any flaking of the galvanizing metal, or roughness on the mesh, as either could seriously injure the parrot.

The aviary wire should be applied to the surface of the frame which will eventually form the inner face of the flight. The method used is similar in all

GUIDELINES FOR CHOOSING WIRE MESH

WIRE GAUGE	MESH SIZE	SUITABILITY
19G	12.5 × 12.5 mm (½ × ½ in)	Waxbills and small softbills
19G	12.5 × 25mm (½ × 1 in)	Larger seedeaters, budgerigars + grass parakeets, pigeons
16G	12.5 × 12.5 mm (½ × ½ in)	Lovebirds, conures, other small parakeets
16G	12.5 × 25 mm (½ × 1 in)	Bigger parakeets, e.g. Alexandrine, magpies + similar-sized softbills
14G	25 × 25 mm (1 × 1 in)	Amazon parrots, dwarf macaws, grey parrots
12G	50 × 50 mm (2 × 2 in)	Large macaws, and cockatoos

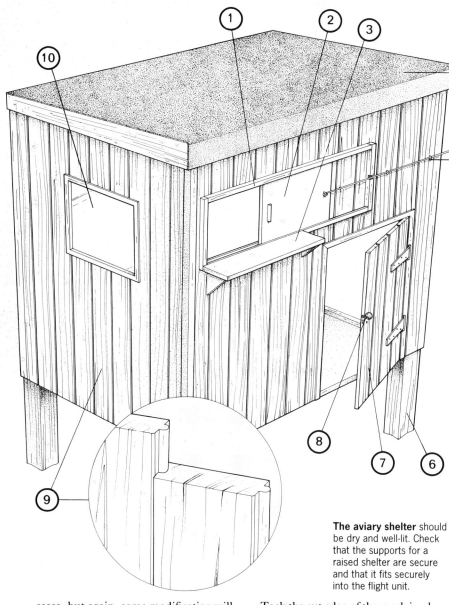

A raised aviary shelter: (1) door rails; **(2)** sliding plywood door; **(3)** platform; **(4)** sloping roof; **(5)** rod for closing shelter from outside the aviary; **(6)** supporting legs; **(7)** door; **(8)** door fastening; **(9)** tongue-and-groove construction; **(10)** window.

The aviary shelter should be dry and well-lit. Check that the supports for a raised shelter are secure and that it fits securely into the flight unit.

thin 25 x 12 mm (1 x ½ in) battening, so there will be no risk of the birds becoming caught up on the loose strands and injured.

In parrot aviaries however, a slightly different approach is to be recommended, in view of the birds' destructive habits. Most species will strip off any battening without difficulty, and are then liable to start on the woodwork behind, when they will be exposed to the sharp ends of mesh. This can be prevented by extending the mesh on to the adjoining face, at the top and bottom of the frame, which will then be out of the birds' reach, once the panels are assembled. Some psittacines, notably Goffin's Cockatoos are adept at removing netting staples, but this method will help to ensure that the mesh is not stripped off the framework, creating a hole through which the birds could escape. Even so, make regular inspections.

ATTACHING THE PANELS

Fix the panels to the perimeter foundations by means of bolts, positioned between the masonry vertically and at regular intervals, approximately 45 cm (18 in) apart. The bolts must have set firm in the mortar before the frames, with corresponding pre-drilled holes, are lowered into position. Washers and nuts should be used so that, with regular oiling, the structure will remain fully sectional. Adjoining frames also need to

cases, but again, some modification will be needed for aviaries that are destined to house parrots. First, the panel should be laid on flat ground, and the mesh unrolled over the surface of the framework. At this stage, an extra pair of hands will be of great assistance, to ensure that the mesh is kept square and taut on the framework. This will contribute greatly to the final appearance.

Tack the cut edge of the mesh in place at the top of the frame, using netting staples, before working down the sides, keeping the wire taut throughout. Then fix the bottom edge before separating the mesh from the rest of the roll, using a hacksaw or wire cutters. Then place additional netting staples all around the frame, at intervals of about 50 mm (2 in). Cover any jagged ends of wire with be attached together by bolts, which weather better than screws. Masonry nails can be driven through the frames into the base, to give the structure extra stability, if required.

SAFETY PORCHES

An entry door to the aviary is often included at the end of the flight furthest from the shelter. To prevent any birds escaping when this door is opened, there should also be a safety porch – a small enclosed area – so that it is possible to close this outer entry door, before opening the inner one leading into the aviary itself. The porch is generally built on the same lines as the flight, but its door opens outwards, whereas the door into the aviary is hinged in the reverse direction.

SHELTERS

The aviary shelter may form part of a larger birdroom, or be a self-contained unit. In the latter case, you will require a similar framework to that constructed for the flight, but with sloping sides, to form a basis for the roof. It must be sufficiently light to encourage the birds

A planted garden aviary should have some clear areas, to permit access to the flight.

This sliding door enables the aviculturist to close the birds into the shelter, or the flight, from outside the aviary: (**1**) staples for guiding rod; (**2**) metal rod; (**3**) rod connected to centre of door; (**4**) runners; (**5**) sliding door. The handle extends outside the aviary mesh. There is no risk of the birds closing the hatch, or injuring themselves, as could happen if a flap system were used.

to enter, so it will be necessary to have a window in the door at the back of the shelter. This should be wired over, to stop the birds attempting to fly through the glass, or escaping if the window is removed in hot weather. A fixed side-window is also useful in increasing the amount of light within the shelter.

The sides of the structure are made of tongued-and-grooved wood, or marine plywood, both of which are efficient draught-excluders. Plywood can also be used for the roof. Once the joints have been filled in and tarred, cover the roof with roofing felt to ensure that the interior remains dry.

In addition to a connecting door, a separate entrance hole and a landing area, suitable for the birds concerned, will be necessary to link the shelter with the flight. It can be useful to be able to close the birds in or out of the flight before entering the aviary. For this purpose, runners for a thin piece of plywood should be included in the design. Then by means of a stout length

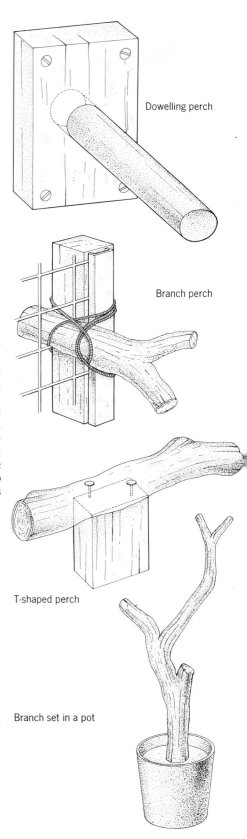

Dowelling perch

Branch perch

T-shaped perch

Branch set in a pot

of wire through the mesh and extending outside the aviary, the plywood can be pulled across the entrance hole as required. A simple piece of plywood fixed by a bracket beneath, to the side of the shelter, will act as a landing platform in front of the entrance hole. This may need to be replaced at intervals if it is "attacked" by the birds.

PLANTS FOR THE AVIARY

A wide range of plants are suitable for growing in an aviary, although the choice out-of-doors must be influenced by the climate. Flowering hibiscus, for example, although very attractive in indoor heated surroundings, will not thrive outside throughout the year in temperate regions. Red flowers are especially attractive to nectar-feeders such as hummingbirds, so fuchsias are a popular choice for aviaries housing such birds. Fast-growing dwarf conifers and other bushes provide plenty of cover and perching sites. Creepers need to be viewed with caution, because in an overgrown flight they may disguise, or even enlarge, a hole in the netting.

Annuals can be sown at the appropriate time of year, and even if they are in boxes or tubs, they can provide maximum ground cover in the aviary, as well as attractive flowers. Nasturtiums are especially suitable, because they often attract aphids, usually at the peak of the breeding season, and for many species, including waxbills and other seedeaters, such insects are of great value in rearing healthy chicks. There are climbing or trailing varieties of nasturtiums, which will thrive even in poor soil, when they will produce more flowers than leaves. Certain plants such as lupins should be avoided however, because their seeds could be poisonous if they are eaten by the birds. For a more detailed list of **useful plants in an aviary setting**, see Glossary pp.152-3.

PERCHES

Apart from those provided by any plants in the aviary, some additional perches will be needed by the birds. The size required obviously depends again on the particular species concerned, but some variation in diameter is desirable, as this will serve to exercise the toes and thus reduce the risk of pressure sores developing. Supple branches are preferred for many softbills, especially the smaller species, and should be renewed when they dry out. Some aviculturists use perches made of string for such birds, simply tying it taut across the flight, as an additional precaution against foot problems. Sycamore, willow or ash perches are quite suitable for general usage, as are apple and elder wood, providing none has been subjected to recent chemical spraying. It is always advisable to wash off the perches before use, in case they have been fouled by wild birds.

The branches should be suspended at a reasonable height, across the flight rather than lengthways. For toucans and similar birds, the perches need to be set low enough for the bird to catch its food, having thrown it into the air, as described on page 113. In addition, the perches must not be so close to the side of the aviary that the bird is unable to land or turn round without hitting its beak against the netting.

Dowelling of the appropriate diameter is frequently used to create perches in the aviary shelter, but this is unsuitable for nectivores, because of its hardness. When used for other birds, such as budgerigars, some lengths should be planed flat, to create two opposing surfaces, thus altering the shape and relieving pressure on the birds' feet.

Perches of this type can be fixed in place by glueing them into a suitable hole drilled in a flat piece of wood, which is then screwed on to the sides of the shelter or flight. Of course, it is possible to wedge branches in place through the aviary mesh itself, but over a period of time, this will serve to weaken the wire, so that holes develop in the netting. This method is particularly unsuitable for larger, heavier species, because the perches, and the mesh, will be jarred

Ionizers will improve the environment of a birdroom by removing dust, pollen and infectious particles.

given to the provision and location of removable or opening windows, in addition to doors, while ensuring that the birds will not be exposed to draughts. It is possible to adapt the system used in greenhouses, for opening and closing windows automatically on the basis of the environmental temperature, and utilize it in the birdroom. The principle is very simple, with a gas expanding or contracting as a result of the temperature, and is extremely reliable. All windows should be wired over with aviary mesh, as recommended earlier. Although relatively expensive, an extractor fan is useful not only for ventilation, but also for removing the dust which can build up in an atmosphere where seedeaters especially are being kept. Such fans need to be placed in a mesh box, so that if a bird escapes, it will not be sucked in accidentally, with dire consequences.

IONIZERS
Another piece of equipment which can improve the environment within a birdroom is an ionizer. It will remove dust, infectious particles and even pollen from the air, by the production of negative ions. These combine with the aerial debris, and precipitate it, resulting in a cleaner, more sterile atmosphere. The effectiveness of ionizers with farm livestock has been confirmed in numerous studies worldwide, and this apparatus is becoming increasingly appreciated by all bird-keepers. Special designs are now available to cater for this growing market.

every time a bird flies on or off a branch. A more satisfactory method is to coil wire loops very tightly around each end of the branch, and extend these to a nearby support, where they can be attached by netting staples.

Other options include T-shaped timber perches, actually set into the floor of the flight, or tree-like branches fixed firmly in pots. The latter type is most suitable for the smaller passerines. The flight should never be cluttered with perches however, particularly when keeping active birds such as Australian parakeets. In most instances, just two perches positioned either end of the flight will be adequate, with two more in the shelter.

BIRDROOMS
A birdroom gives the aviculturist much more potential to keep and breed birds successfully. It is also useful for exhibition purposes. Budgerigars, for example, can be housed in individual pairs when breeding, with young stock kept separate, while ample space is also available for storing show cages and training birds. In the case of foreign birds, indoor flights, with controlled heating and lighting ensure that even the most delicate species can be kept safely through the winter before being released into outside flights during the following year. There should also be adequate space for seed bins and feeding utensils. In well-equipped birdrooms, a sink and food preparation area for softbills may be included.

VENTILATION
A bigger structure does however have its potential problems. Ventilation in birdrooms is often neglected, but will be particularly important if softbills are being kept. A stagnant atmosphere, particularly if the humidity is relatively high, is likely to encourage the development of moulds and fungi which present a very serious danger to the birds' health.

Careful thought should therefore be

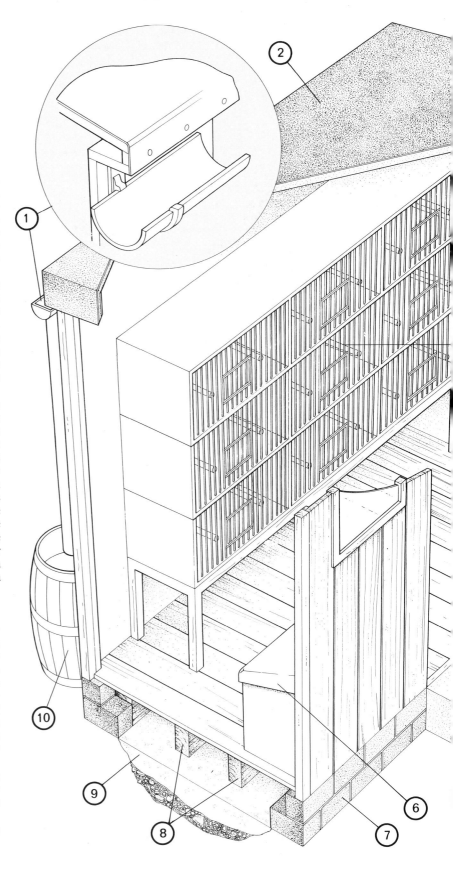

The ion probe is shaped rather like a fluorescent light, and generally connects to a standard light socket. It emits a steady stream of the negative ions from its tip, and for maximum effect, needs to be left on constantly. It uses as little as 0.3 W of electricity, so running costs are negligible. There is even a model operating off a car battery, if a direct electrical supply is not available.

The unit should be sited close to the roof, in the centre of the birdroom, and away from large metal objects such as seed bins, which will attract the ions. The particles will settle close to the probe, and can be removed with a damp cloth. The only servicing that the probe requires is a weekly cleaning of the delicate tip with a matchstick.

The presence of an ion probe in the birdroom will also directly help the birdkeeper, particularly if prone to chest ailments, because the level of dust will be dramatically reduced. This is significant, since a few people actually develop an allergy to their birds, with dust from the feathers and droppings acting as a trigger. Air-movement in the birdroom will help to circulate the negative ions, but unfortunately, if the structure is divided in any way, another probe will be required for maximum efficiency. A partition will act as a barrier to the free movement of ions.

HEATING AND LIGHTING
Electricity also provides the only reliable and safe means of heating a birdroom or aviary shelter. Tubular heaters, available in various sizes, can be used in conjunction with a thermostat to maintain the temperature economically at the required level. In the case of acclimatized birds, this level should be in the range 7-10°C (45-50°F). The thermostat should be positioned in a dry locality, as with all electrical apparatus. Fan heaters are a possible alternative to the tubular type, but prove considerably more expensive to operate, and the motor is readily clogged up by dust. Tubular heaters, being cylindrical, are totally sealed.

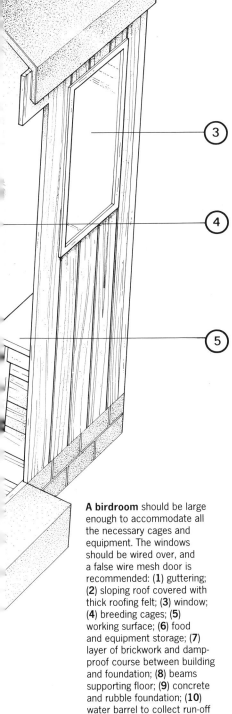

A birdroom should be large enough to accommodate all the necessary cages and equipment. The windows should be wired over, and a false wire mesh door is recommended: (1) guttering; (2) sloping roof covered with thick roofing felt; (3) window; (4) breeding cages; (5) working surface; (6) food and equipment storage; (7) layer of brickwork and damp-proof course between building and foundation; (8) beams supporting floor; (9) concrete and rubble foundation; (10) water barrel to collect run-off from roof.

Lighting can be provided by bulbs or fluorescent tubes. The wide-spectrum tubes which mimic daylight are said to be particularly good for birds kept indoors. The ultra-violet component falling on the plumage ultimately results in the synthesis of Vitamin D_3 (although this can be provided in the diet). Studies with poultry suggest that exposure to three-quarters of an hour of sunlight daily is sufficient to meet their body's needs. That is, to control calcium and phosphorous levels and distribution within the body. The rays responsible for the chemical process are largely filtered out by glass and plastic.

COST-EFFECTIVE GADGETS
Time switches can be used to turn the lights on or off automatically, while a dimmer in the circuit will gradually alter their intensity. This allows darkness to fall gradually so the birds can settle down to roost, as would occur in the wild, rather than being plunged into sudden darkness. Similarly, when the lights are turned on, the reverse occurs. Refined dimmers incorporate a light sensor, and react to natural daylight as a result. They are positioned on a window, and will only turn on the artificial illumination when the external light intensity falls below a certain level. Therefore, in spite of their increased cost, units of this type can actually reduce electrical costs, as well as improve the birds' environment.

SAFETY FIRST
In many places electrical regulations require an earth leakage trip switch to be fitted to installations external to the normal house wiring. It is sensible, therefore, to seek professional assistance to sort out the electrical matters, if in any doubt whatsoever. Apart from the obvious danger of electrocution, bird-room fires resulting from electrical faults are not unknown. All wiring must be kept out of the birds' reach, and along with the equipment itself, should be covered by a mesh cage if located inside the aviary.

FINISHING TOUCHES
The interior of the structure can be lined with oil-tempered hardboard or thin plywood. Protect any exposed edges in aviaries for parrots, since such materials can be rapidly destroyed. It is safe to use light-coloured emulsion paint to cover the chosen lining. Once dried, the surface can be wiped over with a damp cloth quite safely, without fear of warping. If particularly messy birds are being kept, plain light tiling is worth considering, because although relatively expensive, it will be simple to keep clean.

Outside guttering is useful to remove rainwater running off the shelter, and it can be connected to a suitable water-butt. Translucent plastic sheeting will need to be fixed for at least 90 cm (3 ft) on the roof and sides of the flight, extending from the shelter outwards on to the flight, to give the birds some protection in bad weather. Even for hardy stock, it is sensible to cover a large area during the winter, taking care not to reduce the ventilation excessively. A framework of 25 mm (1 in) square timber, made to fit inside the flight frame panels, should be clad with plastic sheeting. Catches can be installed as required to keep these protective frames in place. Then it is possible to move them in and out when necessary, without difficulty.

CAGES IN THE BIRDROOM
Flight cages for all birds are generally constructed on similar lines to the outside flight, although the timber need not be treated with a preservative. Breeding cages are also likely to be required in the birdroom; these can be used for housing birds outside the breeding season. Such cages are normally arranged on a tiered basis, raised some distance off the ground to facilitate cleaning.

A slightly different approach is now being used increasingly to breed parrots indoors in cages. This system may be particularly useful in urban areas, as the birds' harsh calls can be masked by the

building itself. Cages constructed from mesh, held together with clips, are favoured for the purpose, but the dimensions of the mesh across the base of the cages should be as wide as possible, so that droppings and seed husks fall through on to the floor beneath. Parrot droppings tend to be rather tenacious, and readily stick on to mesh, making cleaning difficult. The cages usually rest on a wooden frame.

The same design has also been used on a larger scale out-of-doors, to provide suspended aviaries. Since the parrots cannot come into contact with the ground, they are less likely to succumb to parasitic worm infestations and, in theory, diseases. Yet in view of their larger dimensions, aviaries of this type frequently prove very hard to clean, with feathers and other debris rapidly accumulating on the false floor. Replacing perches can also prove difficult, and the overall stability of the structure may be a cause for concern, particularly in areas where high winds can be anticipated. The sides under the flight will need to be covered in with plywood, in order to exclude vermin attracted to spilt seed, and cats, which will undoubtedly scare the birds.

CONSERVATORY AVIARIES

An aviary built within a conservatory can be made very attractive with suitable plants and, when heated, provide a useful means of overwintering the more delicate species in a relatively large area. A flight built within the conservatory can be dismantled in the following spring if required. The main drawbacks of this environment, however, include the likelihood of excessive temperature differences arising between daytime and night, as well as the high humidity which may be generated therein during the colder months of the year, resulting in widespread condensation on the glass.

The system of opening windows described on page 31, as well as air vents included in the structure will help to counteract some of these difficulties. In addition, painting the panes of the roof white and perhaps the sides as well, will deflect some of the sun's energy, lessening the heat build-up in the structure during summer. It should also reduce the risk of the birds being disturbed by cats on the roof of the conservatory. Scrupulous hygiene is vital, because moulds soon develop under conditions of relatively high humidity.

ALTERNATIVE OPTIONS

Both birdrooms and aviary shelters can be made of brick or blockwork, but these will prove more costly than a timber structure. In addition, construction is likely to require the assistance of skilled labour, and may be more protracted. During both summer and winter, the temperature within the building will be cooler than in an equivalent wooden structure, which could necessitate additional heating costs. Nevertheless, in tropical areas, where termites frequently attack woodwork and the relatively inert nature of the materials is actually advantageous in lowering the internal temperature, brick or blockwork construction may well be considered desirable.

ALUMINIUM FRAMEWORK

Aviary manufacturing firms, especially in mainland Europe, have produced several ranges of flights, and whole aviary systems based on an aluminium framework. These look most attractive, but are relatively costly in the first instance. Nevertheless, they need virtually no maintenance, and have a long potential lifespan. However, aluminium is a soft metal, easily damaged by a parrot's beak. Evidence from the United States indicates that regular

ingestion of aluminium particles over a period of time is harmful, and may be responsible for feather-plucking in some parrots. If there is a risk of such birds being able to damage the framework an **alternative option is preferable**, even if it appears more rustic.

TIMBER DESIGNS

Among the various timber designs produced commercially, are relatively small, octagonal structures, which have become much more popular during recent years. Birds housed in such accommodation are far more exposed to the elements than those kept in a trad-itional rectangular structure with an attached shelter. If a model of this type is chosen, it is vital therefore, especially during the cold winter months, that adequate protection is provided, in the form of plastic sheeting covering the majority of the aviary's sides.

A greenhouse aviary can be very attractive, and breeding results with many species of softbill are likely to be better in surroundings which offer more cover, and also encourage insects. Ensure that the plants are suitable for the birds, and do not overcrowd the aviary, if both plants and birds are to thrive.

An octagonal aviary with a shelter attached. This will be suitable for small seedeaters, but should be in a sheltered location. Plants will create a natural setting for the birds, but will require watering.

FEEDING GUIDELINES

A balanced diet

Cereals and seeds

Grit and cuttlefish

Greenfood and fruit

Softfoods

Pellets and livefood

Nectar and colour foods

In aviculture, birds are divided into various groupings on the basis of their feeding habits. The majority of species, typically finches and parrots, are classified as seedeaters or hardbills; others are categorized as softbills, so emphasizing that they do not subsist essentially on seed. Within the general terms of this latter description, there are further sub-divisions. For example, there are the *nectivores* (including hummingbirds and sunbirds), and the *frugivores*, such as fruitsuckers and toucans.

Although these categories provide useful guidelines for the dietary needs of the various species concerned, they are misleading if interpreted too literally. Finches, for instance, consume not only seeds, but other items such as insects and greenfood, particularly during the breeding season. Nectivores also require insects to keep them in good health, while no bird could survive on a diet of fruit alone, as the bald description of "frugivore" might imply.

A BALANCED DIET

The individual needs of particular species are discussed in Chapter 8. However, the guidelines below and the detailed tables on p. 38, will enable you to provide a balanced, healthy diet for all your birds. Cereals generally contain a relatively high proportion of carbohydrate. When this has been split down into glucose, it is used to meet the body's energy requirements. The protein levels of these seeds are quite low, and while this may not be so crucial outside the breeding season, protein is required in larger amounts when the cells of the body are actively synthesizing, during reproductive and growth phases, as well as in the moulting period.

Proteins are complex molecules, comprised of individual amino-acid residues. Some of these cannot be synthesized in the body and therefore must be present in the diet if a deficiency is not to occur. Animal protein generally contains higher levels of these essential amino-acids than does plant protein.

This is why many seedeaters become omnivorous during the breeding season, often consuming large numbers of insects.

Fat provides an efficient means of storing excess carbohydrate, as well as having important functions in its own right. For example, it helps to protect the body organs against traumatic injury. At a microscopic level, fatty compounds are vital ingredients of individual cell walls, preventing a potentially disastrous breakdown of their membranes. However, excessive dietary fat can have serious consequences for birds, and certain species are particularly prone to obesity. Even so, the relative level of fat is increased in the diet of some birds living outside during cold winters, to help them maintain their body temperatures. Fat provides a very concentrated source of energy for this purpose. Hemp seed (*Cannabis sativa*) is typically added in larger quantities to the seed mixture given to Australian parakeets and the Cockatiel for this reason, especially if the birds are not being offered sunflower seed.

CEREALS

Millets can be recognized easily in a seed mixture; they are always round and vary in colour from yellow through to red. The various strains of these grasses are grown in most warmer regions of the world. Generally, the smaller varieties such as panicum, sold either loose or as sprays, are preferred by birds to larger types such as Pearl White. Giving birds a mixture of millets will help to compensate for potential nutritional shortcomings that may be present in seed

which is grown in one particular area.

This advice also applies to canary seed (*Phalaris canariensis*), which is another cereal crop produced commercially in countries as far apart as Canada, North Africa and Australia. This seed is always oval in shape and light brown in colour. It may be confused with paddy rice, which is sometimes fed to larger seedeaters such as Java Sparrows and certain parrots. However, paddy rice is broader, yellower and has distinct striations along its length. Oats are cylindrical in shape, and, with the husks removed, are known as groats. These can be fed to many birds.

The other cereal seed of major significance as bird food is maize. The yellow form is particularly valuable as a source of Vitamin A. It is frequently given to newly-imported and young psittacines, having first been boiled until it is soft. Maize can be offered in its dry state only to larger parrots which will be able to crack this hard seed. In the form of kibbled (coarsely ground) maize, it also features in some pigeon mixtures.

SUNFLOWER SEED

The high vegetable oil content of sunflower seed is important to commercial growers, as this is a vital ingredient for margarine production. For the birds, the protein content is equally significant, and for this reason, white sunflower seed is preferable. It has a relatively high level of protein, and less fat than either the striped or black

varieties. Unfortunately, the yield of white sunflower is lower, so that it is correspondingly more expensive. The outer casing of striped sunflower seed varies in size, but the kernel within is fairly consistent in this respect, so that purchasing larger grades is often false economy, since it simply means that there will be more husk wasted.

GROUNDNUTS

Sunflower seed is the major ingredient of parrot seed mixtures. Among other seeds of this type which may be included are peanuts, also known as groundnuts. These can be obtained in their shells, or as loose kernels. However, a fungus may develop on their surface, if the kernels become damp, and its toxins will have lethal effects in the body (of both birds and humans), particularly on the liver. For this reason, peanuts sold in health food stores for human consumption are probably the safest option. They can be added to sunflower seeds in small quantities as required. Salted peanuts should *not* be offered to birds, because of their high salt content.

Avian diet
From the top: peanuts, millet, rape, sunflower seed and mixed cereals.

OTHER SEEDS

The majority of seeds used as bird food are cultivated, but pine nuts are harvested from the wild, and consequently supplies can be irregular. Since being introduced to the market during the 1970s by specialist seed merchants however, the problems with supply now appear to have been eradicated. Large grade pine nuts are most suitable for the bigger psittacines. The smaller type, originating from China can be offered to stout-billed finches, such as hawfinches, as well as to parrots. Pine nuts are considerably cheaper than larger nuts and compare favourably with sunflower seed in this respect. Their protein content is also superior. The other small oil seed often included in parrot mixtures is safflower, which is white rather than brown in colour. This is grown in the

VITAMINS: FUNCTIONS AND SOURCES

VITAMINS	FUNCTIONS	SOURCES
Vitamin A	Protects mucous membranes against infections, such as candidiasis.	Seed contains only low levels. Provide seedeaters with carrot and greenstuff, and use a supplement as directed. Vitamin A is stored in the liver, so deficiencies will not become immediately apparent.
Vitamin B Complex	Important in the metabolism of foodstuffs, and thus for growth and healthy plumage. Deficiency of thiamine (Vitamin B1) can cause nervous disorders.	Sprouting seeds are a valuable source of B vitamins, as are yeast-based products. Some B vitamins are synthesized by intestinal bacteria, notably folic acid and Vitamin B12. Excessive use of antibiotics can have a harmful effect on the synthesis of these vitamins.
Vitamin C	Helps to ensure a healthy skin, and protects against infections.	The vast majority of birds synthesize their own vitamin C. The known exception is the Red-eared Bulbul (*Pycnonotus jocosus*), and possibly some other frugivorous species which normally obtain supplies from fruit. This vitamin is normally included in most supplements, so deficiencies are unlikely to arise.
Vitamin D3	Essential for the mobilization and movement of calcium stores around the body, in conjunction with phosphorus.	Naturally synthesized by the ultra-violet component of sunlight falling on the feathers. Birds need the D3 form, which can be given artificially in a supplement. It is also possible to obtain 'natural lights', which serve to replace the role of sunlight.
Vitamin E	Popularly regarded as important for fertility, but this is not proven in the case of birds. It plays a role in metabolism and growth.	Can be supplied in the form of wheat germ oil, or as part of a food supplement.
Vitamin K	A vital role in the blood clotting process.	Synthesized by intestinal bacteria, but now available quite widely in an artificial form. Appears to be vital for certain birds, notably the fig parrots, (*Psittaculirostris* and *Opopsitta* species) and possibly the *Bolborhynchus* parakeets from South America.

United States, Australia and China.

The following seeds are generally too small for psittacines, but feature prominently in the diets of finches, notably canaries. Rape seed forms a major ingredient of seed mixtures for these birds; the red variety of rape seed is commonly used in this way. Black rape is usually soaked prior to feeding. A third type, German Rubsen rape, is traditionally offered to singing canaries, such as roller fancy birds. Canaries are wasteful feeders though, and often seem to ignore linseed or flax seed present in a mixture. This is brown in colour, elliptical and flat in shape.

TONIC SEEDS

The other oil seeds are essentially tonic seeds, usually fed to birds at particular times of the year. For example, niger is highly valued for feeding to hens immediately prior to the breeding season, since it is thought to reduce the risk of egg-binding. This thin, black seed is grown over the Indian sub-continent. Teasel seed is often recommended as a rearing food for the chicks. Blue maw, a small, bluish seed derived from poppies is popular for weaning purposes, encouraging the young birds to start feeding on their own.

FEEDING SEEDS

Various seed mixtures are marketed, but it is also possible to purchase the individual components. To reduce wastage, some breeders offer the different seeds in separate pots, as this allows the birds to make their own choice. All seed used must be as clean as possible, that is, free from dirt, dust and animal droppings. Contaminated or mouldy seed is especially likely to lead to illness and even death. Only samples which meet these criteria, and flow freely through the hands, showing no signs of fodder mites, should be purchased. Even so, it is impossible to assess the actual feeding value of seed by sight.

Reliable seed merchants advertise in most avicultural journals, and may despatch larger orders by road or rail, while sending smaller quantities by post. Discounts on whole bags are also offered by many pet stores, who will sometimes take birds in exchange for seed. However, their range of seed tends to be more limited.

SOAKED SEED

This is a valuable addition to a diet comprised largely of dry seed. Having been stimulated to germinate, its protein levels will have risen and it is more easily digestible. To prepare soaked seed, simply take a small quantity of seed and immerse it in a bowl of hot water, then leave it to stand for about 24 hours. Next, tip the seed into a sieve and wash it very thoroughly before feeding it to the birds. As an alternative, it can be encouraged to sprout by being spread out on damp blotting paper or tissues and placed in a warm environment. Various pulses, such as mung beans, can be offered similarly. Whether sprouting seeds or pulses always rinse them thoroughly under running water before feeding them to birds.

Only a limited amount of seed should be soaked or sprouted at any time, because it provides an ideal medium for the growth of moulds and fungi. Most fanciers prepare sufficient for a day, offering it in the morning and then taking the container out in the evening after feeding. Soaked millet is a very popular rearing food for many finches, but there is no reason why such seed cannot be fed throughout the year, to benefit the birds.

GRIT

Seedeaters require an adequate supply of grit, to assist in the breakdown of hard seeds present in their gizzards. By pulverizing the seeds in the acid medium of this organ, and preventing the grains from becoming stuck together, grit allows the digestive enzymes access to a large surface area of the food. The complex components present in the seed are thus broken down into relatively simple substances such as individual amino-acid residues. These can then be absorbed through the wall of the small intestine.

The grit ingested by seedeaters falls into two basic categories: insoluble flint-type grits remain for a relatively long time in the gizzard. More soluble lime-stone grits, such as oystershell, break down quite quickly. These can act as a source of minerals for the bird. Crushed charcoal, recognizable as black pieces of a lighter texture, is added to grit as it is thought to offer some protection against digestive upsets.

CUTTLEFISH BONE

In conjunction with phosphorus, calcium is an important mineral, particularly during the breeding season. It forms the major part of the eggshells and ensures that the chicks have a healthy bone structure. Deficiencies may become manifest by a relatively large number of soft-shelled eggs, or subsequent skeletal weaknesses in chicks which hatch from normal eggs.

Cuttlefish bone is widely used throughout the world to supplement the calcium intake of seedeaters. It can be obtained from seed merchants, or simply picked up on a beach, depending on the location and time of year. Such bones can vary from only a few centimetres in length to over 45 cm (18 in) in Australia, but their size is not really significant. The cuttlefish bones must be uncontaminated by oil, however, and thoroughly cleaned before being offered to the birds.

PREPARATION

Any remnants of flesh adhering to the bone should be cut off. This is a smelly task, so do it at the beach if you can. Back at home, scrub the bones with a clean brush, then leave them to soak in clean water for a week or so, before drying them out completely. Use the oven for this purpose, if necessary. Once dried, they will keep indefinitely, whereas the feeding value of seed falls off progressively in storage over the course of several years.

Cuttlefish bones should be given to

the birds with the softer, powdery side readily accessible. It is often advisable to scrape off chunks into a seed pot using a sharp knife, as some finches find it difficult to gnaw at a whole bone. They may otherwise become deficient, even though a supply of calcium is available. The eggshells of domestic hens used to be provided instead of cuttlefish, but there is a significant risk of introducing disease via such shells, even if they are heated in an oven beforehand.

Another important mineral source, an iodine nibble, can be purchased with seed. It is particularly vital for budgerigars, which are prone to iodine deficiency, resulting in an enlarged thyroid gland, described as a goitre.

GREENFOOD

The provision of some form of greenfood on a daily basis will be of great benefit to most birds, including certain softbills. Chickweed (*Stellaria media*) is a particular favourite of many species, especially when it is young and leafy. Seeding grasses of all types are popular, and a sunny area of a garden will support a small crop of cereal seeds. Seedheads can be offered to the birds in an unripened condition or left to mature and then harvested.

In Britain, seed sown about September generally yields the best results, as it can develop a good root system before the maximum growth period in the following spring and early summer. Rows should be spaced about 23 cm (9 in) apart, with a distance between individual plants of approximately 12 mm (½ in). The seed can be sown slightly thicker than this however, and covered to a depth of approximately 12 mm (½ in), with the seedlings then being thinned out as required.

When grown under these conditions, the seed should be ripening well by July. Once the seedheads turn brownish, the whole stems should be cut and hung upside down in a dry environment, to complete the ripening process. Species such as weavers which build nests, will take full advantage of the stems whether they are provided with the seedhead attached, or removed.

PREPARATION

Lettuce has a bad reputation with some bird-keepers as it can cause digestive upsets, but small amounts of fresh crisp lettuce will do no harm. In terms of nutritive value however, dandelion leaves and cress are vastly superior. The latter can be grown easily indoors, and is thus useful for pet birds. It can prove difficult to obtain a supply of greenfood through the winter months. Cabbage of any kind is best avoided, since it contains a component which depresses the activity of the thyroid glands. This may adversely effect the whole of the bird's metabolism, especially if large quantities are fed. Spinach beet is a viable alternative however, being a hardy crop, easily raised from seed. Parrots in particular enjoy gnawing the thick stems of spinach beet.

A row of spinach can be cultivated in any garden, so an uncontaminated supply should be guaranteed. If possible, choose a strain containing low levels of oxalic acid, since this chemical can interfere with the body's absorption of calcium. Another vegetable of considerable value is the carrot, and there are varieties which contain high levels of Vitamin A. These are valuable, since the Vitamin A content of seed is generally low. Carrot can be provided either cut into pieces, or grated for smaller birds. Fed daily it can help to maintain the colour of certain species, since it contains a natural colouring agent.

All greenfood should be washed off thoroughly before being used, in case it has been fouled by other animals or contaminated by chemicals. Roadside verges are likely to prove especially hazardous collecting sites, because the vegetation may also contain excessive amounts of lead from vehicle fumes, and over a period of time, this chemical will accumulate in the body. In addition, such locations are often treated with weedkillers, residues of which may remain with grass.

In the winter, frosted greens are probably best not fed until they have thawed out. Otherwise they may cause a severe chill in the digestive system.

During the breeding season, it is sometimes necessary to restrict the supply of greenfood to certain species such as zebra finches, which may use it to build on top of nests already in use. As an alternative, all greens can be cut into very small pieces on a chopping board to

overcome the problem. Apart from greenfood, the various types of fruit offered to softbills (see below) may also be taken by seedeaters, especially those living in a mixed collection.

FRUIT

A wide variety of both cultivated and wild fruits can be offered to softbills and other birds. Apples form the basis of many feeding mixtures, partly because of their ready availability throughout the year, and relatively cheap price. Eating varieties are preferable to the more bitter cooking apples. All fruit should always be washed before feeding, and apples and similar fruits are often peeled for fear of chemical residues present on the surface.

As a source of essential nutrients, fruit tends to be very low in protein, with no fat and only small amounts of vitamins, while containing a high proportion of water. Even the frugivorous softbills therefore, require more than fruit to keep them in good health. Larger softbills, such as toucanets, can be fed whole stoned fruits such as grapes and cherries, as the birds will void these seeds without difficulty. However, it is generally easier to remove stones, especially if the fruit has to be diced, which is necessary in the majority of cases.

Banana is not popular with many softbill keepers, on the grounds that it is sticky and excessively fattening. But this view is not borne out by analysis of the fruit. Perhaps more significantly, bananas are generally ripened artificially, and this may affect their digesti-

bility when fed to the more delicate species. Nevertheless, providing the fruit is not excessively ripe, it can be fed quite safely to many softbills (apart from the smaller ones, perhaps) as part of a mixture. The chemical changes which accompany ripening are likely to render fruit of all kinds, especially pears, a hazard once they start turning soft.

There can be considerable variation in birds' preferences. Tomatoes, fed in limited amounts, are usually popular with toucans, and provide a valuable source of Vitamin C. Apricots are often another particular favourite of these birds and will also be consumed whole by the larger species. Out of season, apricots can be purchased in a dried state from health-food stores. Soak them overnight and give them a thorough rinse, before adding them to a mixture of fruit. Because of their higher calorific value, which may be three times that of the fresh fruit itself, other dried fruits, especially currants and sultanas are fed in a similar manner, mainly during the winter months, to birds living in outdoor accommodation.

SOFTFOODS

Softfoods of many kinds are prepared commercially for both seedeaters and softbills. Some aviculturists still prefer their own recipes, but these are time-consuming to prepare and probably have little advantage over packeted mixtures. Softfood is generally fed to

seedeaters only when they are breeding and contains a relatively high level of protein, including some of animal origin. A few brands require mixing with water, while others can be fed direct from the packet. Commercial egg-food with its high protein content is used primarily for canaries, but is also beneficial for finches if they will accept it.

The majority of softfoods are intended to form the basis of many softbills' diets. They are often graded accordingly, the finer brands being offered to the smaller species. Most birds appear to develop a taste for a particular variety, so changes to the diet should be gradual. The ingredients of such foods do vary, but most generally contain a mixture of dried insects, meat and bone meal, along with powdered biscuit and flour mixed with honey.

The manner in which these softbill mixtures are fed to the birds will vary according to the species concerned. Most starlings, including mynah birds, soon adapt to taking softfood loose on its own whereas other species, such as those which are predominantly frugivorous, will require this food to be well-mixed with their fruit. If wholemeal bread soaked in a 50:50 mixture of milk and water is offered, either as a rearing food or to largely nectivorous species such as sugar birds, then the softbill mixture can be sprinkled on top.

PELLETS

In America particularly, mynah pellets are popular, being used for a variety of softbills. Indeed, in the case of toucans and related species which cannot eat loose insectivorous mixtures because of their feeding habits, such pellets are an essential addition to the diet.

Although softbill pellets can be fed dry, it is preferable to soak them in sufficient water to just cover the desired amount, for up to an hour before feeding. They will swell considerably in size, but should not break up and disintegrate, if handled carefully. Any remaining water must be drained before mixing the pellets in with fruit. Soaking is advisable because there is evidence to suggest that similar complete foods fed dry to dogs and cats may be hazardous, especially if there is any impairment of kidney function, and insufficient water is available. These diets can also be used in a similar way for birds, if mynah pellets are unavailable. Some brands prove much more palatable than others.

Pelleted diets are also produced for seed-eating birds, but initially they are not often taken readily. Hand-reared parrots however, will be more likely to sample such foodstuffs. In some cases, both maintenance and breeding pellets are marketed, the latter containing a higher level of protein. These products offer a more balanced diet than one comprised of seed alone, but can prove wasteful, if the birds develop a taste for crushing the pellets rather than eating them. Initially, mixing pellets in with the seed should encourage the birds to sample this unfamiliar food.

ANIMAL PROTEIN

As suggested earlier, animal protein in some form must be offered to all softbills, as well as to many seedeaters. At one extreme, certain hornbills require a large intake of such food. Other species such as mynahs, which are more omnivorous, readily accept livefood and minced meat as part of their diet. Even the most frugivorous barbets will take animal protein if it is offered, as do other species commonly classed as "fruiteaters".

The erroneous belief that feeding meat to softbills will turn them savage, as quoted even in contemporary works, is a fallacy. Lean, raw minced beef is of value for predominantly carnivorous species. The free-flow type of mince sold in certain supermarkets is preferable, because the pieces do not stick together, and so there is much less wastage. It also appears more acceptable to birds. Indeed, an imported pair of red-billed hornbills which refused ordinary mince took to this alternative form readily, as they could pick out individual pieces, rather than solid, sticky chunks.

Raw minced beef heart can be added to the diet as well, but also needs to be fed in moderation. It is favoured because of its relatively low fat content, but can predispose to a Vitamin B deficiency, and like mince, has a significantly raised calcium:phosphorus ratio, of the order 1:60, instead of the required 1:1. Other useful meats include cooked lamb and chicken cut into small pieces. Some softbills may even take canned dog or cat food, whereas parrots will often gnaw cooked bones in order to extract the marrow and obtain additional protein.

CHICKS AND SMALL RODENTS

The natural diet of bigger species of softbill, such as red-billed magpies, often include chicks and small rodents. Dead animals of this type provide the birds with essential nutrients and roughage. Chicks and rodents can be purchased loose or in packs from specialist suppliers, or hatcheries which produce surplus chicks. If deep-frozen, they must be allowed to thaw out completely before being fed to the birds, and never re-frozen. Day-old mice, known as "pinkies" because of their naked appearance, are especially popular due to their relatively small size.

INVERTEBRATES

The choice available will depend to some extent on the area concerned. In Australia for example, white ants (termites) can be gathered in certain areas, whereas fruit flies are outlawed as pests in many agricultural regions. It is possible to collect quite large numbers of insects by dragging a muslin net through undergrowth, especially during the summer months. The net can then be placed in the aviary with its purse-string top loosened, so the birds will be able to help themselves. Vegetation in the aviary itself also serves to encourage insects, particularly valuable for birds which normally "hawk" their food on the wing. These, including flycatchers, are usually the hardest species to transfer to artificial diets. Such traps also provide a useful means of supplementing the large insect intake required at breeding time by all softbills. However, most softbill keepers do need to rely on commercial supplies of various insects, which are outlined below in alphabetical order, with their breeding requirements where applicable.

CRICKETS

Crickets (*Gryllus domesticus*) have only become more widely-available to aviculturists in recent years, but they are generally cheaper than locusts as live food and considered less difficult to maintain satisfactorily. Crickets do need to be kept warm however, in a temperature between 21-27°C (70-80°F). For short-term storage, they can be kept in similar surroundings to mealworms (*see p.44*). For breeding purposes, they should be transferred to an aquarium tank with a suitable hood, or special locust-type glass-fronted cages, heated by means of a lamp. A variety of greenfood, especially grass, as well as apple and flour, will form the basis of their diet. Their housing should include a shallow dish of water to help to maintain the humidity at about 70 per cent.

The females, which can be recognized by their larger abdomens, lay eggs in pots of damp sand or peat. This should be at least 10 cm (4 in) deep. The eggs are kept in a temperature of 27°C (80°F), and must be sprayed daily to prevent them from drying out. They should then hatch after about a fortnight. The young crickets, known as instars, undergo five successive moults before they, in turn, commence breeding at the age of just over six weeks. There is a tendency for older crickets to eat their younger offspring, which should therefore be separated off if possible. Hatchling crickets, barely one millimetre in length, can provide useful variety in the diets of nectivores.

FRUIT FLIES

Fruit flies (*Drosophilia*) are tiny insects bred in either winged or vestigial winged forms. They are essential for the smaller nectivores such as hummingbirds and sunbirds, and ideally should be provided in a conservatory or glass-fronted cage from which they cannot escape. Alternatively, the flies may be kept in a jam jar, with holes in its lid through which they will gradually emerge, to be caught by the birds.

A culture is simply started by leaving banana skins in an old coffee jar outside in the summer. The skins will attract the flies, and once the larvae are seen the top should be placed on the jar. Subsequently, a week after pupation, the adult flies will emerge. Some can then be transferred to other jars to start new cultures. Banana skins are preferred to other fruit, because they remain relatively dry, and so can be removed and replaced as necessary. The flies breed well in a temperature of about 23°C (72°F) feeding off the skins, although supplementary mixtures of sugar and yeast are often provided in laboratories, where fruit flies are popular subjects for genetic research.

HONEY BEE LARVAE

Although not widely used, and not available commercially, bee larvae (*Apis mellifera*) have proved especially valuable for breeding softbills. Used in the hand-rearing of delicate species such as fly-catchers, their Vitamin D level is approximately ten times more than that of cod-liver oil and they have a relatively low fat content, compared to similar foods such as mealworms. In addition, bee larvae are easily digestible, possessing a very soft cuticle.

Collecting them can be time-consuming however, and may weaken the productivity of a bee colony, especially if it is carried out on a regular basis. Having removed the frames containing larvae from the hive, the capping of the cell must be cut off with a knife. Immersing the combs in chilled water beforehand for a short time will help. Then each larva can be removed with forceps. It may be possible to dislodge more at one time by hitting the edge of the frame against a block, with a suitable catchment area in front, or running the comb under a jet of water.

The best time to remove larvae is between ten and 11 days before they are sealed in the comb by the worker bees. It is certainly easier to collect them at this stage, but a considerable weight loss will result. This may total nearly 100 g (4 oz) per comb. Although such larvae are only available during the spring and summer, and should be fed fresh if possible, they can be stored frozen for later use. No special preparation is needed.

LOCUSTS

Locusts require very similar accommodation and management to crickets, the young in this case being known as "hoppers". First stage instars emerge from the egg after ten days and will breed when approximately two months old. Some mortality will occur in the young locusts however; one study suggests only one-third may survive to reproduce in a colony. If the creatures and their droppings turn red they may be affected with *Nosema*, a unicellular parasite found predominantly in the gut. All livefood containers must be cleaned out thoroughly between batches, which is an advantage of using plastic containers. Check there is sufficient ventilation to prevent condensation.

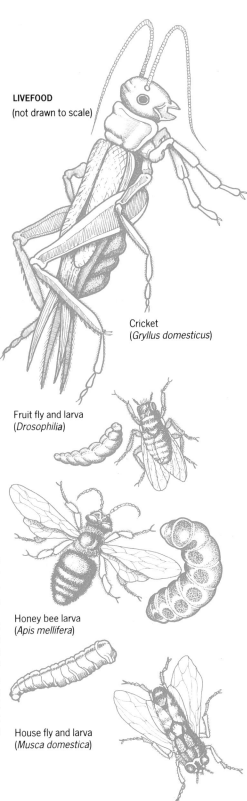

LIVEFOOD
(not drawn to scale)

Cricket
(*Gryllus domesticus*)

Fruit fly and larva
(*Drosophilia*)

Honey bee larva
(*Apis mellifera*)

House fly and larva
(*Musca domestica*)

MAGGOTS

Housefly (*Musca domestica*) and Blowfly (*Calliphora erythrocephala*) larvae are suitable for feeding to many birds, but the risk that they could transmit botulism, which is usually fatal, must never be overlooked. A minimum of three days should be allowed for cleansing, by transferring the maggots to bran (not sawdust, which could be dressed with potentially harmful wood preservatives). This minimum period should enable the larvae to empty their guts of the rotting meat on which they feed.

Since maggots can be purchased without difficulty from bait shops, and in view of their unpleasant breeding habits, most people prefer not to set up a culture for these flies. In a warm environment however, the life-cycle is relatively fast. The maggots often emerge as rapidly as 24 hours after the eggs were laid, and grow to their maximum size before pupation in a fortnight. Adult flies emerge approximately five days after the maggots pupate, and can also be fed to the birds.

MEALWORMS

The mealworm (*Tenebrio molitor*) is simply the larval stage in the life-cycle of the Meal Beetle and is not, in fact, a worm. Mealworms are probably the most widely-used livefood for birds, being freely available and without the unpleasant characteristics of maggots. Their life-cycle is much longer however, with newly-hatched larvae taking four months, at a temperature of 25°C (76.5°F), to develop into mature laying beetles.

As a food source, too, mealworms are not without drawbacks. Their chitin external covering is relatively indigestible. For this reason, moulting mealworms which appear white rather than yellowish-brown, are strongly recommended for the smallest finches and softbills.

The feeding value of mealworms depends on their own diet. This may only consist of bran in many cases, in which case, the mealworms will be deficient in calcium, and have an imbalanced calcium:phosphorus ratio of the order 1:2. Bran also contains a component called phytic acid, which is a chelating agent responsible for binding calcium and thus reduces even further the availability of this vital mineral. For the same reason, wholemeal flour is not recommended as an additional source of calcium. White flour, which has this chemical added by law in Britain, should be mixed with the bran.

Apart from being low in calcium, mealworms are considered to be a poor source of essential fatty acids which, like the corresponding amino-acids, cannot be manufactured in the body. They may also be deficient in certain vitamins, particularly Vitamin A. Thus it is recommended that a vitamin and mineral supplement, in powder form, should be added to their food.

A variety of containers can be used to house mealworms successfully, provided that they are escape-proof, with a lid, and yet ventilated satisfactorily. Empty plastic ice-cream containers, with small holes punched in the lid, make ideal storage or breeding quarters as the mealworms will not be able to climb the sides. The bran mixture should be sprinkled in the bottom to a depth of several centimetres, and a small quantity of oats added to the surface. Chicken meal can be used in place of the more traditional bran, and will provide a more balanced diet. Slices of apple will be consumed by the mealworms, and also serve to increase the humidity.

If the atmosphere becomes too dry, cannibalism will commonly occur. The mealworms' growth overall will be restricted, although not their food intake, at a relative humidity of 13 per cent. Research has shown that there may be a difference of as much as 50 mg in weight between mealworms kept at 30 per cent, compared with those living at 70 per cent relative humidity, which would appear to be the optimum level. Above this value, moulds become a problem in the containers. A hygrometer can be used to measure the level of humidity in the container if required.

For breeding purposes, the beetles should be placed in a container, in a temperature of about 25°C (77°F), and left alone, apart from checking their food. Within six weeks, the young larvae should emerge from their eggs, and after a further three to four weeks, when about 25 mm (1 in) long, they can be fed to the birds. It is often difficult to collect the mealworms from a deep container of bran, particularly towards the end of a batch. Placing a soaked piece of hessian sacking on top of the medium about an hour beforehand will attract the mealworms upwards, provided the container is placed in the dark. Otherwise, the light will have a detrimental effect, encouraging the larvae to remain buried. If it is not intended to breed with them, lowering the temperature will ensure that the mealworms do not change to pupae before they can be used. Various sizes of mealworm are now marketed, including a giant form as well as small mini mealworms, and are generally quite widely available from livefood suppliers.

OTHER LIVE FOODS

Redworms (*Dendrobina rubica*), a popular coarse fishing bait, are also useful for smaller softbills such as sunbirds, which cannot cope with locusts or the larger crickets. If these worms are maintained in a sterile medium, such as peat, they can be fed quite safely without prior cleansing. Place the worms in a shallow box, and the birds will soon start picking them out, ensuring there is no wastage. In addition, if kept at a temperature of 5-10°C (40-50°F), the worms will live for weeks and are even appreciated by larger species such as hornbills.

However, there is a risk attached to feeding other similar invertebrates, since earthworms, as well as molluscs, are the natural intermediate hosts of various wild bird parasites, including gapeworm. These infections can be passed to aviary stock via live food. Subsequently they may prove very difficult to eradicate, necessitating regular and repeated treatment of the birds and their quarters. For this very good reason it is probably safer not to use earthworms, slugs or snails for feeding to aviary birds.

NECTAR MIXTURES

Considerable advances have been made in the field of avian nutrition during recent years, and nowhere is this more apparent than in the field of nectar substitutes. Complete ranges of diets, each geared to the specific needs of the birds concerned, are now quite widely available. These simply need to be mixed with water as directed.

Hummingbirds require a relatively high level of carbohydrate to meet their energy needs. Other nectivores, such as sunbirds or zosterops can manage with less carbohydrate. The protein level is significant in each case however, since there appears to be a correlation between high protein diets and gout, as explained on page 59. Some aviculturists prefer to prepare their own nectar solution, usually with honey or sugar as an energy source, dissolved with a human convalescent food in water. In some cases, pollen granules are also added to provide a source of natural vegetable protein. The granules are available from health food stores, and can be offered whole to parrots, being sprinkled over the surface of cut fruit.

Certain psittacines, notably the lories and lorikeets, as well as hanging parrots, naturally feed on pollen as well as nectar. Their tongues are adapted for this purpose. A fresh nectar solution should always be available to them, but does not substitute for drinking water. It is vital with all nectivores, but particularly these psittacines, that their diet is not changed suddenly. Otherwise, they may suffer the rapidly fatal gut disorder known as enterotoxaemia. In areas where bees are prevalent however, it may be preferable to substitute sugar for honey in a nectar mixture, over a period of time. Bees may cluster around a nectar feeder, and even sting the birds if they approach too closely.

COLOUR FOODS

It has long been recognized that many birds with areas of red or orange plumage tend to lose this coloration over the course of successive moults. Psittacines however, are a notable exception. Research has shown the paler plumage arose from the loss of carotenoid pigments, especially canthaxanthin. Supplementation with carrot juice used to be the most effective means of improving the birds' colour, and was supplied just prior to and during the moult, when the feathers receive a blood supply.

More effective synthetic carotenoid derivatives are now widely used by canary as well as foreign bird fanciers. By this means, it has proved possible to maintain the natural coloration of birds as diverse as flamingos, weavers and cocks-of-the-rock. Canthaxanthin is an extremely safe compound. However, if accidentally fed to excess, it will cause the birds' droppings to become tinged with red, while their plumage coloration will be distorted. But no long term harm will result. Prolonged overdosage can lead to a fat soluble vitamin deficiency. Studies undertaken at the Wildfowl Trust, Slimbridge in Gloucestershire, England on flamingos, which moult from April through to December, have shown that large amounts of the colour pigment are also lost via crop secretions to young birds. This may well apply to other species, also. Some aviculturists therefore prefer to feed the colouring agent in reduced amounts on a permanent basis. You can follow the directions given on the packet. Canthaxanthin is converted to the active chemicals astaxanthin and phoenicoxanthin at the site of feather development. Certainly in the case of flamingos, it has been shown that poor coloration leads to disappointing breeding results, although the reason for this is not clear at present. An interesting, but not necessarily significant, observation concerning trout, which are also colour-fed, is that they require an adequate level of carotenoids present in the diet to ensure fertility of their semen.

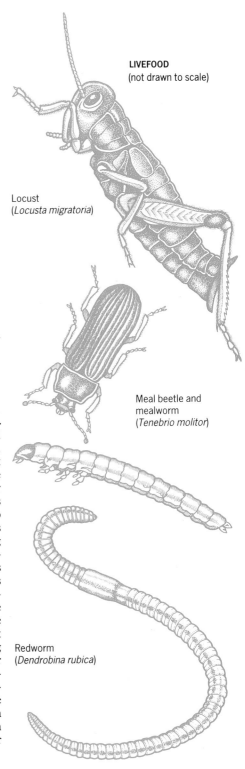

LIVEFOOD
(not drawn to scale)

Locust
(*Locusta migratoria*)

Meal beetle and mealworm
(*Tenebrio molitor*)

Redworm
(*Dendrobina rubica*)

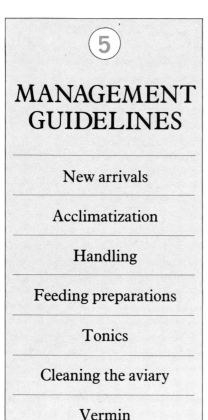

The birds will need regular, daily attention throughout the year. The amount of time required will vary, according to factors such as the species concerned, its feeding habits and the prevailing weather conditions. The birds' requirements will be greater during the breeding season, and in bad weather if they are living outside. Every aviculturist soon devises an individual routine for looking after stock.

NEW ARRIVALS

New birds should be kept in isolation for a fortnight, and preferably housed in individual quarters so that a check can be made on their health, appetite and food preferences. This applies particularly to recently imported stock. Sudden changes in diet should be kept to a minimum at this stage, especially in softbills. Otherwise, there can be an alteration of the bacteria in the gut, so that disease-causing strains may suddenly proliferate, when the bird is faced with this additional stress. It can also be advisable to deworm the birds at this stage, especially if they are Australian parakeets.

If there are no problems during the initial period, the birds can be released into their outdoor quarters as soon as the weather is favourable. If they are to be housed in a mixed aviary, their introduction should be monitored closely, taking place preferably at a week-end or when someone is likely to be close at hand. This will help to ensure that no injuries result from fighting.

The provision of adequate feeding stations is very important at this time, and extra containers should be added alongside new birds. Indeed, several pots positioned around the aviary are to be recommended as a matter of course, in case a dominant individual begins to monopolize a single food source. This behaviour can also apply to nectar and water containers.

Fighting is especially likely to develop during the breeding season, and so no introductions should be made at this time. Otherwise, the pre-existing peck-ing order in the community will be disturbed, and losses may extend to both eggs and chicks. Single birds are generally more likely to be bullied than pairs, and such persecution may develop following the loss of one member of a pair. If this occurs, the only option will be to remove the odd bird concerned, with the minimum of disturbance.

ACCLIMATIZATION

Some species are considered hardier than others, but this is only a relative difference, depending on the area concerned. Birds which may be kept safely in outside quarters during a mild winter will not necessarily be able to survive a prolonged spell of cold weather. The endurance of the bird should never be tested under such circumstances. The aim must always be to keep the bird comfortable. If there is any doubt, it is preferable to err on the side of caution and move the individual to warmer quarters for the duration of the winter.

Thought should be given to winter accommodation for a particular species before it is acquired. This will ensure that any necessary arrangements can be made in advance:

■ Heating in the aviary shelter is the simplest means of maintaining the temperature at about 10°C (50°F) for smaller birds, as discussed on page 32. They will need to be confined in their heated quarters at night, only being allowed out during the daytime when the weather is favourable.

■ Additional light will also be necessary, to allow them sufficient time to feed and thus maintain their body temperature. Approximately ten hours light in total each day will be adequate. The alternative to this system is to bring the birds indoors for the colder months of the year, preferably housing them in a large flight cage, if no birdroom is available.

Imported birds will require additional care with regard to acclimatization, and no species should be expected to over-winter successfully out-of-doors in northern latitudes unless established in their quarters by June at the latest. They should only be released into outside flights once the risk of frost and snow has passed. However, it is preferable to get imported birds outside as early as is safely possible. This will then give them adequate opportunity to adjust gradually to the vagaries of temperate climates during the most favourable part of the year.

A close watch should always be kept on birds in their first few weeks outside, especially after a heavy summer shower, as they may lack sufficient oil on their plumage to protect against waterlogging of the feathers. Oil is secreted from the preen gland at the base of the tail and spread during the preening process. Some birds are so delighted at the sight of rain that they soon become saturated to the extent that they cannot fly. Then, being deprived of the insulating effect of the layer of air trapped beneath their feathers, they rapidly chill. Spraying of birds housed indoors on a regular basis is useful in preventing this problem, if they do not choose to bathe themselves.

OVERWINTERING
While smaller softbills generally should not be expected to overwinter outside without heat, larger species may be kept in aviaries once acclimatized, if they how no signs of discomfort. Their diet should include:
■ An extra ration of meat and mealworms.
■ Cheese in small amounts, or even with macaroni is also useful at this time of year, since it contains a large proportion of fat, to protect against the cold.
■ Boiled potatoes and carrots can also be fed but often do not prove popular.

An additional threat in cold weather is the risk of frostbite. This can result in loss of toes in severe cases and thus may even cripple the bird. As a precaution, birds at risk should be confined to the aviary shelter at night, and boxes provided for species such as toucanets which prefer to roost in them. In a case of frostbite, the bird will be reluctant to perch on the affected foot and should be

brought into the warm immediately. At first, its limbs must be massaged every ten minutes or so in a bid to restore the circulation. If this fails, subsequent painless loss of the affected toes will occur about a fortnight later.

The likelihood of birds succumbing to frostbite is dramatically decreased if the sides of the aviary are sealed in with panels as suggested on page 33. This will help to overcome the wind-chill factor, which creates an artificially low temperature in its path.

CATCHING AND HANDLING
The method employed for catching the bird will be influenced by the species concerned and its immediate environment. It is obviously easier to catch by hand a finch in a cage, rather than in a planted aviary. In the latter instance, a deep padded net is most commonly used, although on a visit to Australia, I saw a popular and ingenious catching unit for finches.

The mechanism operates simply on the birds' weight, as they are attracted by the seed bait within a wire cup. This swings down when weight is applied, trapping the bird in the restraining cage below. The cup returns to its original

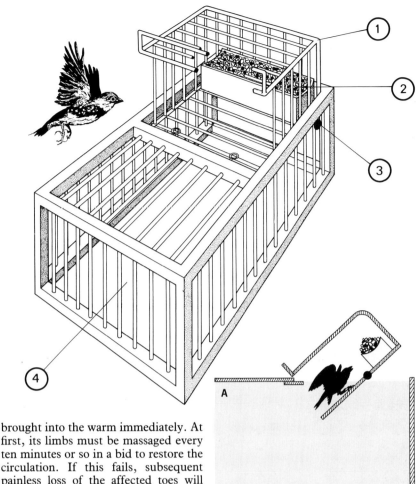

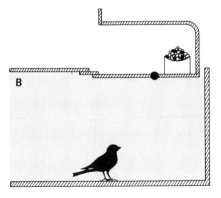

Catching a small bird
A The bird lands on a weighted seed container (**2**) causing the swing cage (**1**) to tip on its pivot (**3**). **B** The seed container returns to its original position, leaving the bird trapped in the restraining cage (**4**). This cage must be deep enough to allow the swing cage to continue operating, without hitting the captured bird.

position in readiness for another bird, and then the process is repeated. All other seed should be removed from the aviary beforehand, with the catching unit placed as close as possible to the usual main food source.

There is no guarantee that a particular bird will be caught at any time, but often several can be taken in succession. The major advantage of this method is that it eliminates the disturbance resulting from the use of a net. Birds can be caught either on the aviary wire or in flight with a suitable net but, even with padding around the rim, care must be taken not to injure the bird during this process.

If a bird shows obvious signs of distress, typically heavy breathing, it must be allowed to recover before another attempt is made to catch it. Being able to close the birds into their shelter, or confining them out in the flight of the aviary will prevent them from bobbing in and out, thwarting your efforts to catch them. It is also useful to take down any loose perches which will only be a hindrance. Larger softbills can often be caught directly by hand, without the need for a net.

Extra care will be needed when dealing with species which have relatively fragile yet prominent beaks. Notable for this are toucans and their allies, as well as hornbills, which may fly hard and directly at the aviary mesh when their aviary is entered with a net.

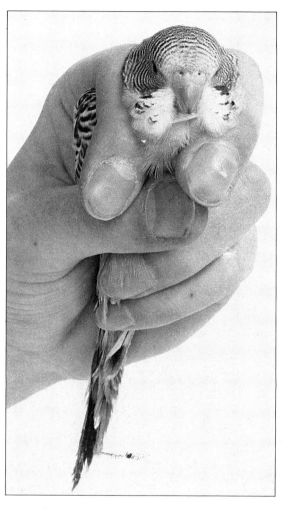

It is important to handle birds safely: the method used will depend to some extent on the species concerned. Restrained in this position, this young budgerigar will be unable to bite its handler. With large parrots, however, it would be advisable to wear gloves, in view of their more powerful beaks.

SAFETY IN HANDLING
Most finches and softbills are not capable of causing a severe bite. Nevertheless, some of the bigger species can inflict a painful nip or stab until they are effectively restrained. For this reason, they should never be held close to the handler's face, within pecking range, unless their beaks are also held carefully, but firmly:

■ Smaller finches can be restrained gently in the palm of the hand with their heads protruding between thumb and first finger.

■ For most softbills, and to allow a thorough examination of other birds, it is most convenient to hold them between the first two fingers of the appropriate hand, which is the left in the case of a right-handed person. Virtually the whole of the body is then accessible, while the bird itself often ceases struggling in this position, with the remaining fingers and thumb gently encircling the body. The grip around the neck must not be too tight however, because otherwise the bird is likely to suffocate.

■ Gloves will be essential when restraining most psittacines, in view of their powerful beaks.

FEEDING
Irrespective of their diet, the birds will need to be fed daily, in the shelter of their aviary. Seed can be provided in open pots placed within reach of perches, or in jam-jar type feeders which operate on a gravity-flow principle. The former means is more reliable, as there is no risk of an outlet becoming blocked, but the seed is likely to become fouled with droppings. Also, wastage is often increased, as the birds scatter the contents of the pot over the aviary floor. Nevertheless, using newspaper as a lining, it is possible to collect spilt seed.

Then, by means of a winnower, the chaff and other debris can be removed and the remaining good seed can be fed back to the birds, provided it is both dry and free from droppings.

Special hoppers are to be recommended for budgerigars, particularly hole-hoppers which allow the bird to insert its head to obtain food. Some designs of flow hopper are suitable for both budgerigars and other seedeaters. The advantage of using this type of feeder is that wastage is kept to a minimum.

SITING FEEDING DISHES

Softbills are fed from open pots or dishes. If these attach to the aviary mesh, then, as with seed containers, they should be located as near as possible to perches. Otherwise, more food will be scattered as the birds fly on to, or away from, the rim of the pot. Many birds are reluctant to eat from the ground if they can avoid doing so. Feed containers may need to be pegged for more mischievous softbills like mynahs,

as well as many parrots. These wily birds soon learn to unhook their pots so that they fall to the floor, scattering food everywhere.

Heavy earthenware bowls positioned on a washable tray stand cannot suffer the same fate. Furthermore, this type of structure prevents mealworms from escaping, and hiding in crevices around the aviary floor. Another advantage is that there is no risk of perishable food-stuffs becoming trapped behind wire netting, as can happen using hook-on food pots. However, this problem can be overcome by fixing long netting staples into a suitable piece of the wooden framework. If these are not driven in completely, the feeding containers can be hooked on to them.

CLOSED DRINKERS

These are widely used for finches, and as nectar containers for smaller softbills like zosterops, because they ensure a constant, uncontaminated supply. As an alternative, the special closed feeders

designed for hummingbirds can be provided for other small nectivores. Hook-on containers used for food can also serve as water receptacles for larger birds, but metal designs should not be provided as any chemicals in the water may react unfavourably with the metal. This type of open water vessel also enables the birds to bathe if they wish, while large-beaked species which could not drink successfully from narrow-tipped containers are able to do so without difficulty.

PONDS AND TRAYS

The provision of a shallow pond as a source of water in an aviary is an attractive alternative out-of-doors, if it can be drained and the water changed regularly without difficulty. The slope of the sides should be very gentle, so that not even the smallest bird is likely to drown in the water. For the same reason, no buckets of water should be left in a birdroom, as a means of increasing the humidity during the breeding season. If a bird

A wide variety of feeding and drinking vessels are available. The drinker and feeder shown are suitable for canaries.

escapes from its cage and accidentally falls into a bucket, it will be unable to get out again. Shallow trays are much safer. They also offer a much wider surface area for evaporation.

FEEDING PREPARATION

When feeding perishable foodstuffs it is vital that the utensils are washed thoroughly each day before being re-used. With species which only eat a relatively small amount of solid food, or when giving rearing foods, it may be easier to provide disposable containers. Clean yoghurt pots or the drink cups dispensed from machines, cut down close to their base, make very adequate receptacles and can be discarded after a single usage.

When washing pots, add a household detergent to the water to remove grease and superficial dirt. Then immerse them in a warm solution of disinfectant. The utensils should finally be rinsed off thoroughly using tap water, and allowed to drain. If they are to be dried, disposable paper towelling will help to prevent re-contamination.

The reason for the two-stage procedure is that many disinfectants do not work effectively in the presence of organic matter, or when mixed in cold water. A pair of rubber gloves is useful to prevent hands chapping and cracking as the pots will have to be washed on a regular basis. Bottle brushes are recommended for tubular nectar containers particularly, as they can remove all traces of the food material from the top of the vessel.

As far as possible, food must be prepared fresh, although a nectar solution mixed in the morning and kept in a refrigerator will be safe to feed that evening if allowed to warm up to room temperature beforehand. Nevertheless, the containers must be clean and never just topped up with a new solution, as this provides ideal conditions for bacterial and other harmful micro-organisms to become established.

In the case of a honey and convalescent food mixture, it is useful to blend these together in the bottom of a measuring jug with a little cold water, before adding a small quantity of hot water to dissolve the ingredients. Then top the solution up to the required level with cold water. Pollen granules will also dissolve successfully if added to the mixture from the outset. When prepared in this way, there is less tendency for the solid food component to separate out to the top of the mixture in the tube.

ADDING TONICS

A variety of tonics can be given via the food or water. Water-soluble preparations are commonly added to a nectar mixture or the drinking water. These serve to supplement the fat-soluble vitamin intake, especially of A and D_3 which are only present in low levels in seed. Vitamin A helps to prevent infection while Vitamin D_3 is important in controlling the calcium stores of the body. The Red-vented Bulbul and certain other frugivorous softbills cannot manufacture Vitamin C (ascorbic acid) so this must be supplemented also, using a suitable preparation, with fruit in their diet. Prolonged overdosage with tonics can have harmful side-effects, so it is better to give a small quantity if in doubt. The fat-soluble vitamins are stored in the liver, so a regular intake serves to augment and maintain this reserve.

Similar preparations are also available in powdered form, and can be given to seedeaters on greenfood or fruit. They tend not to adhere readily to dry seed, and so are likely to be wasted if administered in this way. Food supplements containing all the essential amino-acids, in addition to the usual vitamins and minerals found in tonics, are most valuable. Although quite expensive, they are particularly beneficial for parrots and other seedeaters which are reluctant to sample animal protein.

MODERN AIDS

A deep freezer is of great value when keeping softbills and parrots, as it enables fruit to be purchased in season at a relatively cheap price and then stored for use throughout the year. However, not all fruits freeze well in their natural state without special preparation. Some varieties of apples are better than others, and it is advisable to carry out a test with a small amount before purchasing a box of the same variety for freezing. The apples can be diced before freezing them to save time in preparing them at a later date. In many cases however, it is possible to store the apples in their natural state for some months, in a suitable cold environment, and these are more palatable than frozen apple.

Grapes are well-worth freezing, as out of season they tend to become prohibitively expensive. Only firm fruit should be selected and, after removing them from the stems, the grapes must be washed off and dried on a towel before being frozen. It can be useful to spread the grapes out on a tray in the freezer at first. They can then be packed in disused ice-cream containers or plastic bags, and since they will not be stuck together, any amount may be removed for thawing overnight as required. Other fruits can be treated in a similar way, including cherries and plums, and will give useful variety to the birds' diet throughout the year.

In a large birdroom, a food preparation area with a sink and hot water supply will be valuable. Even then, the daily washing of a large number of dishes can be quite a chore. With just six individual pairs of softbills, their water and food containers may well take one hundred hours per year to wash daily by hand! So the acquisition of a reliable second-hand dishwasher will be a welcome, if somewhat luxurious, acquisition. It is often possible to acquire a suitable machine for less than the cost of an individual bird, through a local newspaper. A further advantage of a dishwasher is that it will almost guarantee that the pots are sterilized by the heat of the water, and thoroughly rinsed.

AVIARY MANAGEMENT

The aviary must be cleaned out at least

weekly, and feeding in the shelter is always preferable in any aviary, since the majority of waste food will accumulate where it can be swept up and removed without difficulty. Newspaper is probably the best covering for this area, since it is relatively absorbent and easily replaceable. In addition, spilt seed can be recycled using a winnower as described on page 49.

Cleaning of the flight itself will also need to be frequent. Species such as lorikeets, mynahs and other large softbills produce copious droppings. In mixed aviaries where some birds spend a relatively large proportion of time on the floor, and certainly if quail or similar birds such as rail are included, the floor of the outside flight should be covered with a layer of peat. Droppings can be removed from from the peat as necessary by means of a trowel. Also, the abrasive action of sand particles in the concrete on the birds' feet, which can cause bumblefoot infections (*see p.58*), will be avoided. At intervals, the layer of peat should be scraped off, and the floor washed and disinfected. However, keep disturbances to an absolute minimum, if the birds are breeding.

LONG-ACTING DISINFECTANTS
Prior to disinfecting the concrete base of a flight, wash it as clean as possible. The chosen disinfectant, mixed in strict accordance with the manufacturer's instructions, should then be applied over the whole area. The synthetic group of phenolic disinfectants, based primarily on chloroxylenol and terpineol are useful for this purpose. Some brands retain their activity even where the environment is heavily contaminated with organic matter, and will be effective against a whole range of micro-organisms, from viruses and bacteria to moulds and fungi as well as parasitic worm eggs.

A disinfectant of this type will destroy the bacterium *Staphylococcus aureus*, which builds up in the environment and is the major cause of bumblefoot. Wash perches in softbill aviaries with this disinfectant if they are not changed at regular intervals. The birds' feeding habits cause debris to accumulate quickly, and can precipitate foot ailments. All surfaces exposed to disinfectant should be hosed off thoroughly afterwards, although this particular group of chemicals is considered relatively non-toxic.

AUTUMN CLEAN-OUT
It is preferable to clean and disinfect the aviary thoroughly in the autumn after the breeding season, in preparation for winter. Some bacteria such as *Yersinia* soon flourish under cold conditions in a dirty environment, and should be destroyed before they can do so. In a planted aviary, remove annuals and dead leaves and prune any bushes. Also, check the framework of the flight and netting, and carry out any necessary repairs without delay. It is not possible to give the woodwork another coat of preservative unless the aviary occupants can be removed for at least a fortnight to enable it to dry out thoroughly. If the birds are confined to their shelter on a permanent basis, this procedure is best left until winter sets in.

On freezing days, check the water at least twice daily, to ensure the birds have a drinkable supply still available. Water containers should not be filled completely though, since their contents will expand on freezing, and may well cause the vessel to crack, and start leaking once it is thawed out. In really severe weather the fruit in softbill mixtures may itself become frozen. It is particularly important at such times to ensure that birds living outside have adequate, or preferably additional time to feed before darkness falls. The perches must also be cleaned of snow, and kept as dry as possible. This will reduce the risk of frost-bite when the birds rest on them.

RODENTS
These pests can wreak havoc in an aviary of small seedeaters, but may fall prey to larger birds, such as hill mynahs and toucans. Nevertheless, the problems associated with their presence far outweigh the rodents' possible advantage as an additional source of food. If it is desired to feed mice, obtain them from a reputable supplier, where they will have been reared under clean conditions. Then the risks of them introducing diseases such as pseudotuberculosis are negligible.

The safest and most reliable method of removing rodents from an aviary is to use a live trap which can catch several in the course of a night. Poisoning is particularly dangerous if there is any chance that the birds may consume mice, even if the birds do not have direct access to the poison themselves. Metal spring-loaded traps can be placed in aviaries containing larger softbills, if the traps are enclosed in budgerigar-type cages from which one of the feeders has been removed. This will allow rodents but not the birds to enter. Make sure that the trap is placed in the centre of the cage so that there is no chance of an inquisitive bird managing to reach the trap and get caught by accident. This method is obviously not safe for use with finches, whatever precautions you take.

Rats present a bigger hazard than mice since they are more likely to eat the birds, their chicks and eggs. Seek advice from a pest control officer as soon as their presence is suspected. Also, sulphur fuses should be put down their tell-tale burrows immediately. They will have more than one exit, so before inserting the fuses all other holes in the vicinity must be found and sealed with a soaked cloth (to prevent the gas escaping from the burrow). Wedge the cloth in place with a brick. Once lit, the fuses should be positioned as far as possible down the one remaining entrance. Then seal off this hole with a soaked cloth. Hopefully, the rats will be killed quickly and efficiently by this means. As a further precaution however, leave the burrows shut off, and keep a close watch for the appearance of any new excavations in the soil. Continual vigilance is obviously very important.

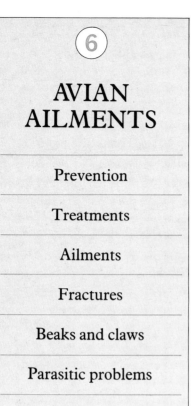

All of the birds covered in this book should thrive without difficulty, provided they are offered a suitably varied diet, and kept in clean surroundings. Illness however, is much more likely to develop in newly-imported or recently-acquired stock. These birds will have less resistance to infections, partly because of the stress of movement imposed upon them. Furthermore, in the case of softbills especially, they are often faced with adapting to new foodstuffs, some of which may not be immediately acceptable. A temporarily lowered food intake coupled with an unbalanced diet increases the chances of disease developing.

PREVENTION

Guidelines for the successful acclimatization of foreign birds have already been discussed, on page 46. Cleanliness, as always, is of paramount importance, while keeping new birds in separate quarters for a fortnight after their arrival will help them to settle down, without the risk of bullying from already established stock.

Check on all birds twice daily, to ensure that there is nothing amiss:
- A lack of vitality and fluffing of the plumage are often the first indications that an individual may be poorly.
- Usually there is a loss of appetite.
- There may also be staining of the feathers around the vent and laboured breathing.
- The first moult may prove a difficult time for some softbills, and a closer watch for signs of illness should always be kept during the moulting period.

DEALING WITH SICK BIRDS

Warm surroundings are vital for all sick birds. Indeed, a finch which is neither eating nor moving, and thus not producing body heat, will soon succumb from the effects of cold, by virtue of its small size. A hospital cage, heated with a thermostat control, is of great value when dealing with such birds. The temperature should be controlled at about 32°C (90°F), and then gradually decreased as the patient's condition improves, until it is fit for release back into its usual quarters. Metal cages of this type can be purchased, but, unfortunately, are not suitable for larger birds, because of their small size.

Even without a hospital cage it is possible to provide heat which will be of value. Remove the sick bird from its companions and transfer it to an all-wire cage, kept warm by an infra-red lamp bulb. This is conveniently suspended over the cage by means of an angle-poise lamp, as most bulbs will fit into a standard socket. If possible, obtain the type of infra-red bulbs produced for use with livestock generally. These emit heat, not light, and are quite durable, with a ceramic rather than a glass covering. A reflector is also recommended, to concentrate the heat source, with the temperature within the cage being checked by means of a thermometer.

It is important that food, and water especially, are within easy reach of the sick bird. If it is not perching, suitable containers should be placed on the floor of the cage (away from the rays of the infra-red light).

TREATMENTS

There is a range of antibiotics and sulphonamide drugs which can be used for treating avian ailments, but in Britain they are available only on veterinary prescription. Veterinary advice should be sought immediately because, in the case of an infection, treatment must begin as early as possible in order to be effective. A veterinarian will be qualified to decide on the most suitable antibiotic. Some of these drugs, such as lincomycin and pencillin, are largely active only against the Gram-positive group of bacteria, whereas others act predominantly against the Gram-negative group. Antibiotics will not combat viral infections, and only a limited number are effective against fungi.

It is possible to culture bacteria, and test their sensitivities to individual antibiotics, although this takes time. An investigation of this type may be recom-

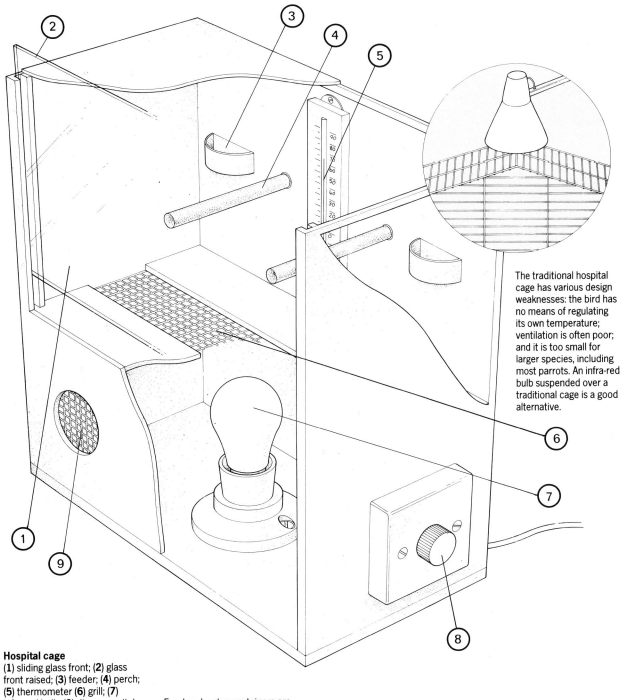

The traditional hospital cage has various design weaknesses: the bird has no means of regulating its own temperature; ventilation is often poor; and it is too small for larger species, including most parrots. An infra-red bulb suspended over a traditional cage is a good alternative.

Hospital cage
(**1**) sliding glass front; (**2**) glass front raised; (**3**) feeder; (**4**) perch; (**5**) thermometer (**6**) grill; (**7**) infra-red bulb; (**8**) dimmer switch; (**9**) ventilator. This is the conventional type of hospital cage that is widely used for smaller birds. The heat is supplied from below, by means of a bulb. The temperature within the cage is regulated by thermostatic control.

Food and water containers are near the perches, but if a bird is unable to perch, heavy earthenware pots should be placed on the floor. Be careful not to spill water on the floor, as it could penetrate to the heating unit underneath.

mended by a veterinarian however, particularly when there is an outbreak of disease affecting a number of birds. It is usually carried out in conjunction with post-mortem examinations. Fresh carcases are the most likely to yield significant results, and should be sent direct to the laboratory as soon as possible after death. They must be packed in accordance with current postal regulations, so you are advised to check these before despatch. Background information which is useful at such times includes:

- The number of birds affected.
- Their origins and diet.
- The length of time they have been ill.
- Possible contacts with other birds.

Treatments are available in several forms:

- For most seedeaters, canary seed impregnated with a drug often proves beneficial, in conjunction with a powder preparation dissolved in the drinking water. The latter means of administration will be essential for species which depend largely on nectar as the basis of their diet.
- Tablets are generally too large to be given easily to many birds, but it is sometimes possible to dose pigeons, mynahs and other bigger softbills by this means. A fixed amount of the drug is thus ingested, whereas the other methods are often not so reliable. Nectar feeders for example, seem to find most of the water-soluble preparation bitter, and thus drink correspondingly less.
- Actual injection of an antibiotic when necessary will be carried out by the veterinarian. This means of dosing is most appropriate for larger psittacines. Whenever treating sick birds with antibiotics and similar medicines, the accompanying instructions should be followed implicitly. Harmful, even lethal, side-effects are likely to result from over-dosing. Prolonging therapy unnecessarily can be equally hazardous, giving rise to resistant strains of bacteria. Always consult your veterinarian for advice if you are concerned about a bird's progress.

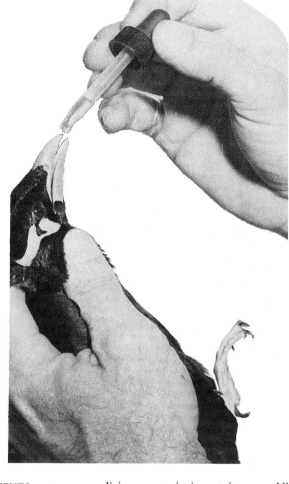

A dropper can be used to administer medicine, but the result is often not very satisfactory. Veterinarians prefer to pass a tube, which is connected to a syringe, down the bird's throat and directly into the crop. In this way, there is no risk of choking the bird.

BREATHING AILMENTS

It is possible to assess the state of breathing by noting the tail movements when the bird is resting. Exaggerated or irregular movements suggest a breathing problem, which may be accompanied by wheezing, and sometimes worsens after flying. Many of the infections which affect the respiratory system have effects elsewhere in the body however, and so the signs are often not specific. There may be a general picture of ill-health and malaise though, and the affected bird will be less active than its companions.

Fungal infections of the airways, often by *Aspergillus fumigatus*, may show initially only as a gradual loss of appetite with an accompanying weight loss, over a period of time. These are often difficult conditions to diagnose without an internal examination, and no reliable cure is available at present, although ketoconazole, a drug used in human medicine, can assist in certain cases. All fungal infections of this type are especially likely to occur in birds housed together in poorly ventilated surroundings, under conditions of high humidity.

When faced with an outbreak of aspergillosis, cleaning the birds' quarters with a strong solution of washing soda, using hot water, should help to eliminate any surviving spores, while the general standard of management will need to be reviewed. Gloves must be worn while the aviary itself is being treated, because of the caustic nature of the soda solution. All surfaces should be hosed down thoroughly before re-introducing birds to such quarters. Species such as *Pionus* parrots and red-vented cockatoos, seem particularly prone to aspergillosis.

Pasturella: Whereas the above mentioned fungal infections can often be traced to mouldy food or droppings, bacteria capable of causing severe breathing ailments may be spread to aviary inmates by feral birds and rodents. *Pasturella* for example, is often a killer, with an acute onset. Birds can die very quickly, showing few symptoms apart from laboured breathing and occasionally diarrhoea, with bacteria being present and multiplying in the bloodstream. Youngsters appear especially susceptible, but if the condition is recognized in the very early stages, antibiotic treatment can be successful.

Newcastle Disease (also known as Fowl Pest), is an important viral illness in poultry, which can affect the respiratory system of other birds. Although outbreaks are thankfully rare, quarantine measures are enforced in Britain and elsewhere because of the economic significance of the disease. No treatment is available, and all birds from a consignment in which Newcastle Disease is diagnosed have to be slaughtered. The risk of spread is considered greatest from psittacines, but the last outbreak in Britain was traced to feral pigeons, which had probably received the infection via racing birds from mainland Europe.

It is impossible to cover all the likely reasons for breathing problems, although infectious causes are probably most common. Tumours should be considered, especially in older birds, because when located in an adjoining area of the body, a growth of this type may compress part of the airway causing respiratory distress, particularly after exercise. Alternatively, in the case of budgerigars, on a diet low in iodine, the thyroid glands in the neck may enlarge tenfold, from a normal size of about 2 mm. The glands then press on the trachea, and interfere with breathing. A parasitic infection can be responsible in other cases. Air-sac mites can be found, notably in certain finches.

It is always a wise precaution to separate an individual afflicted· with a breathing complaint, and seek qualified advice as soon as possible.

BREEDING AILMENTS

Egg-binding is the most serious and common problem encountered during the breeding season. This occurs when a hen is unable to lay an egg, causing a blockage in the reproductive tract. It generally happens sporadically but the factors detailed below appear to predispose to the problem, so it can become more widespread.

The body's calcium stores are very significant with regard to egg-binding, being utilized both to form the eggshells and also for the muscle contraction necessary to expel the egg from the oviduct. Cold weather depresses muscular activity, while young birds have a high calcium requirement to ensure a healthy skeleton. Breeding during the colder months of the year with immature birds is therefore almost certain to result in an increased incidence of egg-binding, as will continuous breeding, which does not allow the hens to replace their calcium stores.

During the nesting period, a close watch should be kept for possible cases of egg-binding. The first indication of an egg-bound hen is often when she has left the nest, and appears fluffed-up and unsteady when perching. It may be possible to locate the egg by feeling carefully between the legs, close to the vent.

Rapid treatment is required, and heat is the first step towards assisting an egg-bound hen. She must be kept warm, preferably in a hospital cage set at 32°C (90°F). This alone often results in the egg being passed within an hour or two. If there is no improvement however, it is sometimes possible to remove the egg by gentle manipulation, using olive oil to lubricate the vent, but this is a hazardous procedure, especially with a small finch. Apart from the actual stress of prolonged handling, there is a risk that the egg will break inside the body, and lead to a fatal peritonitis. It is better therefore to engage a veterinarian who will be able to administer an injection of calcium borogluconate, or even operate. Consult one without delay.

Eggs which have to be removed by such means are sometimes abnormally large, or more often have soft shells, giving them a rubbery texture. During the subsequent convalescent period, hens must be gradually re-acclimatized before being placed back in a flight, when the weather is favourable. They should not be allowed access to breeding facilities for a minimum of four months, and preferably not until the following spring. Egg-binding is not confined to paired hens however. Occasionally, it may strike a pet bird living on its own.

DIGESTIVE AILMENTS

"**Enteritis**" is the term popularly used by many fanciers for digestive disorders, and literally means inflammation of the intestines. There are many possible causes.

The most obvious sign of a digestive upset is that the droppings are altered in consistency, and may range in colour from white through to reddish-brown, if there is blood present. It must be remembered though, in the case of softbills, that their food will influence the colour and state of their excrement. For example, toucans fed black grapes or cherries will pass darkish red faeces, which is quite normal. The whitish component of their droppings is uric acid, which corresponds to a mammal's urine. In the case of a sick bird however, the feathers around the vent often become stained, and its appetite usually goes into a rapid decline.

Candidiasis: many generalized infections will affect the digestive tract, whereas candidasis tends to localize here, often in the mouth. It may also spread lower down into the crop and beyond in severe cases. It results from infection by a yeast organism known as *Candida*. Newly-acquired nectivores such as sunbirds are particularly susceptible to candidasis, and their feeding utensils must be kept spotlessly clean for this reason. An early sign of infection is a bird sitting with its beak open, and tongue protruding. Candidiasis can also affect lories and lorikeets, and requires specific antibiotic treatment. The whitish areas in the mouth are painted with the medication, using a small clean paintbrush for the purpose. High levels of Vitamin A during this time will also be of assistance, as a dietary deficiency of this vitamin predisposes birds to the condition.

Sour crop: In budgerigars, *Candida* can also be isolated from some cases of sour crop. Recent research has also revealed an underlying protozoal involvement in this condition, and appropriate treatment with the drug dimetridazole has proved successful in eliminating the protozoa responsible, and preventing any recurrence of the symptoms. Birds afflicted with this complaint attempt to retch, and vomit mucus, which stains their heads. On closer examination, the crop is found to be full of gassy froth. Remove this by holding the bird upside down, and gently massaging the crop, in the direction of the head, before commencing treatment. Sour crop is also occasionally encountered in peach-faced lovebirds.

Salmonella: Dirty conditions are always likely to lead to infections developing in all stock, with an outbreak of disease often depending directly on the numbers of bacteria digested. When these reach a certain level, illness is inevitable as the body's defences are overwhelmed. Salmonella bacteria, often spread directly by rodents, or from seeds contaminated with their droppings, are a major hazard, with some strains presenting a danger to human health.

Strict isolation of the bird, coupled with thorough cleansing of the perches and food pots in the aviary is a sensible precaution to reduce the risk of other inmates succumbing with the infection as well. Antibiotic therapy, in a warm environment with water close at hand is often successful in saving affected birds. The appetite of many finches can be rekindled at such times, by offering seeding grass-heads suspended within easy reach of their perch.

Botulism or limberneck is a serious disease as losses can be very widespread in an outbreak. The most common source of infection for birds in collections is maggots which have consumed putrid meat, and are then offered as food without being thoroughly cleansed. The disease itself results from a bacterial toxin, often type C, which is absorbed via the gut, and then affects the nervous system, causing a varying degree of motor paralysis.

Birds suffering from botulism usually remain motionless, and have increased difficulty in breathing as the respiratory muscles cease to function effectively. Death results from breathing or cardiac failure, often within a few hours of the symptoms first appearing.

The early administration of botulinum antitoxin may assist recovery in some cases. When outbreaks have occurred in zoos, sick birds have also been fed glucose and protein hydrolysate via an oesphageal tube, since they are unable to swallow, in a bid to keep them alive until the effects of the toxin wear off completely.

EYE AILMENTS
A discharge from one or both eyes may be a sign of a localized infection, or a symptom of a more serious generalized illness. In parrots, it can be indicative of **sinusitis**, especially if the nostrils are blocked as well. The eyelids often appear swollen in such cases. Affected individuals must always be kept separate, and the perches washed off, because birds rubbing their heads along the branches to ease the irritation may spread the infection to others.

An antibiotic ophthalmic ointment should be applied three or four times daily, as it is constantly being washed out by the tear fluids. The bird must also be restrained for a few moments after application, so the medication can

Paralysis is not a common condition, but may occur after injury, such as when a bird flies directly into an obstruction and hits its head. Paralysis can also be connected with egg-binding, internal tumours in budgerigars, and other conditions. For an accurate diagnosis, consult a veterinarian.

Feather disease is most commonly associated with psittacines. This budgerigar is showing the characteristic signs of French Moult. The symptoms are extremely variable, but in this case, the bird is showing loss of both flight and tail feathers.

dissolve, rather than being wiped off immediately. These ointments are generally rather firm in nature, so run the tube under a warm tap to help soften the preparation before the bird is actually caught. Alternatively, eye drops can be used, but these are more difficult to administer satisfactorily.

FEATHER DISORDERS

Psittacines generally are very prone both to plumage ailments and to feather plucking.

French Moult is the most common plumage condition, with the signs becoming apparent in young budgerigars just at the stage when they are leaving the nest. Other species, including lovebirds, ring-necked parakeets and cockatiels are also occasionally afflicted.

The primary flight feathers of the fledglings are dropped, often with some blood loss, and in more serious cases, the tail feathers are lost too. In some instances, replacement feathers will grow apparently normally; in other cases, affected birds will never be able to fly properly.

Ever since the disease first appeared in the large commercial budgerigar breeding units in France during the last century, arguments have raged over its likely cause, and possible treatment. Latest research from the United States has gone some way to solving this enigma. Virus particles have been isolated from the feather follicles of affected birds, and these are now known to be a form of papovavirus, christened budgerigar fledging disease virus.

It appears that this virus may also be implicated in deaths of chicks up to the age of three weeks old. The infection is probably spread directly from bird to bird. No treatment is available at present, although research is continuing into the possible production of a vaccine. Good hygiene should help to prevent the spread of the disease, and the presence of an ionizer in a birdroom is said to reduce the incidence of French Moult in chicks. This suggests that the virus could be airborne.

Feather rot: A progressive feather disease is known to affect cockatoos, notably the Lesser Sulphur-crested, although Australian species may also succumb. The condition is sometimes described as "feather rot". The plumage of such birds becomes increasingly tatty and fragile, over the whole body, and in the latter stage of the illness, the beak and nails become soft. The Cockatoo Feather Maturation Syndrome appears to be more common in younger birds, but the actual cause of the disease is presently unknown. The most likely causes seem to be either depressed thyroid gland activity, or a viral infection. The adrenal glands may also be involved, but whether this is a cause or an effect of the disease is not clear at present. Some cases do respond, for a period of time, to doses of synthetic thyroid hormone, available from a veterinarian, but no treatment has proved completely effective.

Feather plucking: In cases of this nature a variety of factors may be implicated. The vice is most often seen in the larger parrots being kept on their own as pets, and tends to become increasingly common in birds once they mature, from around three years of age onwards. The breast and lower abdomen are the usual sites from which the feathers are first removed, and in severe cases, the parrot may transfer its attention to the wings. New feathers are likely to be plucked out as they emerge through the skin, but in other respects, the bird usually appears healthy.

Boredom and a poor diet can be at least partially responsible for such behaviour, as may a desire to breed. Feather plucking in parrots tends to become habitual, so that even when the original stress is no longer present, the parrot persists in destroying its plumage. Once the signs are clearly apparent, it can be very difficult to remedy completely. Although some improvement may be obtained, relapses are not uncommon. For example, the behaviour may recur if the bird's owner goes away for a period, leaving the bird in a strange environment.

Various preparations are marketed to counteract feather plucking, but they do not provide an answer to the underlying stress or nutritional shortcomings which first precipitated the behaviour. As a last resort, the bird may respond if it is paired up and given the opportunity to breed.

In the case of finches and softbills, feather plucking is generally only seen when the birds are housed in overcrowded conditions. Once released into an aviary, given a good diet and allowed to moult out, the vice will rarely reappear. There is a likelihood though, that if the birds are kept short of nesting material, some plucking will occur, to correct this deficiency. Such behaviour is seen quite commonly in zebra finches. Later during the breeding cycle, a build-up in the number of ectoparasites may also lead to renewed feather plucking because of the irritation caused.

This **cockatoo** is seriously affected with the disease known as feather rot. The cause is almost certainly a virus akin to that causing French Moult in budgerigars, although its effects are more severe.

FEET AILMENTS

Feet disorders are relatively common in many softbills, especially the smaller species, being usually associated with poor management. Pressure pads, confined to the undersurfaces, especially in the vicinity of the ball of the foot, appear as skin thickenings and are caused by the constant trauma of hard perches of similar diameters.

Bumblefoot: Joint swellings on the toes may result from a localized infection, typically by the *Staphylococcus* bacterium, giving rise to the condition known as "Bumblefoot". Dirty surroundings which enable droppings to build up on the feet will allow the bacteria to gain access through the slightest skin wound. The resulting swelling can come up very quickly, and may track up the leg, affecting other joints. There is a risk of a generalized infection, also, if the bacteria are transported round the body via the bloodstream.

Anything that predisposes to a puncture wound, such as overgrown claws, sharp ends of wire or splinters from woodwork can cause the initial injury. Birds with long toes, such as waders, are especially at risk, both from bumblefoot and frost-bite.

Successful treatment of bumblefoot is possible, provided it commences early. Surgery may be required so that the site of the infection can be treated with antibiotics, and in some cases, cryosurgery may be recommended. This entails using a special probe to freeze the diseased area to a very low temperature and kill the affected tissue. This tissue will slough off over a period of time, with luck, to be replaced by healthy skin. It is vital that the region is clearly defined and treated, because otherwise the whole toe may be lost. This can also happen in advanced cases of bumblefoot, where the blood supply to the toe is restricted by swelling, resulting in gangrene.

Articular gout is the term used to describe accumulations of urates and similar compounds in the joints. This may be confused with bumblefoot at first glance. The swelling usually develops much more slowly however, and is relatively hard, because of the crystals formed from the by-products of protein metabolism. Under normal circumstances, these toxic by-products are excreted via the kidneys, and so cannot build up in the circulation and become deposited in the tissues.

Hummingbirds are susceptible to gout, if their diet contains an excessively high level of protein. Occasionally, the condition is also seen in budgerigars, usually older birds, and may be indicative of declining kidney function. Unfortunately, there is no effective treatment for gout in birds. As with bumblefoot, loss of toes can occur.

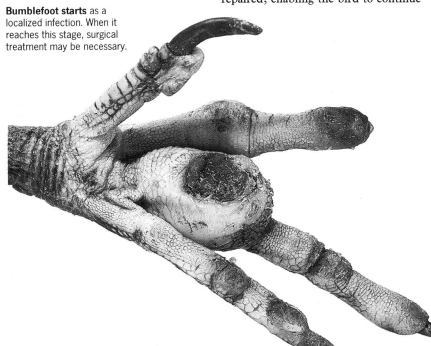

Bumblefoot starts as a localized infection. When it reaches this stage, surgical treatment may be necessary.

FRACTURES

Rough handling or getting caught up in the aviary may lead to fractures in the smaller passerines. A reluctance to use the affected limb and swelling at the site of the fracture are the most obvious immediate signs. The chances of a successful recovery are governed by the type of fracture, and its location.

Allow the bird to recover from the shock of its injury in quiet surroundings with food and water nearby, and seek veterinary advice. If splinting is possible it should be carried out fairly soon after the event. The immobility provided by a splint should ensure that the opposed ends of bone have the maximal chance of joining together successfully. In the case of some leg fractures, slight shortening of the affected limb may occur during the healing process, but the bird will not be unduly handicapped as a result.

Beak fractures are generally rare, but toucans and their near-relatives may suffer this problem. It is likely to occur if the bird is frightened suddenly, and flies hard into the mesh at the end of an aviary. Again, specialist attention will be necessary, so that the beak can be repaired, enabling the bird to continue eating without difficulty. Pinning of such fractures is difficult, but in some instances, if a piece has actually broken off, false tips have been constructed and attached by various means to the remaining stub of the beak.

OVERGROWN CLAWS

The claws of some species of finch, particularly mannikins and weavers, become long and spindly, and require regular trimming. In a bird with a lightly-coloured claw, this is a relatively easy procedure, once the blood vessels running down the claw have been located. Using a stout pair of scissors, or preferably bone clippers, the cut is made a short distance away from where the vessels disappear, to prevent bleeding.

When dealing with black claws, it is often impossible to identify the blood supply, so extra care must be exercised. If the claw does start to bleed, a styptic pencil should be applied to the cut end, or else it can be dabbed with a solution of cold potash alum, which is available from pharmacies.

OVERGROWN BEAKS

Beaks rarely need cutting back as often as claws, unless they are malformed. Remember that their length varies according to the species concerned. In some aracaris for example, there is a prominent downward-pointing tip on the end of the upper mandible. This is quite normal and under no circumstances should it be cut off.

PARASITIC PROBLEMS

Ectoparasites are those which lie outside the body of the host. In the case of aviary birds, **red mite** (*Dermanyssus gallinae*) is the most significant parasite in this group. These mites suck blood, giving them their characteristic colour, and so may cause anaemia, especially in nestlings. Red mites actually live in dark corners of a cage or aviary and thus proliferate when the birds are using a nestbox, as a ready supply of food is accessible to them. Conversely, they can also survive for months without feeding, even over-wintering from one breeding season to the next.

There are various safe preparations available in the form of special aerosols to kill these and other avian ectoparasites. Other products can be used to wash or powder the birds' quarters. It is important to use these as directed, to kill all stages in the lifecycle. This applies also to lice, which, in contrast to red mite both live and multiply on the birds, feeding on the feathers and skin debris.

Air-sac mites (*Sternostoma trachea-colum*) as their name implies, live in the birds' airways. Many species can be infected but gouldian finches are especially susceptible, and fatalities are relatively common. Control entails separating healthy birds from those which are showing signs of respiratory distress. It has been suggested that the infection may be transmitted in the nest, via regurgitated food offered to the nestlings by their parents.

Some authors recommend the use of a dichlorvos strip in the birdroom to combat air-sac mites. However, this is a potentially toxic chemical, to which the birds will be constantly exposed. Individual treatment should consist of placing the bird in a small box, and puffing in 5 per cent malathion powder through an opening every minute for five minutes only as directed. The procedure will need to be repeated each week for a month, and is apparently safe for birds as young as six weeks old. A new class of compounds, known as the avermectins can also be effective against air-sac mites (*see pp. 152-3*).

Scaly-face mites (*Knemidocoptes pilae*) are relatively common on budgerigars, but they can also affect other birds. Kakarikis are highly susceptible to these minute parasites. In most cases, the first signs are likely to be snail-like tracks on the beak, especially just below the cere (the wax-like membrane at the end of the beak). These will develop into the typical coral-like encrustations if left untreated. The mites can spread on to the legs, and even over the body in severe cases. This is particularly likely to occur in kakarikis.

Treatment should begin as soon as possible. Otherwise, the beak will start to grow abnormally, and is then unlikely to regain its former shape. A proprietary remedy obtainable from a pet store, or even vaseline applied to the affected areas will inhibit the breathing of the mites, although it may be several weeks before a full cure is obtained. It is likely that these mites spread by direct contact, so any birds showing signs of infection should be isolated. In a severe outbreak, the perches should also be changed if possible, because birds suffering from scaly-face frequently wipe their faces on perches and may transfer mites in the process.

Parasitic worms or helminths: A wide range of these parasites have been recorded in various finches and softbills, but they are much more commonly reported from psittacines, particularly Australian parakeets. These birds are often affected with roundworms, notably *Ascaridia*, which has a direct life-cycle. The eggs are passed via the bird's droppings, and after a short period of time, these will be capable of infecting other birds.

The vast reproductive potential of the parasites ensures their survival, particularly in an aviary with a grass floor, where hundreds of thousands of eggs may survive. The birds descend to feed on the floor, and inadvertently consume the worm eggs. The damp conditions and the grass help to protect the eggs from dessication and ultra-violet light. Earthworms may also assist the survival of these parasites by ingesting the eggs, and then depositing them back on the surface in an earth cast several months later.

Regular treatment of the birds will not therefore be sufficient to overcome the infection, unless hygiene within the aviary is improved. Concrete floors are most suitable in this respect, as they can be washed off using an appropriate disinfectant to kill any worm eggs. It is very difficult to deal with parasitic disease of this type in an aviary with a grass base. The surface of the soil can be treated with a blow-torch, but there is

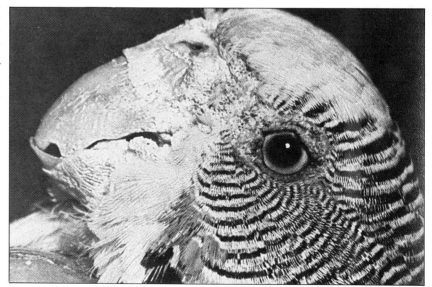

Scaly-face is an unpleasant parasitic disease caused by mites, which can bore into the beak and surrounding tissues.

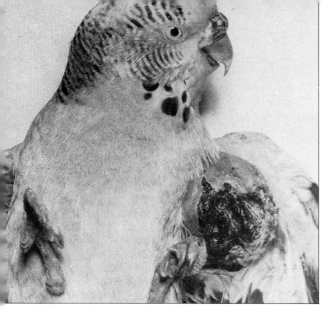

Budgerigars are particularly prone to tumours, which can occur either superficially, as shown here, or internally, where their presence is unlikely to be suspected until they are well-established.

no guarantee that this will eradicate all the eggs.

Dirty food and water pots soiled by droppings can also spread the infection. Young parakeets are particularly at risk, and fatalities in this group because of helminth infestations are not uncommon. Administration of medication via the drinking water tends to be unreliable, as the birds may not drink sufficient of the drug in solution for it to be fully efficacious. Direct treatment is therefore often recommended, and a veterinarian will assist if required.

Since the gut of psittacines becomes more narrow posteriorly, it may be advisable to give a laxative at the same time as the anthelmintic to remove the parasites. Otherwise, in a severe infestation the worms may be dislodged only to create a potentially fatal blockage lower down the intestinal tract, which might be prevented by a laxative.

Tapeworms, in contrast to round-worms, tend to have indirect life-cycles. This makes their control more straight-forward. They are flattish and segmented in appearance. The segments contain the eggs, and these must then be consumed by an invertebrate host, such as a beetle or snail, attracted to the birds' droppings. Only when this creature is in turn consumed by a bird will the young tapeworms be able to complete their development.

This group of parasites are not very common in psittacines, but they can be a problem in lories and lorikeets. Presumably, these birds take invertebrates while they are feeding on nectar and pollen but they will rarely express any interest in livefood when living under aviary conditions.

Tapeworms are more frequently encountered in pigeons and doves, and even the fruit-eating species can carry a heavy burden. Other, more insectivorous softbills are also at risk from tapeworm infections.

Pigeons can be dosed satisfactorily using proprietary remedies produced for racing birds. In other cases, it may be possible to administer tablets directly, or dissolve them in nectar. A new group of anti-parasitic drugs, known as the avermectins, are effective against intestinal helminths, but have to be given by injection. They can also control air-sac mites, which are often difficult to eradicate by more conventional means.

Protozoal parasites can also be encountered in aviary stock, but are relatively symptomless in certain instances. The most common disease caused by protozoa is probably coccidosis, which can lead to bloody diarrhoea. Sulphur-based drugs will often overcome infections of this type. Other microscopic protozoa can be transmitted by invertebrates, rather than by direct contact. Red mite, for example, may spread *Lankesterella* which attacks the birds' white blood cells, and can prove fatal.

Protozoal disease may be very localized. In certain areas of England, for example, birds can be at risk from black flies belonging to the family Simuliidae, (not the aphids of the same name). These, like red mite, feed on blood and may transmit the protozoan called

Leucocytozoon from wild birds to aviary stock. The parasite will form cysts in skeletal and heart muscle, leading to sudden death, without any prior signs.

Disorders of this type can only be found by means of a post-mortem examination which in turn, can help to save other birds. In this instance, the aviaries will need to be covered by mosquito netting, to exclude the flies during the high-risk period in later summer.

TUMOURS

Growths of this type are generally rare, except in budgerigars. Over a third of these birds are likely to be afflicted with tumours, some of which are benign, others malignant (cancerous). There are three common sites for tumours in budgerigars:

■ When the reproductive organs are affected, the colour of the cere is often altered, and turns brownish in cock birds, and bluish in hens. Behavioural changes may also be apparent, with the bird showing some of the characteristics of its acquired sex. Gradual weight loss will occur, the budgerigar becoming progressively weaker because of the tumour.

■ Weight loss, causing distinct hollows either side of the breastbone, also becomes evident in the case of a kidney tumour. In this instance, the bird will suddenly be unable to use its legs, and is then unable to perch, due to the pressure of the growth on the spinal cord.

There is no effective treatment available for either of the above tumours.

■ In the case of the benign tumour of fatty tissue, known as a lipoma, surgery may be both practical and desirable, depending upon where it has occurred in the body. A growth of this type will discourage the bird from flying, and so it may tend to put on more weight, creating a vicious circle. Lipomas appear to have a nutritional link, certainly in the case of the Galah Cockatoo. These birds should be kept on a low fat diet comprised essentially of cereal seed, with little sunflower seed being supplied.

7
BREEDING
AND
COLOUR

Sexing

Nesting

Breeding

Ringing

Breeding problems

Fostering

Hand-rearing

Species such as the Budgerigar and Zebra Finch have been domesticated for a long period (see page 130), and in recent years there have also been very considerable developments in the breeding of other birds under controlled conditions. For example, the number of psittacine species that have been bred successfully in aviary surroundings has risen from 127 in 1966 to 241 in less than two decades. Now 84 per cent of all parrots known to aviculture have reproduced in captivity, and a vast amount of information has been obtained about this family as a result.

Both in public and private collections, considerable success has also been achieved with other birds that are seriously declining in numbers in their wild habitat, such as the Bali Mynah. The establishment of viable breeding groups of such birds is vital in maintaining species which otherwise have a very bleak future. And the ability of aviculturists to propagate many of the Australian parakeets and finches in Europe and elsewhere over the last 20 years or so, since their export from Australia was prohibited, has ensured that successive generations will be able to appreciate these beautiful birds.

Increasing restrictions on the movement of birds for various reasons make it inevitable that other species will become unobtainable, unless they are more intensively bred in collections. The whole group of weavers and whydahs, currently quite common, are especially vulnerable in this respect. In some cases this is partly because of their parasitic breeding habits. As an example, Fischer's Whydah lays its eggs in the nests of violet-eared waxbills, which then rear the chicks. For successful breeding in aviary surroundings therefore, both pairs of birds must nest together.

SEXING
The problem of obtaining true pairs can be a major obstacle to successful breeding. This applies especially to the more expensive species, which are also often in short supply. It is not always possible

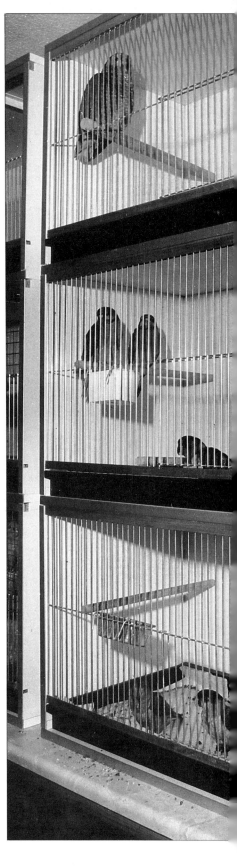

Commercial breeding units for parrots are becoming more common. Good hygiene is absolutely vital in breeding programmes on this scale, as disease can spread rapidly via feeding equipment.

to purchase several birds and allow them to pair themselves, although this is the ideal way to start a serious breeding programme. It gives the maximum chance of obtaining a compatible pair. Odd birds can be kept as replacements should anything happen to one member of a pair, and at a later date to breed with their offspring. In this way the developing strain is not handicapped from the outset by potential problems, such as poor hatchabilty, which arise from being very closely related.

SURGICAL SEXING
Surgical or laparotomy sexing is now being used with monomorphic species, which cannot be sexed by obvious differences in their external appearance. An increasing number of veterinarians offer this service, which is generally quite reliable in mature birds because the sex organs are viewed directly, by means of an instrument inserted through a small incision in the abdominal region. Although currently more widely adopted for parrots, the method has been applied especially to larger softbills, such as touracos, which have then gone on to breed successfully. It does necessitate anaesthetizing the bird however, so there is always a slight risk attached, even in experienced hands. Laparotomy is also used in diagnosing diseases within the body, such as aspergillosis, and enables the state of the reproductive organs to be assessed.

FAECAL STEROID ANALYSIS
Other means of scientific sexing, which do not involve surgery will be of great value, once perfected and generally available at a realistic price. Faecal steroid analysis, based on the differences in the levels of the major sex hormones present in the droppings, was tried out on birds of known sex, but results proved disappointing. Chromosomal karyotyping involves direct visualization under a microscope of the chromosomal pattern. The chromosomes present in all living cells include a pair of sex chromosomes which code the individual's gender. In the case of female birds, the Y chromosome of this pair is shorter than the other member. As this distinction is not seen in cock birds, it provides a totally reliable means of separating the sexes. But it is expensive, and not universally available in Britain at the time of writing.

ANALYSING PLUMAGE STRUCTURE
The most exciting breakthrough in sexing monomorphic species is very recent. It began as a science project, that went on to win the first prize in the veterinary studies category at the International Science Fair, in 1983. The student concerned, Todd Jarman of Roy, Utah, in the United States, wanted to find a reliable means of distinguishing between monomorphic cock and hen birds. He started searching for any differences in blood samples and by chance, part of a feather fell on the slide he was preparing. When this was placed under the microscope, a difference in the structure of the plumage between male and female birds became apparent. In cocks, the feather structure is less ornate; the barbicels or barbules running at right angles off the barbs predominate in hens.

Working with feathers taken from the centre of the bird's right wing, Jarman's studies have proved startlingly accurate in birds ranging from condors to parrots and pheasants. The impact of his discovery could revolutionize sexing of monomorphic birds. It should be possible to sex even young birds without difficulty, and anyone with access to a basic microscope could carry out the procedure. Or, a feather could be sent by mail to a centre for examination. There would be no risk to the bird, as is the case with anaesthesia, or the accompanying surgical procedure.

NESTING SITES

A wide variety of nesting receptacles are available, ranging from plywood boxes to wire cups. The choice depends to some extent on the species concerned. Boxes are a common adjunct to breeding cages, and are also often provided in an aviary of finches. Wickerwork baskets are another popular alternative, while wire cups act as a basic support for species which generally construct their nests in the open, reducing the risk of nests falling apart and the contents being lost. In a mixed aviary, include a variety of such receptacles, so the birds can choose their own nesting sites.

In the case of larger softbills, boxes are required by toucans and their allies, as well as starlings. Others, such as tanagers, may prefer to build a loose nest in a suitable bush. Barbets should be

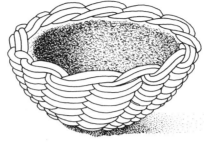

Open container (generally plastic), used as a base for canary nests.

offered hollow or soft, rotten logs, into which they can tunnel with their powerful beaks to excavate a breeding chamber.

A few softbills have rather specialized requirements which must be met if breeding is likely to be successful. Motmots tunnel into banks of earth to create a nesting site, so an appropriate open bunker, packed with firm soil (sandy soil could cause the burrows to collapse) will encourage these birds to nest. Leave one side open for their excavations. In addition to a suitable box or hollow log, hornbills must be provided with a container of damp clay. This will be used to

Some designs of nesting container are more suitable than others. The choice will depend on: the species concerned; whether the box has a side-hatch for inspection purposes, and whether the container is easy to clean.

(Drawings not to scale)

Beer barrel, suitable for macaws and cockatoos.

Artificial bank for tunnelling and digging birds. It should be quite large.

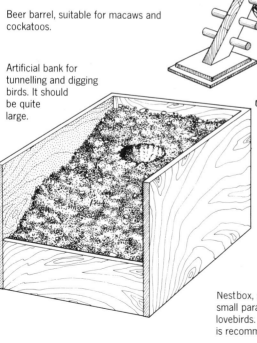

Nestbox, suitable for small parakeets and lovebirds. A side-hatch is recommended.

seal the female in her nesting chamber.

Parrots almost invariably nest in boxes or hollow logs, although very occasionally, they may prefer to lay on the ground. A solid and substantial nestbox is to be recommended, and for most species this should be constructed of plywood at least 25 mm (1 in) thick. In the case of more destructive psittacines, such as cockatoos, it may be necessary to reinforce the entrance hole with sheet metal, knocked flat around the exposed surfaces of wood. It is vital that the birds cannot cut themselves on the sheeting, or get their claws trapped between the sheeting and the wood. The roof of the nestbox should be detachable, and it will be useful also if the top part of one side can be opened. This will give easier access to the nestbox once it is in position, without any fear of eggs or chicks falling out.

Oak beer casks are occasionally provided as nesting chambers for macaws, and prove relatively sturdy. They should be laid on their side rather than positioned vertically, to give more floor space. However, the trend towards countering the destructive habits of the larger psittacines by converting metal dustbins into breeding sites is to be deplored, since the birds are unable to gnaw and this could increase the likelihood of chicks being plucked. More significantly, the temperature within the dustbin can rise to fatal levels in a short space of time.

NESTING MATERIAL

Nesting material of various sorts may need to be provided, both for species building their own nests and for those which prefer to make a lining in artificial receptacles. Placing such material in boxes or baskets often serves to stimulate the birds' interest. Strands of wool cut into short lengths should help to insulate the finished nest, and clean feathers are often taken to form a base on which the eggs are laid. Dried moss, available from florists, is another useful material, while short sticks will be appreciated by some larger softbills. Some breeders also provide hay, but this can be dangerous. It is frequently contaminated with fungal spores which, especially under damp conditions, may cause an outbreak of aspergillosis in the birds and currently there is no reliable cure. Two safe alternatives are hamster bedding or canary nesting material, both of which can be purchased from pet stores.

The majority of psittacines do not build a nest, although lovebirds and hanging parrots are exceptions. They will strip bark off suitable twigs, such as elder and hazel, and carry pieces back to the nesting site, either in their beaks or tucked in among the plumage of their rump, depending upon the species concerned. Some *Neophema* parakeets will also take nesting material, but this is rare. Yet the nesting site must have a suitable lining if the eggs are not to be rolled about and damaged. In the case of budgerigars, wooden or plastic concaves are used for the purpose. It is vital that these fit snugly into all corners of the nestbox, otherwise young chicks may be lost down the sides.

Other psittacines prefer more natural surroundings, and preparation of the nest site in the wild may take place over several months, reinforcing the pair bond. Gnawing and chewing are a vital part of the breeding cycle at this time, and even hen budgerigars become more destructive, destroying sandsheets or newspaper placed in their cage. Damp peat is a traditional lining material for parrot nestboxes, provided in the hope that the moisture from the peat will maintain humidity within the box. Yet most birds dislike peat. They will eject as much as possible through the entrance hole of their nestbox and any remaining soon dries out, becoming dusty. A better alternative is to provide small pieces of soft but dry wood, to enable the parrots to create their own nest lining. They will use their strong beaks to create an absorbent nest, with no risk of fungal spores and other harmful micro-organisms being introduced, as is likely if soft, rotting wood is supplied for the purpose.

AVIARY BREEDING PERIOD

Birds should be encouraged to breed when conditions are favourable. This will be influenced by climatic factors and hours of daylight. During this period, any plants in the aviary will also be growing, ensuring adequate cover for the birds. Without this cover, success is unlikely with many species. In the case of those which cannot be housed successfully in a planted flight, their nestbox or other receptacle should be positioned in a quiet, secluded part of the flight, under cover. Sadly, many chicks are lost each year by being drowned in their nests during a rainstorm. So cover the roof of the flight, and water the plants carefully from outside the aviary to prevent such losses.

With mixed collections, at breeding time a close watch should be kept for any outbreaks of fighting. Birds which live alongside each other in apparent harmony for much of the year, may grow to resent their companions as they establish a breeding territory. It very much depends on the individuals concerned and their housing. For this reason lists of "compatible" species should not be interpreted rigorously, but rather in the light of observation.

Many larger softbills need to be housed in individual pairs as do parrots, but some finches, such as java sparrows, will often breed more successfully if kept in a group and given a choice of nesting sites. Much squabbling can be eliminated by providing twice as many nesting receptacles as pairs of birds in the aviary. Distribute them all round the flight, at the same height. Most birds prefer to nest in the highest available site if there is a choice, and this can lead to serious fighting.

While many finches and softbills start carrying nesting material at the onset of the breeding season, parrots spend increasing periods of time in their nestbox during the day, prior to laying. To secure its substantial weight, their nestbox must be fixed firmly in place using brackets attached to the aviary framework. In contrast, pigeons and doves will adopt a simple shelf as a nesting site. This should have rimmed sides, to prevent eggs or chicks being lost from the nest. In a mixed flight, small species will readily take to nesting in a canary nestpan.

BREEDING IN CAGES

This method ensures that a chosen pairing has the maximum chance of producing youngsters of a particular colour or type for exhibition purposes. For this reason, budgerigars, canaries, zebra and bengalese finches are commonly bred in cages. Other Australian finches, especially gouldians, are also kept in cages for breeding purposes throughout much of Europe, but are often housed communally in their homeland. Although many species such as the singing finches will also breed successfully in cages, results are generally better in aviaries, where more privacy is available to the birds.

Suitable breeding cages can be purchased ready for use or the cage fronts may be obtained separately. Designs for budgerigars, canaries and finches have slight differences in bar spacing, and design. The cages are usually constructed of plywood, although hardboard can be used for canaries and finches which are not as destructive as budgerigars. The box design incorporates the front, with a gap of 12 mm (½ in) beneath the supporting bar. This accommodates a sliding tray to facilitate cleaning; simply line the tray with newspaper and change this when necessary.

The interior of the cage may be lightened by a coat of white emulsion paint. Two perches should be fixed firmly across the cage, to facilitate entry to the nestbox. Attach this to the outside of the cage, either at the front or on the side.

Regular cleaning of the box is required in the case of budgerigar nests, so convenient siting is important. Most finch nestboxes are fixed inside the cage, like canary nesting pans. They do not need to be elaborate and can be made out of thin plywood. The completed box should be a 12.5 cm (5 in) cube, with a

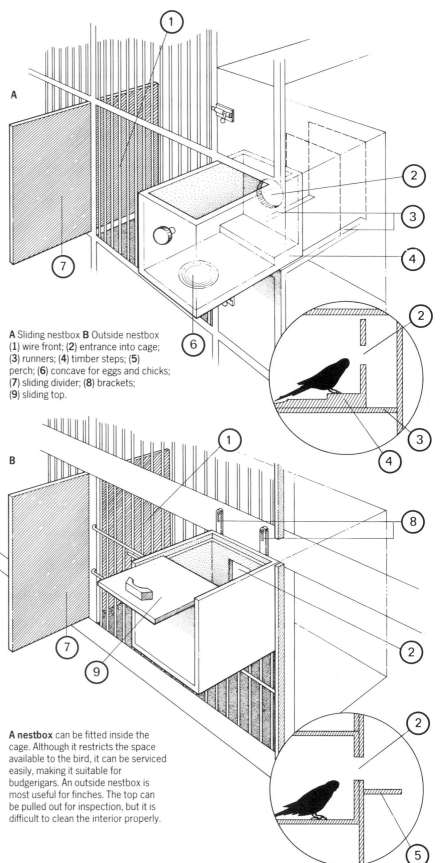

A Sliding nestbox **B** Outside nestbox (**1**) wire front; (**2**) entrance into cage; (**3**) runners; (**4**) timber steps; (**5**) perch; (**6**) concave for eggs and chicks; (**7**) sliding divider; (**8**) brackets; (**9**) sliding top.

A nestbox can be fitted inside the cage. Although it restricts the space available to the bird, it can be serviced easily, making it suitable for budgerigars. An outside nestbox is most useful for finches. The top can be pulled out for inspection, but it is difficult to clean the interior properly.

rectangular opening made in one side.

Although plastic nestboxes have never become very popular, increasing numbers of breeders are adopting the very attractive cage systems produced in mainland Europe. These very flexible designs can be converted easily to stock cages outside the breeding season. The epoxy resin coating ensures that they have a long lifespan, and are easy to keep very clean. Some designs are free-standing, others can be fixed to a wall.

BASICS OF BREEDING

The birds may not sit tightly when the first egg is laid. This behaviour is quite normal and fertile eggs will remain viable for several days after being laid. In fact, this characteristic is utilized by canary breeders. They remove the eggs for storage until the clutch is complete, to ensure that the chicks will be of a more equal size when they hatch.

Care needs to be taken with some of the larger parrots, notably amazons and cockatoos, which can turn aggressive during the breeding season. Tame birds in particular will attack anyone who enters their aviary. However, if the nestbox is located under cover in the outside flight, it should be possible to enter the shelter as usual, and to feed and water the birds in safety.

Once the chicks hatch and begin to grow, so the food consumption of their parents will be increased, and a higher level of protein in the diet is necessary, as detailed on page 42. It will do no harm to glance into the nestbox if the adult birds are both out of the nest, but do not disturb the parents while they are in the box. Otherwise, they may trample their chicks, and damage eggs.

As the young birds gain their feathers, so the adults will spend less time with them during the day. In the case of cockatoos, be watchful at this stage, since often the adults will neglect their youngest chick. The crop, clearly visible below the neck in an unfeathered bird, will tend to be slack in such cases, even at night, and the chick's growth rate becomes progressively stunted unless it

is removed from the nestbox for hand-rearing.

The fledging period is a critical time in the life of a young bird. Pigeons and doves frequently leave the nest before they can fly properly, and are likely to end up on the aviary floor. There, they could become saturated in a heavy rainfall. Some birds will rapidly attack, and even kill their young once they have left the nest. This applies particularly to species which breed repeatedly. Most starlings and Australian parakeets are the worst offenders. Therefore, their fledglings should be removed from the aviary as soon as possible. When transferred to separate quarters, such as a large flight cage, the youngsters should start eating on their own, particularly if food is sprinkled on the floor.

RINGS

Ringing is carried out for several reasons, but primarily to identify a particular bird. Those bred in cages are most commonly ringed, for exhibition purposes, using special closed aluminium bands produced by the appropriate societies. Since the ring guarantees an individual's age and origin, it enables the birds to be entered in breeders' classes. Similar rings, numbered sequentially, can be purchased from ring manufacturers and usually feature the year and breeder's initials. However, manufacturer's rings are not acceptable for show purposes.

Closed rings must be applied while the chicks are still in the nest, before their feet become too large for the circular band to be passed over. Detailed instructions for applying the rings are usually sent with an order. First pass the ring over the three longest toes, and slide it backwards. This will trap the short back toe, which is then freed by very careful manipulation. As a result, the ring should slide freely up and down the leg, between the foot and hock (knee) joints.

In the case of both zebra and bengalese finches, ringing is carried out when the youngsters are about seven days old.

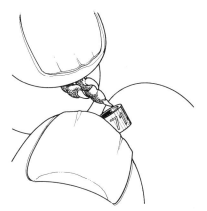

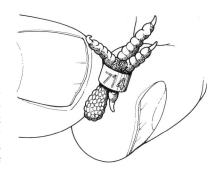

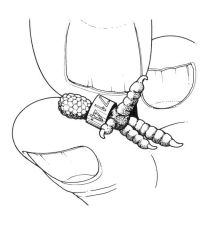

Close-ringing (1) Group the three largest toes together. **(2)** Gently slide the ring over the foot and the fourth toe, which should be parallel with the leg, until the band is on the lower part of the leg **(3)**.

Disturbance to the nest should be kept to a minimum, with only one chick being removed at a time, while the parents are distracted with greenfood or a soaked millet spray. No problems should then result. But breeders of non-domesticated species are loathe to ring their chicks in the nest, for fear of causing the adults to desert, or mutilate their offspring in attempting to remove the shiny rings from their legs. As a precaution against this, rub damp peat over the ring to discolour it a little.

Split celluloid rings provide an alternative means of identifying seed-eaters and the smaller softbills, and simply clip over the same part of the leg as the closed ring. They must be closed properly however, or the bird may become trapped by its leg in the aviary. Various identification schemes can be devised with these rings, as they are available in a large number of colours and combinations.

Split rings of any type give no guarantee of a bird's age or origin however, as they can be applied at any time. When ordering rings from a supplier, it is very important to state not only the type of ring, but also the species for which they are intended, because various sizes of ring are produced.

BREEDING PROBLEMS

There is always an element of luck in having a successful breeding season, whatever the species concerned. In spite of the most meticulous preparations, unexpected difficulties may arise. For instance, a hen may become egg-bound, or a cat may disturb birds nesting in a planted flight. Nevertheless, careful preparations will minimize the risk of poor breeding results. As a deterrent to cats, four strands of thin (18 gauge) wire can be fixed around the aviary and extend about 30 cm (1 ft) above the roof. This should help to discourage cats from climbing up on to the roof.

At the outset, it is important that both members of a pair are fit and ready to breed. For example, introducing a newly-imported hen softbill to an estab-lished cock in the spring is almost certainly courting disaster. She will be in no condition to breed and yet will be chased relentlessly by her intended mate. Once a pair have gone to nest, disturbances should be kept to a minimum, throughout the incubation and rearing periods with most species. Some individuals will tolerate interference more than others, but with non-domesticated species particularly, there is a considerable risk that the adults will then abandon their nest.

FAILURE TO HATCH

Only a proportion of the eggs laid are likely to hatch, and failure may result from various causes:

■ The eggs may not have been fertilized, and are thus referred to as 'clear', because in a good light it is possible to see through them.

■ Chicks which actually die in the egg may have failed to hatch because of an infection entering through the shell. Typically this occurs if the shell is soiled, or there are deficiencies in the diet of the hen, or incorrect humidity - this is considered the major cause by many breeders.

Losses resulting from the latter reason are most likely in the case of birds breeding indoors. As a precaution, nestboxes can be sprayed on the outside during hot weather. The humidity can be measured by means of a hygrometer, and special humidifiers are available for birdrooms where a low level of humidity is a constant problem.

DIET AND MORTALITY

Deaths of chicks after hatching can result from an inadequate diet, especially insufficient livefood, which is vital for many species which may be classed primarily as seedeaters when not breeding. Indeed bengalese do not make such good foster parents for waxbills, as waxbills become very insectivorous when rearing chicks, compared with the grassfinches and bengalese. Species which rely on vast quantities of smaller insects are often the hardest to breed successfully unless virtually unlimited supplies of fruit flies or hatchling crickets are available during the rearing period. Mealworms are far too big for most young chicks, but in an emergency, moulting larvae can be cut into very small pieces after being killed. At this stage, their skins are soft and easily digestible. Alternatively, it is possible to scald non-moulting mealworms and remove the hard outer skin.

RESUSCITATING CHICKS

Chicks are sometimes found on the floor of the aviary, having been thrown out or dragged out of the nest. There is always a chance that they may not be dead, even if they appear lifeless, so hold them in cupped hands for a minute or two, to see if they will show signs of reviving. If this is the case, keep the young bird warmed in the hand for several minutes more, then replace it carefully. The parents should return and feed it.

This problem is more likely to arise in a mixed collection, as other birds may disturb the breeding pair, even entering the nest in some cases. Pekin robins have a bad reputation both for thieving eggs from nests and for disturbing the breeding pair.

After fledging, remove the young chicks as soon as they are seen to be eating independently, as the adults may attack them, particularly if they are going to nest again.

"GOING LIGHT"

A difficulty encountered in newly-weaned Australian finches, especially gouldians, is the phenomenon known as "going light", characterized by weight loss either side of the breastbone. There are various possible causes for this condition, but it may be simply that the birds are not eating adequately on their own. A slight weight loss is normal just prior to fledging, but the distinctive signs of "going light" can be noticed rapidly. Such birds become dull, with ruffled feathers and, if left, will eventually die. As a precaution therefore, offer the youngsters soft food through the weaning period until they have adapted fully to a diet of seed alone. Infections of various kinds can give rise to similar symptoms however, so veterinary advice should be sought, especially if a number of birds are affected.

FOSTERING
In an emergency, it may be necessary to foster eggs or chicks to another pair of birds. For example, if a hen dies suddenly in the nest. The situation is less critical if a cock bird is lost, since the hen may rear the chicks on her own, although she is less likely to continue incubating a clutch of unhatched eggs.

Certain birds, notably budgerigars, are habitual egg-eaters. Consequently, if it is desired to breed from them, the eggs should be taken away as soon as they are laid, unless the vice can be overcome. Canary breeders place dummy eggs in the nest as a deterrent.

Feather-plucking is a similar problem. It can be particularly bad in the case of some lutino cockatiels, whose chicks will leave the nest almost totally bald. They will grow more feathers eventually, but it may be preferable to transfer eggs to a pair of normal greys, if they are laying at the same time. Or you could swop clutches, should this be preferred.

CHOOSING FOSTER PARENTS
Nowhere is fostering for economic purposes more widely practised than in the case of many Australian finches, particularly gouldians. The use of bengalese as foster parents for such birds is controversial, with valid points both in favour of and against this method of breeding. Zebra finches could serve the same purpose, but are rarely used. The concept of total fostering, is perhaps most widely practised in Japan, whose birds gained a poor reputation in Europe for their fecundity as well as their general health. The practice is frowned on by many aviculturists because it converts Australian finches into little more than egg-producing machines, whose chicks are, without exception, reared by bengalese.

Nevertheless, many fanciers do keep several pairs of bengalese as a safeguard during the breeding season, in case a pair of Australian finches fail to rear their chicks from a first round, or one of the birds becomes ill or dies. A more conservative approach is to take away the first clutch of eggs, and then let the Australians lay again, rearing their own chicks.

Using bengalese is no guarantee that success will result though, as not all pairs make satisfactory foster-parents, after the eggs have hatched. The chocolate varieties generally have a good reputation with breeders, but strains do vary in this respect. Some effort should be devoted to establishing reliable feeders, otherwise no advantage is to be gained from the system. Rather than discarding eggs from proven pairs of bengalese, it is preferable to substitute them under less reliable pairs as they will foster their own breed more successfully than they would finch chicks. In this way the reliable feeding trait is hopefully maintained in the young bengalese. In this respect, their type is unimportant.

The maximum number of eggs transferred to a nest should not exceed four, because although bengalese may rear additional chicks successfully, the primary aim should be to produce good quality youngsters. Bengalese will raise chicks of more than one species in the same nest, but all the eggs transferred should have been laid at approximately the same time. This will ensure that the young hatch as close together as possible, maximizing their chances of survival. In order to keep a check on the transferred eggs, a marking system can easily be devised, using dots, or crosses, of different colours applied to the eggs by felt-tipped pens.

WHAT CAN GO WRONG?
The major objection to fostering in the short-term is that chicks reared under these circumstances will identify more closely with their foster parents rather than with their own species, and so be unable to reproduce satisfactorily. This does not seem to be the case however, especially if the youngsters are brought together after weaning. Indeed, the parasitic whydahs which never rear their chicks, leaving the task to various waxbills, do not suffer from this vice. Nor does the cuckoo.

In the case of total fostering, however, there is a danger that over a period of time the birds will lose their instinct to incubate and rear their chicks, if they are never given the opportunity so to do. Provided this is borne in mind, the judicious use of foster parents can still provide a useful means of raising additional, quality chicks each season.

When failures do occur, they can often be traced to poor feeding, as the ability of the birds to rear chicks will be influenced by the available food sources. As with all seedeaters covered in this book, bengalese should be offered additional foodstuffs with relatively high levels of protein. For example, egg-food or insectile mixture can be sprinkled on wholemeal bread first soaked in a 50:50 milk and water mixture. Greenfood sprinkled with a vitamin and mineral powder can also be given daily.

INCUBATORS/HAND-REARING
Game birds such as quails have long been bred in incubators, with the resulting chicks being independent on hatching, but artificial incubation and subsequent hand-rearing of psittacines is a relatively new phenomenon. It is a fascinating, albeit time-consuming process. Although the eggs can be transferred to an incubator as they are laid, many breeders prefer to let the adult parrots hatch and rear their chicks for the first few days of life. After this time, it is easier to incubate them successfully. The hen will normally lay again within a short time of the eggs or young chicks having been removed, and this technique is described as double-clutching. Clearly this can have considerable appeal both for those working with endangered species in captive-breeding programmes, and commercial breeders,

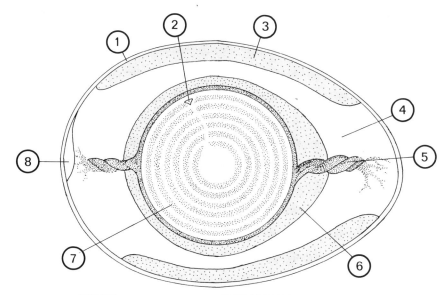

since more chicks are likely to result from any pair in a given period.

Incubators fall into one of two basic categories:
■ Forced air machines, which are easier to operate and more reliable overall.
■ Those operating on the still air principle.

It is also important to select an incubator which features an automatic turning device, since the eggs will need to be turned several times daily, up to the point of hatching. Detailed operating instructions are supplied with incubators, but it may be necessary to obtain a separate thermometer, and a hygrometer to measure the relative humidity during the incubation period.

WATER LOSS

As the chick develops, water is lost from the egg. The rate of loss must not be too rapid, and water is present in the incubator for this reason. The loss can be assessed by weighing at a set time each day. Excessive handling of the egg is not to be recommended however, since this can kill the developing embryo during the early stages of incubation. Clean hands are vital at all times when working with eggs, since infections can enter via the shell. Indeed, dirty eggs are unlikely to hatch if they are heavily soiled. It may be possible to remove faecal material by gently chipping it away (very carefully) with a finger-nail. Eggs which are cracked can be patched using nail-varnish and they may then hatch successfully.

Towards the end of the incubation period, the loss of sufficient water leaves an air space. The chick will gain access to this when it cuts through the inner shell membranes, to breathe atmospheric air for the first time. This phase, known as "internal pipping", takes place about a couple of days before hatching. If the egg has not lost sufficient water to create a suitable air space, hatching is unlikely to be successful, and the chick will die trapped in the shell. With an incubator it is possible to dry out eggs that may not otherwise

THE EGG

The egg forms a protective shell within which the embryo can develop. If the shell is heavily soiled however, bacteria can gain access and infect the embryo, often with fatal results.

1 Shell over two membranes
2 Germ cell
3 Outer liquid
4 Albumen
5 Chalaza
6 Inner liquid
7 Yolk
8 Air space

DEVELOPMENT OF THE EMBRYO

A
1 Fused chorion and allantois
2 Amnion
3 Yolk sac
4 Allantoic cavity
5 Remains of albumen

B
1-3 Visceral arches
4 Mandible
5 Maxilla
6 Mid-brain
7 Limb bud
8 Wing bud
9 Heart

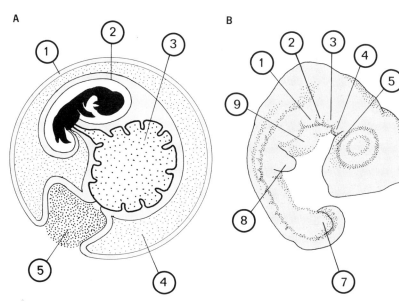

hatch, by running the unit with no water present. In other cases, where the air space was restricted in size, soggy hatchlings are likely to emerge. These can prove difficult to rear, initially lacking the usual vitality associated with healthy young chicks.

EARLY CARE OF CHICKS

The newly-hatched birds should be kept at incubation temperature, 37°C (100°F), for the first few days of life. Then the level should gradually be reduced. If they are too hot, the chicks will separate and appear generally distressed, holding their wings away from their bodies. If the temperature is too low, they will group together tightly.

A clean environment is vital. Disused plastic ice-cream containers, cut down in size if necessary, and lined with paper tissues, are ideal. Wood shavings are not suitable, particularly with older chicks kept on their own, since they tend to eat the shavings and this can lead to a fatal blockage in the intestinal tract.

A wide range of rearing mixtures have been used successfully, many being based on the complete foods marketed for human infants. The chicks still possess some reserves of food in their yolk sacs on hatching and need only very liquid food for the first couple of days. Mix the food with water to form a thin paste, preferably prepared fresh at each feed. It should also be given warm, never hot. A small spoon with vertically bent sides is most suitable as a feeding instrument. Syringes have a relatively high output pressure which is more likely to choke the chicks. A dropper may be useful for very young chicks. Any food adhering to their mandibles must be wiped off with a tissue because if it sets hard, malformation of the beak is likely to result.

Young parrots generally need feeding about every two hours, with a slightly longer gap at night, up until the age of a week old. Then the interval between feeds can be gradually increased to four hours. The crop, at the base of the neck is a useful indicator of food intake. At the end of a feed, it should be relatively full, and normally will slacken prior to the next feed. If it remains full, this is a sign that all is not well, and the crop contents should be gently removed by holding the bird upside down. It may not be an infectious problem; chilling can delay crop emptying. However, when in doubt, feeding utensils should be kept separate. A solution of sodium bicarbonate (baking soda, *not* caustic soda) can help to resolve any crop trouble in chicks.

LATER STAGES

As the young birds grow, ground sunflower can be added to the feeding mixture. The most effective way to monitor the progress of the chicks is to weigh them once a day. The weaning period may prove difficult, with the fledgling parrots tending to refuse food offered on a spoon, and yet not taking seed on their own. Some weight loss occurs naturally at this time, before the birds are fully independent.

With chicks such as eclectus and macaws, which take a relatively long time to develop, in the latter stages a vitamin and mineral supplement should be added to the hand-rearing mixture, with powdered cuttlefish providing an additional source of calcium, to guard against skeletal abnormalities (*see page 39*). Chicks should be reared together if

C

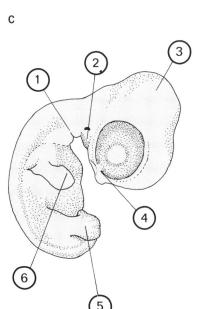

D

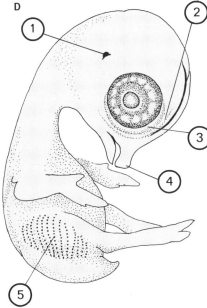

C
1 Visceral arch
2 Mandible
3 Mid-brain
4 Maxilla
5 Toe plate
6 Digital plate

D
1 External auditory opening
2 Eye lid
3 Nictitating membrane
4 Egg tooth
5 Feather germs

possible. If not, they should be introduced to other members of the same species as soon as possible after rearing, so they can relate to other birds.

HAND-REARING SOFTBILLS

While the greatest strides in the field of hand-rearing have been made with psittacines, there is no reason why similar success cannot be anticipated with softbills. Their chicks obviously cannot be fostered successfully under domestic finches, but it has proved possible to rear by hand even small species, such as sugar birds. As an example, one breeder lost the hen of a pair with youngsters which were barely a day old, and the cock appeared unable to rear the chicks alone. They were transferred to an incubator with a minimum night temperature of 34°C (93°F), and readily called for food when their nest was tapped or a quiet whistle was made in their vicinity. Their diet consisted of chicken or beef made into a pulp, to which a corresponding volume of rice pudding was added, after being liquid-

ized in a blender. Subsequently, scrambled egg was also added to this mixture, and the chicks were carefully fed by means of a tooth-pick. Nectar was given at the end of each feed which took place between five and six times every hour, over a 15 hour period.

As hen sugar birds are believed to feed their offspring small quantities of food at least every five minutes, there was always a risk of suffocating them with relatively large amounts of food, especially if it was given too fast.

Sadly, this attempt at hand-rearing ended in disappointment, with the chicks dying a week later, not from suffocation, but from a bacterial infection. This emphasizes the equally vital importance of good hygiene throughout a hand-rearing process.

There is little data on the hand-rearing of many such species, simply because it has seldom been carried out. Even if an attempt fails, however, it is useful to weigh the chicks daily and keep a log of their progress. Thus avicultural knowledge is constantly being ex-

panded, thanks to such attempts being carefully logged, and written up for publication in a magazine. Trial and error must play a part in hand-rearing but, as a guide, the chicks should be fed frequently on demand, rather than a large quantity given less often. When involved in a specific case, advice can usually be obtained from other aviculturists, zoological collections or a veterinary surgeon if necessary.

END OF THE SEASON

Once the birds have finished breeding, their quarters should be thoroughly cleaned as described on page 51. Old nests and nesting material should be destroyed, to prevent parasites such as red mite becoming firmly established, and undergoing a population explosion if the birds use the same nest in the following year. Nestboxes and cages must be washed using a suitable treatment to kill mites, and repainted where necessary, in preparation for the next breeding season. In the case of exhibition studs, training and selection of the

The rearing cabinet must be absolutely clean. Plastic containers lined with paper tissues are ideal for the young chicks.

An eclectus parrot chick
being fed with a rearing
mixture paste.

They are likely to be conspicuous and thus increasingly at risk from predators. More significantly, most mutations are of recessive inheritance. This means that when a mutant bird mates with a normal one, all the chicks will resemble the normal bird in appearance. Nevertheless, they carry the mutation in their genetic constitution, referred to as the genotype. Further mutants result only if these birds breed together, or with a mutant individual.

Under aviary conditions, of course, it is possible to nurture and selectively breed such birds, to maximize the production of chicks of a particular colour. The chances of a mutation appearing are significantly higher in stock that is closely-related, since unknown "splits", as carriers of mutant genes are described by breeders, may be paired together by accident.

show team should be well underway for the season ahead. Surplus stock should be sold or given away before winter.

COLOURS AND MUTATIONS

Colour plumage results from a combination of various pigments and the effects of light being reflected back through the feathers. These pigments are surprisingly consistent throughout the avian kingdom. Melanin and its derivatives give rise to black and brown coloration, and the carotenoid group are generally responsible for red, orange and yellow plumage. Exceptions are known however. For example, certain touracos possess a unique copper-based pigment, known as turacin, which gives rise to the crimson coloration on their wings. Blue is created by the effect of light.

A colour mutation occurs when the genes coding for the normal distribution of colour becomes modified. There appears to be a particularly high likelihood of such change in parrots. As a result of genetic modification, colour alterations can be transmitted from one generation to the next. Colour aberrations resulting from metabolic disturbances however, may prove transitory, disappearing at the next moult. Typical examples of acquired coloration of this type are scattered areas of yellow plumage in ring-necked parakeets and *Pyrrhura* conures, and the red speckling in peach-faced lovebirds. The latter effect can be induced by the feeding of excessive

levels of cod-liver oil in a hand-rearing mixture. However, this practice is not to be recommended, as it will probably have ill effects on the health of the birds.

Various colour mutations have been recorded from the wild, including yellow budgerigars and blue-masked lovebirds. Yet in the majority of cases, such birds have little chance of transferring their coloration to the next generation.

THE PUNNET SQUARE SYSTEM

The potential offspring from any pair can be calculated, using the Punnet Square system, provided that the genotypes of the birds concerned are known. The dominant character is written in capitals, whereas the recessive character appears in small letters.

Autosomal Recessive Mutations
Using the example of a normal, green peach-faced lovebird paired to a green split for pastel blue, the following prediction can be made, with the oblique line indicating a split bird. Each parent contributes half the genes to all offspring. These are therefore arranged at right angles to each other as shown:

green (BB)

	B	B
B	BB	BB
b	Bb	Bb

green/pastel blue (**Bb**)

50% green
50% green/pastel blue

Sex-linked Recessive Mutations
The genes responsible for this mutation are located on the sole pair of sex chromosomes. The hen has one shorter chromosome, thus only one gene can be present. In the following example, involving lutino peach-faced lovebirds, the lack of a gene is shown by a dash:

green hen (L-)

	L	-
L	LL	L-
l	Ll	l-

green/lutino cock (**Ll**)

25% green cocks (**LL**)
25% green hens (**L-**)
25% green/lutino cocks (**Ll**)
25% lutino hens (**l-**)

AUTOSOMAL RECESSIVE MUTATIONS

All blue mutations, and most yellow mutations presently known, fit into this category. Following on from the pioneering genetic work of Gregor Mendel during the last century, it is possible to predict the likely percentages of mutant offspring from any pairing. These are average figures however, and are unlikely to apply in every individual instance. It will be impossible to distinguish between normal and splits in cases where both are present in the offspring, without trial pairings.

The potential offspring from any pair can be calculated, using the Punnet Square system (*see box*). In addition, the following pairings involving these colours can be undertaken, and the offspring calculated in a similar way:

SEX-LINKED RECESSIVE MUTATIONS

The lutino is undeniably the most striking of the sex-linked recessive mutations, although some rare forms have an autosomal recessive manner of inheritance. The description of "sex-linked" stems from the fact that the genes responsible for the mutation are located on the sole pair of sex chromosomes. One of these chromosomes is shorter in the case of the hen, so that only one gene can be present because this part of the chromosome is unpaired. Therefore, hens cannot be split for sex-linked mutation. Their visual appearance or phenotype is a true reflection of their genotype.

This lack of a gene can be shown in a Punnet Square (*see box*). The other possible pairings are as follows:

DOMINANT MUTATIONS

Invariably, colours in this category can be bred in the first generation, when a mutant individual is paired with a normal green. Typical examples include the grey and dominant pied mutations in budgerigars, as well as the pied form of peach-faced lovebird. It is impossible to have birds split for dominant mutations, but individuals can be single or double factor, depending as to whether the gene on one or both chromosomes is affected. This distinction can only be made by trial pairings, possibly extending over the course of several clutches.

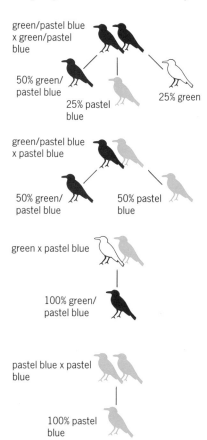

green/pastel blue x green/pastel blue

50% green/pastel blue

25% pastel blue

25% green

green/pastel blue x pastel blue

50% green/pastel blue

50% pastel blue

green x pastel blue

100% green/pastel blue

pastel blue x pastel blue

100% pastel blue

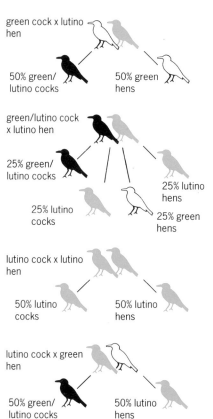

green cock x lutino hen

50% green/lutino cocks

50% green hens

green/lutino cock x lutino hen

25% green/lutino cocks

25% lutino cocks

25% lutino hens

25% green hens

lutino cock x lutino hen

50% lutino cocks

50% lutino hens

lutino cock x green hen

50% green/lutino cocks

50% lutino hens

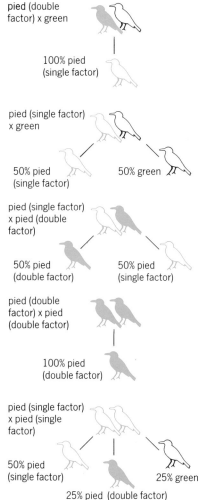

pied (double factor) x green

100% pied (single factor)

pied (single factor) x green

50% pied (single factor)

50% green

pied (single factor) x pied (double factor)

50% pied (double factor)

50% pied (single factor)

pied (double factor) x pied (double factor)

100% pied (double factor)

pied (single factor) x pied (single factor)

50% pied (single factor)

25% green

25% pied (double factor)

THE DARK FACTOR

In the case of the dark factor, presently recognized in both budgerigars and peach-faced lovebirds, it is straightforward to distinguish between single and double factor birds by an obvious difference in their coloration. In both cases, double factor individuals are described as "olives", whereas single factor peach-faced lovebirds are sometimes known as "jades", although now more commonly as "dark greens", like budgerigars. It is also possible to transfer the dark factor to blue series birds, creating cobalt (single factor) and mauve (double factor) colours.

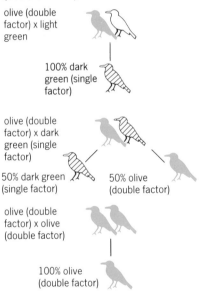

olive (double factor) x light green

100% dark green (single factor)

olive (double factor) x dark green (single factor)

50% dark green (single factor)　50% olive (double factor)

olive (double factor) x olive (double factor)

100% olive (double factor)

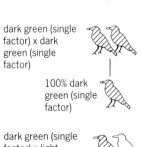

dark green (single factor) x dark green (single factor)

100% dark green (single factor)

dark green (single factor) x light green

50% dark green (single factor)　50% light green

COLOUR FORMS

Working with the various primary colour mutations, it is possible to create colour forms. The following example shows how to breed cremino peach-faced lovebirds, using lutino parents that are split for pastel blue. The starting point is to obtain hens of the desired genotype by pairing a lutino cock with a pastel blue hen. Lutino/pastel blue cocks can be expected from a pastel blue/lutino cock mated to a lutino hen. Then in the next generation, the following breeding results can be anticipated:

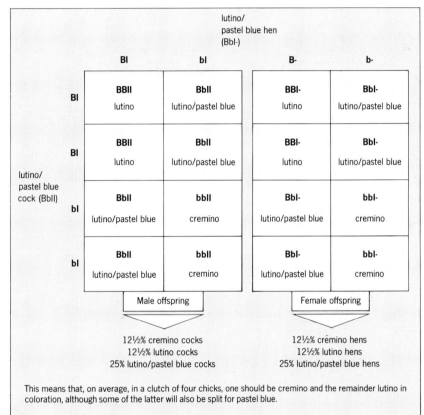

	lutino/ pastel blue hen (Bbl-)			
	Bl	bl	B-	b-
Bl	**BBll** lutino	**Bbll** lutino/pastel blue	**BBl-** lutino	**Bbl-** lutino/pastel blue
Bl	**BBll** lutino	**Bbll** lutino/pastel blue	**BBl-** lutino	**Bbl-** lutino/pastel blue
bl	**Bbll** lutino/pastel blue	**bbll** cremino	**Bbl-** lutino/pastel blue	**bbl-** cremino
bl	**Bbll** lutino/pastel blue	**bbll** cremino	**Bbl-** lutino/pastel blue	**bbl-** cremino

lutino/ pastel blue cock (Bbll)

Male offspring

12½% cremino cocks
12½% lutino cocks
25% lutino/pastel blue cocks

Female offspring

12½% cremino hens
12½% lutino hens
25% lutino/pastel blue hens

This means that, on average, in a clutch of four chicks, one should be cremino and the remainder lutino in coloration, although some of the latter will also be split for pastel blue.

LETHAL FACTOR IN CRESTED BIRDS

The crested mutations are dominant in their mode of inheritance, but crested birds are not paired together, since a proportion of the resulting young will not be viable (the eggs will not hatch or, if they do, the chicks will not survive). A lethal factor associated with the genes responsible for crested mutations prevents the development of double factor crested birds. The pairing illustrated is carried out to overcome the problem as far as possible. "Crested" is the term normally used to describe normals bred from this pairing. Alternative names include "plainhead" and "non-crested".

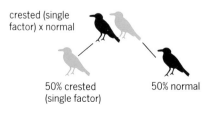

crested (single factor) x normal

50% crested (single factor)　50% normal

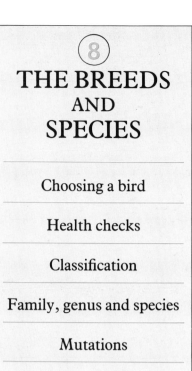

The first priority when choosing any bird should be to ensure, as far as possible, that it is healthy. Quietly looking at the bird from a distance will be of great value. A sick bird is likely to be slightly fluffed up, and less active than its companions. It may sleep for a long period with both feet resting on the perch. Other, more specific signs might include staining around the vent. Closer examination will then reveal if the bird is "light", since the breast muscle wastes very quickly. In a healthy individual, the breastbone should be well-covered. The feet and claws need to be in perfect condition, especially if the bird may be exhibited at a later date. The condition of the plumage itself is not vital, as it will be replaced at the next moult, although in parrots generally, do not purchase a bird showing signs of feather plucking or other disorders.

Indeed, certain points should be looked at especially closely in specific groups of birds:
■ The nostrils of parrots need to be clear, and of an even size. Blocked nostrils are frequently linked to watery or swollen eyes, and an abnormally large nasal opening is likely to be indicative of a long-standing infection.
■ In newly-imported lories and lorikeets, the inside of the mouth should be examined, for any sign of candidasis.

Apart from these very important health checks, there are other specific points you may wish to assess:
■ The gender of a particular bird, may have to be considered. Birds that have been surgically sexed are usually advertised with the initials S.S.
■ The approximate age may also be important, but once an unringed bird has moulted into adult plumage, it is almost impossible to assess its age with any degree of reliability. In canaries as well as other finches and softbills, the scales on the legs tend to thicken in older individuals, which can act as a guide. Even varicose veins may be apparent in some instances.
■ The colour and type of an individual are clearly significant factors when seeking exhibition stock. While few breeders are likely to part with their best adult birds, it may be possible to obtain young stock at a realistic price.
■ It is also worth enquiring about the diet of a particular bird.
■ With foreign birds, check whether they have been housed in an outside flight. The fact that a bird has undergone a period of quarantine is not an indication that it is acclimatized. Purchasing such birds in the autumn means that you will have to keep them indoors, in suitably warm surroundings, for the duration of the winter.

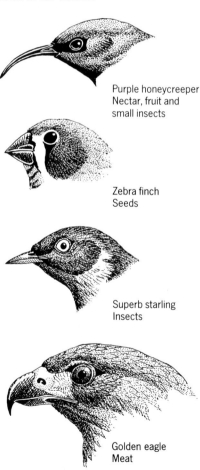

Purple honeycreeper
Nectar, fruit and small insects

Zebra finch
Seeds

Superb starling
Insects

Golden eagle
Meat

Beaks are adapted according to the type of food a bird eats.

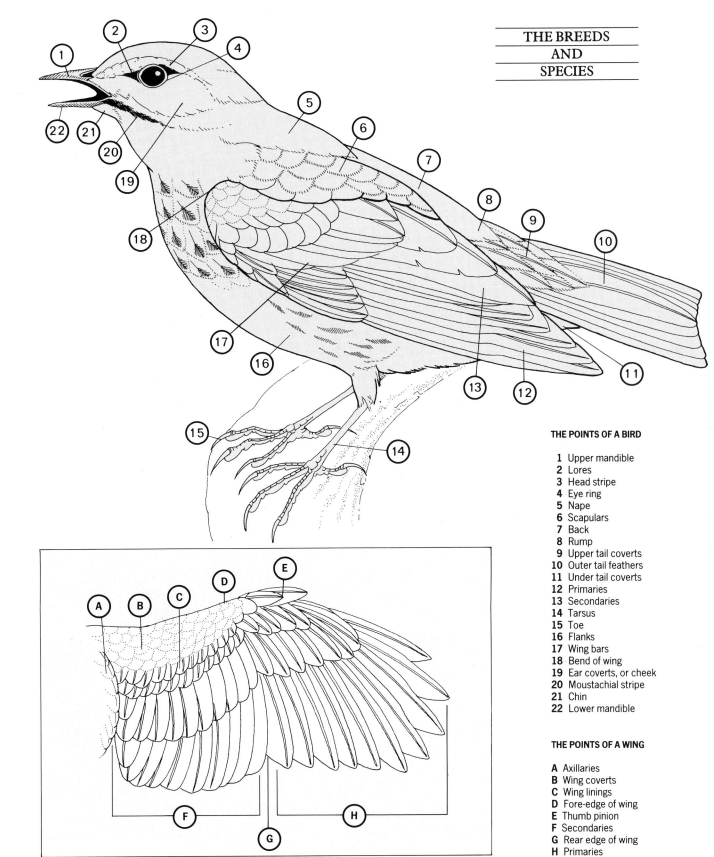

THE POINTS OF A BIRD

1 Upper mandible
2 Lores
3 Head stripe
4 Eye ring
5 Nape
6 Scapulars
7 Back
8 Rump
9 Upper tail coverts
10 Outer tail feathers
11 Under tail coverts
12 Primaries
13 Secondaries
14 Tarsus
15 Toe
16 Flanks
17 Wing bars
18 Bend of wing
19 Ear coverts, or cheek
20 Moustachial stripe
21 Chin
22 Lower mandible

THE POINTS OF A WING

A Axillaries
B Wing coverts
C Wing linings
D Fore-edge of wing
E Thumb pinion
F Secondaries
G Rear edge of wing
H Primaries

This section features approximately 200 species of popular cage and aviary birds, covering a representative selection of the groups that are usually available, and it has been arranged essentially to conform to the scientific scheme of classification. This enables birds with similar characteristics and habits to be grouped together, and provides an invaluable means of recognizing birds that are closely related. As more species have been discovered however, and more studies undertaken, so classification has needed to be revised.

The earliest attempt at arranging all the known creatures in groups was undertaken by the Greek philosopher Aristotle during the fourth century. His scheme relied essentially on functional distinctions, rather than physical differences and thus varies significantly from the scheme now universally adopted throughout the world. Modern classification dates back to the 17th century, and the publication of the work called *Ornithologia* in 1676, actually after the death of its author, Francis Willoughby. This ornithological work featured not only descriptions of the birds themselves, but also identification tables, arranged in sequence so that it was possible to trace an unknown bird through the system to learn its identity, by virtue of its appearance.

Yet the founder of the accepted classificatory system employed today is recognized as being a botanist called Carl von Linné, who is now better known as Linnaeus, with the method he devised being known as the Linnean System. While Linnaeus retained certain aspects of Aristotle's system, he relied essentially on the external physical appearance of the organism, rather than considering anatomical functions as being of prime significance. There is a hierarchy within this system comprised of various ranks. All birds, because of their unique features (*see Chapter 1*), constitute a recognizable class, known as Aves. The class is then sub-divided into various orders, comprising the major groupings of birds, with orders in turn being split

Sir Francis Willoughby (left) was the author of *Ornithologia*, published in 1676. This book made it possible to discover the identification of an unknown bird by tracing it through his system. However, it was Carl von Linné, or Linnaeus, (below) who was the founder of the classification system used today. His most important work, *Systema Naturae*, was published in 1735.

into families. The family is possibly the most useful starting point within the classificatory system. Looking at an unknown bird, it is usually possible to gain some idea of its likely relationships, at the family level.

Consider the case of a pigeon. This is sufficiently distinctive in its appearance to be recognized as a member of the family Columbidae, which embraces all pigeons and doves. The family itself is split into various genera; birds within an individual genus show close physical similarities to each other, typically in terms of size, and possibly markings and colour as well. Indeed, it is quite easy to identify relationships at this level, with the members of a genus being described as species. If there are slight variations within a species, this may be sufficient to establish sub-species, which although virtually identical, do differ in some slight respects from each other. This typically occurs when the species in question ranges over a large area, or has a scattered distribution over a number of islands, where in isolation, slightly different forms have developed. A typical example is the instance of the Rainbow Lorikeet, which occurs over numerous islands throughout Australasia (*see page 143*).

Linnaeus' highly practical scheme also meant that it was possible to ascribe a unique name to each individual organism as it became known, even at a time when many birds were still to be discovered. This is now referred to as the trinomial system of nomenclature, and evolved from the initial usage of this method in Linnaeus' famous tenth edition of his work *Systema Naturae*, which was published in 1758. Here, he added a so-called "trivial name", in order to identify the individual members within each genus. The use of the genus and trivial names together are said to constitute the name of the species, and are written in italics. When the trivial name is repeated, this is indicative of sub-species being recognized by taxonomists. In this instance, it is referred to as the nominate

CLASS	Aves
ORDER	Columbiformes
FAMILY	Columbidae
GENUS	*Oena*
SPECIES	*Oena capensis*
SUB-SPECIES	*Oena capensis capensis* *Oena capensis aliena*

race, being the original "type" specimen. A new sub-species is identified by the presence of a different name following the trivial name. The example illustrated, using the Cape Dove (*see page 126*), draws together these points.

This particular species was first described by Linnaeus himself, in the twelfth edition of *Systema Naturae* which appeared in 1766, when he named it as *Columba capensis*. As it has since been reclassified into its present genus *Oena*, the species description is now written as *Oena capensis* (Linnaeus) 1766. This shows that although Linnaeus was the first person to classify the species, it has since been moved to another genus, as shown by placing his name in parentheses.

The science of classification, known as systematics, is constantly advancing, so that classificatory revisions, notably in the lower ranks, are made from time to time. Whereas the early systematists had to rely essentially on anatomical features, a wider range of tools is now available to those working in this field today. The detailed analysis of specific components present in eggs, and close study of song patterns are two examples of work which has helped to further scientific investigation into the relationships between various groups of birds. A study of their external parasites, notably lice which are relatively host-specific, has also proved useful in this field, confirming, for example, an apparent

affiliation between flamingos and waterfowl.

In the wild, species do not normally interbreed freely, even if they are closely related. Yet such behaviour does occur in aviary birds, and can confirm a close relationship between members of different genera. Some crosses, notably the breeding of canaries with certain finches, are relatively common, whereas other crosses of this nature are considered by some to form a basis for reappraisal of the classificatory position of the species involved. A typical example in this respect concerns the lovebirds, belonging to the genus *Agapornis*. The so-called white eye ring group, although differing noticeably in coloration, will hybridize quite readily, and it has been suggested that they should be grouped as a single species, with the Masked (*A. personata*) as the nominate race (*see pp. 152-3*).

From the avicultural viewpoint however, breeding stock should be kept pure, especially since hybrids of this type are most often sterile, but if fertile, may introduce unwanted characteristics to existing stocks over a period of time. This has happened in the case of the Black-cheeked Lovebird (*A. nigrigensis*), where pure stock is hard to obtain, following repeated crossings in the past with masked lovebirds which were much more numerous and thus often paired with their black-cheeked relatives.

79

CANARIES

Family: Fringillidae

The early history of the canary is obscure, but it appears that the ancestors of today's breeds were brought from the Canaries and possibly other neighbouring islands off the north-west coast of Africa.

SELECTIVE BREEDING

This began in earnest during the early years of the 17th century. Italy appears to have been one of the first countries where this pastime became popular, the birds being exported to Germany and elsewhere. At that time, it appears that colour variants were unknown. Yet, by 1709, when Hervieux, who worked as aviary superintendent for the Duchesse de Berry in France, produced the first comprehensive guide to these birds, entitled *Traité des Serins de Canarie*, both white and yellow forms had been recorded. Hervieux featured 29 varieties, on the basis of their plumage, as distinct from the type breeds recognized today.

This division occurred early in the development of the canary. German breeders concentrated on the song of these birds, whereas elsewhere, notably in the Low Countries, greater interest centred on evolving breeds with distinctive physical features. The regionalization of the canary fancy is still apparent today, both in the names of the breeds and in their distribution.

During the Victorian era, increasing support for the selective breeding of livestock for exhibition purposes gave rise to specialist canary clubs and societies in the 19th century. While some breeds, notably the London Fancy, have been lost during the intervening years, the introduction of a South American finch, the Black-hooded Red Siskin (*Carduelis cucullatus*) to existing canary bloodlines has given rise to a variety of red coloured birds.

Other new coloured canaries have also gained an extensive following in subsequent years, especially in Europe. A recent trend has been an encouraging revival of interest in many of the older breeds which might have been lost if it were not for a few dedicated fanciers.

CANARY TERMINOLOGY

Specific terms have evolved within the canary fancy to describe particular features. Clear canaries are characterized by the absence of melanin from their plumage, and are thus light coloured, whereas birds described as "selfs" resemble the wild canary, being dark greenish or blue. When the birds are variegated, with a predominance of clear feathering, they are known as "lightly variegated". If areas of melanin predominate then these birds are described as being "heavily variegated".

WILD CANARY
Serinus canarius

Distribution: Canary Islands, Madeira and the Azores

The Spanish are credited with introducing these birds to Europe at the beginning of the 15th century. They still occur on the islands today and are closely related to the European Serin (*S. serinus*). They are relatively small dull birds compared with contemporary canaries, but still valued as songsters in their native islands.

In some instances, only a tiny patch of light plumage may be present, and providing this does not exceed 19 mm (¾ in) in diameter, or cover more than three tail or flight feathers, such birds are categorized as "foul". In the reverse situation, dark feathering on a clear bird is described as "ticked".

While yellow can refer to colour in canaries, it is also applied to feather type and pigment distribution, irrespective of that bird's colour. Yellow canaries have relatively coarse plumage, with pigment present throughout the feather.

CANARY: FIFE FANCY

A smaller version of the Border Fancy Canary, these birds are becoming increasingly popular. They are judged by almost identical standards as for the Borders, except with regard to their size. The original meeting held in 1957 at Kirkcaldy, Scotland, agreed that the Fife Fancy should not exceed 11cm (4¼ in) in size, making them 2.5 cm (1 in) smaller than their near relative.

In the case of buff birds, the feathering is softer, and the colour pigment is absent from the edges of the feathers. This tends to create a paler coloration overall.

Such variation in feather type is significant, since excessive usage of buff to buff pairings (known as "double-buffing") will lead to the formation of feather cysts in the resulting chicks. The developing feather, being excessively soft, starts to curl within its follicle and so does not emerge through the skin. A swelling then results and will ultimately burst. The condition is impossible to cure, being an inherited weakness. Sometimes described as "lumps", feather cysts are particularly associated with Norwich Fancy birds although, in recent years, they have also become more common in Gloster Fancies. Buff birds should always be paired with yellows to prevent this problem arising.

FEEDING

Canary mixtures basically consist of canary seed and red rape, with other seeds, such as hemp and linseed being added in smaller quantities. Studies suggest that a single bird will eat on average about 6g (¼oz) of food every day, but adequate variety must always be available. Regular supplies of green-food, especially chickweed, will be readily taken by canaries, along with soft food, which is particularly important during the breeding season. Colour-feeding for exhibition purposes is necessary for Lizard, Red Factor, Norwich and Yorkshire Fancy birds. The actual regulations can vary slightly from country to country in this regard.

CANARY: BORDER FANCY

This bird is one of the most popular canary breeds. Since its original development in the border counties between England and Scotland in the early 19th century, it has increased in size as a result of the introduction of Norwich blood. These birds provide an ideal introduction to canary-keeping, as they are reliable breeders. They are available in a wide range of colours and do not have to be colour-fed, while their lively natures add to their appeal as pets.

CANARY: PARISIAN FRILL

One of the larger frilled breeds, these birds attain a maximum size of about 21 cm (8 in). These birds have naturally twisted claws which are a unique feature. In good quality exhibition birds, these should resemble a corkscrew. The pattern of frills in this breed is especially well-developed. Yet the stance too is significant for exhibition purposes, and a Parisian Frill should stand tall, rather than sloping across the perch.

CANARY: PADOVIAN FRILL

This breed was only officially recognized in 1974, being named after the Italian city of Padua where it was evolved. It resembles the Parisian in type, but also carries the crest factor. While crested birds of this breed are easily recognizable, the plainhead can be mistaken for its French relative, although its mantle is distinctive, since it does not form the characteristic bouquet at its end. This feature also distinguishes it from the Milan Frill.

GENERAL CARE

Canaries are not difficult birds to maintain, and can live for ten years or longer. Although best known for their singing prowess, a very few pet canaries have learnt to mimic some words as well. They can be kept quite safely in a mixed aviary with other smaller finches, or even cockatiels. Although relatively hardy, canaries need adequate protection during cold weather. They often spend considerable periods of time on the floor of their flight, which must be kept clean if the birds are not to succumb with enteric complaints.

BREEDING

The breeding season of canaries is more closely defined than in the case of many other seedeaters. Most birds will be ready to nest in April, in northern climates. Although canaries can be bred successfully in aviaries, cage breeding is more common, and prevents the likelihood of cocks fighting each other. Before hens are placed in their breeding quarters, their claws should be checked, to ensure these are not overgrown. Otherwise, they could puncture eggs or drag chicks out of the nest. Sexing canaries at this time of year is not difficult, since cocks sing repeatedly to attract mates. Also, on closer examination, their vents are enlarged in size.

Various systems of management are used for breeding canaries, and a cock can be run with two or more hens if required. The hens can be caged individually, with the cock bird near at hand. Once a hen is ready to mate, she will start cheeping loudly to attract the cock, and solicits feeding by bending forward on the perch, fluttering her wings.

The birds should then be put together for about a week, after which the cock is removed, leaving the hen to complete the nest and start laying her eggs. Plastic nest pans with felt linings sewn into the bottoms are now widely-used, although nest pans made of ceramic and other materials can still be seen. Special nesting material should be teased out and supplied to the birds (see p.65).

Canary eggs are turquoise, speckled with reddish-brown dots. It is often standard practice to remove these each day as they are laid, replacing them with dummy eggs. They should be stored in a relatively cool environment. Clean, empty margarine tubs lined with paper tissues are useful for the purpose. In this way, clutches can be kept separate until they are replaced under the hen on the morning that the fourth, and probably final egg of the clutch is laid.

The chicks should then hatch virtually simultaneously, about 13 days later.

A suitable rearing food must be offered (there are a large number of brands available), with special feeders being produced to facilitate the provision of this item. The young canaries will have left the nest by the time they are three weeks old, and weaning can then begin in earnest.

Some breeders prefer to leave the youngsters with their parent for a longer period however, maintaining that there is no set-back to growth, as may occur if they are weaned at an early age. To some extent, this will be influenced by the

CANARY: GIBBER ITALICUS

A recent development in the breeding of frilled canaries is the *Giboso Espanol*, which was first bred in Spain. It has a particularly long neck, with an additional vertebra in the cervical region. It has been derived from the *Gibber Italicus*, which only occurs in a yellow feather type. Persistent yellow to yellow pairings have led to a deterioration in its plumage and such birds now lack any feathering over the sternum and upper legs.

CANARY: GLOSTER FANCY

These lively birds date from the 1920s and are derived from Border Fancy and Crested Roller bloodstock. The crested form is described as the "Corona" and the plainhead as the "Consort". An unfortunate recent tendency to double-buff (see p.81) has resulted in an increased incidence of feather cysts and a relative scarcity of yellow type birds. Glosters make good exhibition birds and are easier for the novice to train than Border Fancies.

rearing system employed, and is easier if the cock bird remains with the hen throughout the whole of the breeding cycle. He will then take over the task of feeding the fledglings while she will invariably prepare a second nest. It is unwise to remove a cock bird once the hen has begun incubating in earnest, as this may cause her to desert the nest.

When the young canaries are transferred to separate accommodation, a supply of the rearing food, topped with blue maw seed, should be readily available to them, along with soaked and dry seed in separate containers. A close watch should be kept to ensure that they are all eating independently, especially if they were weaned at a very young age.

The cages used to house the canaries should include soft perches, to minimize the risk of slipped claw. Under normal circumstances, three toes of each foot are directed forward over the perch, with one behind, but in cases of slipped claw this hind toe is deviated forward. This means that the bird cannot perch properly, being unable to grip with the affected foot. If this problem does arise, it may be possible to correct it by using adhesive tape to hold the toe back in a vertical position, parallel with the leg, for about a fortnight. When released, the toe should assume its normal position. If not, try binding it up again.

At the first moult, only the body feathers are replaced, so the birds are described as "unflighted" or "non-flighted". Having passed their second moult, they become "flighted". Until this second moult, therefore, difference in coloration is clearly noticeable in colour-fed young canaries.

CANARY: GLOSTER FANCY

The Corona's crest does not obscure the eyes, as in the case of the Crested Canary, and contributes to the bird's dainty appearance. As with other crested mutations, it is necessary to pair a Corona with a Consort, rather than to another Corona, because of the lethal factor (*see p.74-5*). Both forms of Gloster have been bred in a wide range of colours. This breed usually breeds quite readily without problems, and stock is normally obtainable without difficulty.

CANARY: LIZARD

Probably the oldest surviving canary breed, the Lizard featured in Hervieux's book. The spangled markings are most significant for exhibition purposes, with the old description of "mooned un" referring to the crescent shaped patterning along their backs. Brighter yellows are known as "gold" and the buffs as "silver". Pairs should ideally comprise one of each.

CANARY: NORWICH FANCY

The end of the 19th century saw a radical change in the Norwich Fancy when a fancier used some cayenne pepper as a tonic for an ailing bird that was moulting at the time. When the new plumage appeared, there was a dramatic improvement in coloration. Thus began the era of colour-feeding. Repeated double-buffing saw the emergence of feather-cysts on a wide scale, making healthy Norwich stock difficult to acquire.

SUMMARY OF THE BREEDS

Essentially the Canary Fancy today is divided into three categories. Some breeds are kept primarily for their singing abilities and others are valued for their colour. The third group comprise the canaries bred to conform as closely as possible to prescribed physical characteristics that judges must take into account when assessing these birds on the show bench. In practical terms however, the categories are not mutually exclusive, as all cock canaries will sing and colour is considered in the standards of many type breeds.

SINGING BREEDS

American Singer These birds have been derived from roller canaries crossed with border fancies, the origins of the breed dating back to the 1930s. The major feature of the exhibition standard is the bird's singing ability, as colour is not considered important.

Roller Canary This breed is the forerunner of all other contemporary singing canaries. It was developed in Germany and was already in existence by the end of the 17th century. The singing pattern of the Roller Canary is divided into various distinct components for exhibition purposes. Tapes, or so-called "schoolmaster birds" are used to train young rollers. Their vocal performance can extend over three octaves.

Spanish Timbrado Their name is derived in part from their metallic call note, or *timbre*. These birds are particularly popular in southern Spain, where they are often housed on balconies. This exposure occasionally puts them at risk from pox virus infections transmitted by mosquitoes. In areas where this disease is endemic, it is possible to vaccinate birds at risk. The first evident signs of infection are swellings, typically around the face and on the legs. When these swellings burst or rupture, their contents can spread the disease directly to other birds in the vicinity. No effective treatment is available, but good hygiene is vital to restrict the spread of the infection.

TYPE BREEDS

Belgian Fancy The popularity of this breed has declined during the present century, although it has played an important part in the development of other contemporary breeds, such as the Yorkshire Fancy. Like many other breeds from Europe, posture is an important characteristic and, during judging, the neck and slender head should be extended and the stance must be upright.

Cinnamon Canary This variety was evolved on the basis of a colour mutation, rather than a distinct type breed.

CANARY: YORKSHIRE FANCY

No other breed has undergone quite such a dramatic change in appearance. In the 1860s, the breed was popularly believed to be so elongated it would slide through a wedding ring. It is still a long bird, about 17 cm (6¾ in), but with a much more rounded profile. This probably originated from crossings with Lancashire and Norwich Fancy canaries. It is one of the most difficult breeds to stage successfully. Birds should not be hunched; they must sit erect.

It has since been developed into a breed, although its characteristics are variable.

Crested Canary The history of the Crested Canary dates back as far as 1793. Although crests are associated with various breeds, only these birds, which resemble the Norwich Fancy in type, are recognized independently. The shape, position and size of the crest – it should extend to the level of the eyes – are vital for good exhibition birds.

Frilled Canaries A number of breeds fit into this general category. Their unusual plumage can be divided into three

BLACK-HOODED RED SISKIN
Carduelis cucullatus

The introduction of this South American finch to existing canary bloodlines has given rise to a variety of red coloured birds. The natural appearance of the canaries bred from these hybrids is reddish-orange, rather than pure red. Diet is particularly important in reducing the orange tints. During the moult, birds are fed a diet low in lutein, consisting mainly of niger and groats.

basic components, with additional modifications depending on the particular breed concerned:

- The mantle runs along the back, dividing into two parts, with the sides of the wing being covered with frilled plumage.
- The waistcoat, or breast feathering, curls in towards the midline of the body; it is also known as the "jabot" or "claw".
- The fins occur at the top of the thighs, and these frills extend up to the wings.

Lancashire Canary The original bloodline of the Lancashire canary had vanished by the end of the Second World War, but since then efforts have been made to revive the breed. Yorkshire Fancy birds are being used for the purpose, in conjunctions with Norwich and Crested canaries.

London Fancy In most discussions about the development of the Canary Fancy, the name of this breed will be mentioned, although it has been extinct for about half a century.

Scotch Fancy Belgian Fancy canaries were widely used in the development of these birds during the 1830s. Their unusual stance gave rise to their popular description of "bird o'circle". A good action, known as "travelling", was also essential when they were being judged. Progressively poorer breeding results led to a severe decline in the breed's fortunes, but is now being revived.

COLOURED CANARIES
This group of canaries is bred primarily for coloration and has become increasingly popular. The specimens illustrated give some idea of the variety available.

CANARY: RED-ORANGE COCK

It has now become fully acceptable to colour-feed red factor canaries, but their coloration can only be fully appreciated under natural lighting. Buff birds have whitish edges to their plumage. The descriptions of the two feather types as "buff" and "yellow" have been replaced by "frosted" and "non-frosted", or "apricot" and "red-orange". Colour canaries offer considerable scope for breeders with a keen interest in genetics.

CANARY: RECESSIVE WHITE BLUE OPAL

There are now well in excess of 50 distinctive colour varieties. Unfortunately confusion arises over the correct terminology for a particular individual. This is due to the dual system of nomenclature between Continental and British fanciers. In some instances there is no identifiable similarity. Examples are the Melanin Pastel Cinnamon Dilute (British) and the Pastel Silver Isabel (Continental).

CANARY: FROSTED ROSE AGATE OPAL

One of the composite colours of the New Colour or Colour-bred group. The frosted feather type is clearly apparent in this bird, with the white tips to its plumage creating a frosted appearance. Agate is a Dutch mutation, which tends to be greyish, whereas opal affects the black pigment, causing it to turn silvery-grey. It is a German mutation, which first emerged in 1949.

TRUE FINCHES

Family: Fringillidae

From an avicultural viewpoint, this is a less significant family than the Estrildidae, although certain species are popular aviary occupants.

FEEDING

A general seed diet is required, and should take into account the size of the particular species' beak. Canary seed can be supplemented with small oil seeds such as rape and maw. Greenfood, berries and soft food should also be offered, with livefood being especially important during the breeding season.

GENERAL CARE

Careful acclimatization will be necessary as always, although some species such as the hawfinches are quite hardy once established in their quarters. It may be possible to house finches in groups, depending upon the species. If kept in cages, such accommodation needs to be suitably spacious.

BREEDING

A cup-shaped nest is usually constructed from typical canary-nesting materials and a canary nest-pan frequently forms its base. The hen is largely responsible for nest building and also for the major part of the incubation period, which lasts about a fortnight. The chicks will fledge about three weeks later. Livefood is very important for successful rearing of the resulting chicks and, if possible, the adult birds should be encouraged to take an insectile mixture.

OTHER SPECIES

Apart from the hawfinches with their powerful beaks, those of the crossbills

HIMALAYAN GREENFINCH
Carduelis spinoides

Distribution: Himalayan region

This species is occasionally available, often in the company of the Himalayan Goldfinch (*C. c. caniceps*). Both can be distinguished from their European counterparts, which are subject to legal controls in Britain. A densely-planted flight is to be recommended. The weaning period may be difficult: European Greenfinches are prone to the complaint known as "going light".

BULLFINCH x CANARY MULE
Hybrid

The breeding of native finches with canaries is known as muling. The hybrid offspring show characteristics of both their parents. This particular cross should yield attractive hybrids, which are good songsters. Mules are invariably sterile, and have no reproductive potential of their own. While it is usual to cross a male canary with a hen finch, in the case of this particular cross, the reverse pairing is required.

MASKED HAWFINCH
Coccothraustes personatus

Distribution: Eastern Asia to Japan

Hawfinches are relatively large birds, with equally stout beaks, but they tend to have shy, retiring natures and are best kept on their own, in densely-planted flights. The oriental species, including the Chinese (*C. migratorius*), which is also known as the Yellow-billed Grosbeak, are occasionally seen. In addition to the usual seed mixture, these birds can also be offered small pine nuts.

(*Loxia* species) are also capable of dealing effectively with pine seeds. In this instance however, their beaks are strongly curved for the purpose. Although not often obtainable, crossbills generally make very interesting and rewarding aviary occupants. They soon become very tame, almost to the point where they will feed from the hand. Again, they can suffer a loss of colour if they are not colour-fed from at least prior to the moult to some stage afterwards, where there are no more feathers being moulted. Young crossbills do not have the typical twisted bills seen in adult birds. This feature only develops as the bird gets older. Crossbills can be supplied with fresh pine cones showing no traces of mould, and will readily use their peculiarly shaped bills in order to extricate the seeds within.

Other Eurasian finches include members of the genus *Acanthis*. This includes the Linnet (*A. cannabina*) and Redpoll (*A. flammea*). There are also the bullfinches forming the genus *Pyrrhula*. The siskins are often grouped alongside the greenfinches and goldfinches as members of the *Carduelis* genus, and sometimes on their own.

Among the other serins, the Redfronted (*Serinus pusillus*) is unusual. Rather than occurring in Africa, it ranges into mountain areas of Asia, and is unique in having naturally red plumage. Indeed, it is surprising that this species was not selected for the experimental pairings which led to the development of the Red Factor Canary, because of its closer relationship with the Wild Canary. It may have been because this species is rarely available.

GREY SINGING FINCH
Serinus leucopygius

Distribution: Equatorial Africa, south of the Sahara.

A popular and commonly-available species, frequently included in mixed collections alongside waxbills, although their lively natures tend to interfere with the breeding activities of their companions. Cock birds have an attractive song, and singing finches are potentially long-lived birds.

YELLOW-RUMPED SEEDEATER
Serinus atrogularis

Distribution: From Arabia and East Africa to Angola and southern Africa

This species is very similar in habits to the Grey Singing Finch, with eight subspecies recognized across its wide range. Cock birds may disagree, but outbreaks of serious fighting are unusual, especially in spacious surroundings where there is plenty of cover. Also known as the Black-throated Canary, these finches are lively songsters.

HOUSE FINCH
Carpodacus mexicanus

Distribution: Western parts of North America, ranging south to Mexico

These birds are rather reminiscent of sparrows in some respects, living in small flocks in among human settlements. The vivid red coloration of the cock birds can only be maintained over successive moults by the use of a colour food. Apart from this, they are easy birds to cater for, and appear to breed quite readily.

ZEBRA FINCHES

Family: Estrildidae

The normal wild form of the Zebra Finch was first seen in Europe during the early 19th century. It was named after the characteristic barring present on the chest of cock birds, which resembles a zebra's markings. Hens lack this feature, as well as the coloured ear coverts, and they also have paler beaks.

FEEDING

In the wild, zebra finches, like other grassfinches feed largely on small seeds. They are thus easy birds to cater for in an aviary. A mixture of canary seed and millets forms the basis of their diet. Seeding grasses and other greenfood are also very popular. When breeding, zebra finches will sample soft food, and occasionally take small insects.

GENERAL CARE

Zebra finches can be accommodated satisfactorily either in flight cages or aviaries. They are generally hardy birds, but should be protected from the worst of the winter weather, when they will benefit from lighting and possibly heating in their quarters. Zebra finches are not aggressive birds, either when kept in groups on their own, or as part of a mixed collection.

BREEDING

Zebra finches construct a fairly loose nest, the work being shared between the sexes. Studies in the wild suggest that on average about 300 individual strands are used for this purpose, the smaller pieces being woven to create a lining for the nest. In aviary surroundings, a small nestbox with an open front, or a nesting basket will suit them. Once egg-laying commences, nesting material should be withdrawn to prevent continual building and consequent loss of eggs.

The average clutch is comprised of four or five eggs, but up to ten is not unknown. The birds take it in turns to incubate. The incubation period is not less than 12 days, and can be longer. It depends upon when the birds began to sit in earnest.

The young chicks grow rapidly, their eyes opening when just over a week old. They normally fledge around three weeks of age, but may still return to roost in the nest at night for a further period. The characteristic red beaks start to become apparent by six weeks of age, and they begin to moult for the first time when approximately two months old.

The Zebra Finch matures more quickly than any other species of Australian grassfinch. In some instances, cocks become fertile when only nine weeks old. While pairs under three months of age have bred successfully, it is better to wait until they are least six months old. Hens should be restricted to a maximum of four broods a year; otherwise the risk of egg-binding and related problems is significantly increased. Zebra finches are normally very dependable parents but, occasionally, young birds rearing for the first time may lose chicks because of their inexperience. Avoid any unnecessary interference, and when the birds nest again, the problem may have resolved itself.

ZEBRA FINCH
Taeniopygia guttata

Distribution: Australia apart from some coastal areas, and Tasmania

The nominate race is found on the Lesser Sunda Islands, to the north of Australia. This sub-species can be distinguished because the barring on the chest is either reduced or totally absent in the case of cock birds. Hens of this race are darker than their Australian counterparts. Although often living in large flocks numbering perhaps thousands of individuals, zebra finches form strong pair bonds and remain in close contact with their mates throughout the year. Indeed, it is in wild flocks that some of the popular mutations now kept throughout the world were first seen.

MUTATIONS

In view of the free-breeding nature of these finches, it is not surprising that a number of colour mutations have appeared, some of which originated in wild flocks. The following are the most widely-known colours: **Albino**: An Australian mutation, characterized by its red eyes, which distinguish it from the white form. **Crested**: The crested character can be combined with any colour, although the rules applying to the breeding of other crested birds also need to be observed with this mutation

(*see p.75*). **Penguin**: The body coloration of the cock bird gave rise to the popular name for this mutation, which dates back to the late 1940s. It is an autosomal recessive character, and remains scarce. **Silver**: The dominant form has cream cheek patches, and lighter coloration overall compared with its recessive counterpart, which has orange ear coverts. Combining these two mutations separately with the Fawn has produced cream zebra finches, of corresponding genetic types. **White**: The White was the first mutation to be

established in the Zebra Finch and it dates from 1921. Black eyes distinguish them from albinos. They tend to show traces of grey in their plumage, but repeated breeding of flecked whites will eliminate this fault in some of the offspring.

Perhaps the most unusual colour change relates to beak colour. A yellow, as distinct from the typical red-beaked variety, is now firmly established, and can be combined with any colour. Various other plumage mutations are known, but remain scarce.

ZEBRA FINCH: FAWN

These pale brown zebra finches were among the earliest recorded colour variants. The mutation is believed to have developed from two fawn hens that were caught around a camp fire close to Adelaide in South Australia, although it has also appeared in captive stock elsewhere. It is a sex-linked recessive mutation, and persistent fawn to fawn pairings are not to be recommended, as they produce dark smoky coloured offspring.

ZEBRA FINCH: CHESTNUT FLANKED WHITE

Known in Australia as the "Marked White", this is a mutation that occurred in the wild. In mainland Europe, a slightly different strain appears to have evolved, with such birds being described as "marmosets". Their skin is darker overall, and the cock's black throat markings are more prominent. In this instance, dark flecking is permitted in exhibition birds. It is a sex-linked recessive mutation.

ZEBRA FINCH: PIED

A combination of white and coloured areas characterize pied zebra finches. The pied factor is usually combined with either fawn or grey (for maximum contrast). Unlike some pied mutations, this is of autosomal recessive rather than dominant inheritance. It is impossible to predict the likely markings in any individual, so it is extremely difficult to produce good exhibition birds, where half the normal coloured plumage should be replaced by white.

AUSTRALIAN FINCHES

Family: Estrildidae

None of the Australian grassfinches are talented songsters, but these birds are highly valued for their attractive coloration and markings. Some colour mutations are known, but remain relatively scarce. Many species are domesticated in aviculture.

FEEDING

A seed mixture comprised of the smaller cereal seeds, whenever possible augmented by seeding grasses is recommended. It is important that a variety of livefood should also be offered, particularly when birds are breeding.

Gouldian finches appear to require a relatively high mineral intake. Rock salt, available from many bigger supermarkets, can be provided for them. Cuttlefish bone and iodine nibbles, as well as grit, should be available to the birds at all times.

GENERAL CARE

Gouldians especially have a reputation for being rather difficult birds to maintain and breed successfully, usually being housed in individual pairs in cages for the latter purpose. In Australia however, they are free-breeding when kept on a colony system. In Europe, their accommodation may need to take account of their desire to breed out of season. It is highly recommended that they be provided with heat and lighting during cold winter months.

BREEDING

An open nestbox, partially filled with suitable material is usually provided. It is vital to ensure that hens receive adequate calcium, and if necessary,

RED-HEADED GOULDIAN
Chloebia gouldiae

Distribution: Australia

Three distinct wild colour forms of the Gouldian Finch are known. The Red-headed phase is dominant to the Black-headed, and also sex-linked in its mode of inheritance. The third form, the Yellow-headed, is scarce in the wild and results from the inability of these birds to synthesize the red carotenoid pigment.

BLACK-HEADED GOULDIAN
Chloebia gouldiae

Distribution: Australia

The yellow form is an autosomal recessive mutation, which can affect either red or black-headed birds, those of the latter colour being distinguishable from normal black-headed individuals by the yellow markings at the tips of their beaks. Other mutations have been developed in aviary stock including white and lilac-breasted forms.

DIAMOND FIRETAIL FINCH
Emblema guttata

Distribution: Australia

This species, also known as the Diamond Sparrow, is well represented in collections of Australian finches, in spite of its aggressive tendencies. They can be bred successfully in cages, but are prone to obesity. Compatibility is vital – birds should be allowed to pair off themselves and then be transferred to separate accommodation.

cuttlefish bone should be grated over their food.

As many as six eggs can form the clutch, and the chicks should hatch about a fortnight after the start of the incubation period. They fledge at around three weeks of age, and begin to moult for the first time several weeks later. Losses of youngsters after fledging are not uncommon (in the case of Gouldians), the affected birds going light. A suitably varied diet, and a comprehensive food supplement should help to prevent this problem. Take care to ensure that the young birds can feed themselves adequately.

OTHER SPECIES

Long-tailed Grassfinch (*Peophila acuticauda*): In the wild, two sub-species showing different beak colorations are recognized: *P. a. hecki* with an orange-red beak, and *P. a. acuticauda*, with a yellow bill. Pairing these two races together yields offspring resembling *P. a. hecki*. In common with other Australian grassfinches, these birds will usually include pieces of charcoal in their nests. The reason for this is unclear, but it may be linked to nest sanitation, and a supply of crushed charcoal should be available to them.

Parson's Finch (*Poephila cincta*): These finches often prefer to use a nestbox for breeding purposes, rather than attempt to construct their own nest without any support. Some cock birds prove inveterate builders however, destroying one nest as it nears completion and starting it again elsewhere in another box. When breeding, pairs may prove quarrelsome towards other birds.

BICHENO'S FINCH
Poephila bichenovii

Distribution: Australia

These birds make an ideal introduction to breeding Australian grassfinches. They are usually compatible occupants of a communal aviary and may choose to nest in a small colony. Pairs remain in close proximity to each other at this stage. They can rear chicks without livefood, but this is not recommended.

STAR FINCH
Neochmia ruficauda

Distribution: Australia

Individuals can live well into their teens. They are likely to become aggressive when breeding, but can be housed with other birds in a flight which affords them adequate space. Their nest may be located on the floor of a planted flight, although they can also be bred in cages, using a traditional finch nestbox.

PIN-TAILED PARROT FINCH
Erythrura prasina

Distribution: Australia and South-east Asia

The Parrot Finches comprise a group of ten species, most of which are not available to aviculturists. These birds are invariably shy at first, but will settle down in spacious surroundings. They are normally found close to forests and will need adequate cover in an aviary. They will also take some livefood.

BENGALESE FINCHES

Family: Estrildidae

The Bengalese (*Lonchura domestica*), is totally unique to aviculture, since it does not occur in the wild, and its origins have been researched and debated. Any possible involvement of the Silverbill (*Lonchura malabarica*) in the ancestry of the Bengalese Finch was discounted by Dr Desmond Morris. Most opinion now agrees that Bengalese are derived from the Striated Mannikin (*Lonchura striata*).

Since Bengalese were probably developed in China, it seems likely that the sub-species known as *L. s. swinhoei*, occurring in China itself, and possibly *L. s. subsquamicoelis*, were both involved in its early development. The first Bengalese were seen in Japan about 1700, and introduced to Europe as recently as 1860.

FEEDING

A typical foreign finch diet suits these birds well, although they will often show a preference for millet sprays. While greenfood is popular, Bengalese tend not to consume large amounts of livefood.

GENERAL CARE

Bengalese are hardy birds which live well on a colony basis, and can be kept alongside other small finches in a mixed aviary.

BREEDING

Unfortunately, it is impossible to sex Bengalese by sight out of the breeding season, unless the cock gives voice to the characteristic song. Housing two birds within sight of each other can precipitate this behaviour, but may not necessarily be indicative of two hens if there is

BENGALESE: DILUTE FAWN

As its name suggests, this Bengalese is fawn in coloration. Its beak has a pinkish tinge. Dilute forms have also been bred, where the normal body coloration is diluted to give a paler form than normal.

BENGALESE: SELF CHESTNUT

Chestnut mutations are some of the newer colours, now being bred both in the Self, or pure-coloured form, and in combination with white. The dilute forms are paler in colour. Bengalese of pure white coloration were the first examples of the species to be seen and were initially believed to be a colour variant of the Nutmeg Finch (*L. punctulata*). White Bengalese tend to be smaller than the coloured birds.

BENGALESE: CHESTNUT AND WHITE

Bengalese of this colour are identical to the chestnut variety but should possess equal amounts of white in their plumage as well. The actual distribution of the markings can be highly variable. It is important in exhibition birds that the two colours are clearly delineated, and do not simply merge into a paler area, as this is adjudged to be a fault.

no response from either individual. Once identified, it is worth ringing birds of known sex using split celluloid bands.

Bengalese will breed satisfactorily either in cages or aviaries, and are mature by nine months of age. Their white eggs can number up to eight in a clutch, although four or five is average. The incubation period is about 12 days and the chicks fledge within about three weeks. Pairs are likely to prove prolific, but should be restricted to a maximum of three clutches per year. Various colour mutations have been established.

Bengalese have also been hybridised with other *Lonchura* species. In combination with the Bronze-winged Mannikin (*see p.101*), they have given rise to predominantly black hybrids.

Bengalese make an ideal introduction to the hobby of breeding finches, and they are usually keen to nest, and make very reliable parents. It is for this reason that they have become so widely used as foster parents for the young of Australian finches, particularly the rarer varieties (*see p.69*). Many breeders specialize in Bengalese for exhibition purposes however, and standards are established for these birds. Unlike budgerigars for example, Bengalese are normally exhibited in pairs, with several classes for the various colours and the crested form. It is vital in this instance that the birds correspond as closely as possible to each other, in terms of appearance. This applies especially for those birds with pied markings. Because of their social natures, Bengalese are also known as Society Finches, especially in the United States.

BENGALESE: FAWN AND WHITE

An identical form to the chestnut and white. There is also a chocolate and white combination. In the case of the fawn and white, because of the naturally paler coloration, offset against the white plumage, the distinction between the coloured areas may not be so clearly apparent as in other pied varieties.

BENGALESE: CRESTED CHOCOLATE

Foul marked Bengalese are quite often produced when breeding chocolate Bengalese finches. Pairing self to self over a period of time will enable a pure strain to be evolved. This colour proved dominant over the paler ones. The crested form originated in Japan. It can be combined with any colour, but crest to crest matings should not be attempted.

WAXBILLS

Family: Estrildidae

The waxbills are one of the most popular groups of seedeaters. A number of species are characterized by their dull reddish beaks, which resemble sealing wax in appearance, and this feature gave rise to the common name for these birds.

The estrildids as a family occur exclusively in the Old World, from Africa to Australasia. Many species congregate in large flocks, frequenting grassland or open scrubland. They feed close to the ground, although some are very specialized in their feeding habits, and are unknown in aviculture. Within a flock, waxbills form recognizable pairs, whose members reinforce their bond by mutual preening.

FEEDING
Although they will take various seeds, the majority of species depend mainly on smaller millets as a basic diet. Foreign finch mixtures are available; alternatively, the seeds can be fed separately. In the wild, estrildids frequently feed on green seeds which are significantly softer than those which feature in seed mixtures. As a result, particularly with recently-imported birds, it is useful to crush seeds with a rolling-pin, so that the birds can pick up crushed pieces from the debris which can be eaten whole, rather than dehusking the seeds. Seeding grasses such as canary seed grass, cut while the seed heads are still green, should be given at every opportunity. Soaked millet sprays are also taken readily by these birds.

Most livefoods are too large for the smaller waxbills especially, but hatchling crickets or moulting mealworms

ORANGE-CHEEKED WAXBILL
Estrilda melopoda

Distribution: Senegal and neighbouring countries

These waxbills can be rather nervous, especially when breeding, but given suitably secluded surroundings, they may rear three clutches of chicks in a season. As in other instances, the hens tend to be paler in colour than the cocks.

BLACK-CHEEKED WAXBILL
Estrilda erythronotos

Distribution: East and Southern Africa

Although not as colourful or common as the Orange-cheeked Waxbill, they make attractive aviary occupants. They are not always easy to establish however, being sensitive to cold and more dependent on livefood throughout the year than related waxbills. To compound the problem, many do not relish whiteworm. A pink-bellied form, sometimes classified as a separate species, *E. charmosyna*, occurs in East Africa. Some members of this genus are extremely well known in aviculture, whereas very little has been recorded about others such as the Black-lored Waxbill (*E. nigriloris*). In total, about 16 distinct species are recognized in the genus.

can be provided. Many successful breeders rely on whiteworm (*Enchytraeus*) cultures. These tiny worms are usually sold for tropical fish and amphibians. Colonies can be established very easily in a used margarine tub. Separate the worms into groups, and bury them at the bottom of the tub, under a piece of bread soaked in milk; then cover the bread with damp sphagnum peat. Kept in a temperature about 21°C (70°F), the culture will take about a month to mature. Then the worms can be harvested. Sequential cultures will ensure a regular supply is available, especially during the breeding season, when large quantities will be required.

GENERAL CARE

Estrildids have been kept and bred successfully in cages on occasion. However, the likelihood of successfully rearing chicks will be much greater if, for the warmer months, the birds are kept in a planted aviary where they can forage for livefood. These birds need heated winter quarters in areas where the temperature is liable to fall below zero. They will also need some additional lighting.

When kept under correct conditions, these small birds have a surprisingly long lifespan. For example, cordon bleus may live well into their teens, and gold-breasted waxbills have lived for in excess of 20 years. As a general rule, firefinches tend to be among the shorter-lived species. About 70 per cent of the overall population die each year, according to research carried out in Senegal. The age of adult birds will be unknown; it is best to buy immature birds.

COMMON WAXBILL
Estrilda astrild

Distribution: Africa, south of the Sahara desert

Also known as St Helena Waxbills, these active birds do not differ significantly in their requirements from other related species. The cock's nest is conspicuous and if threatened, the birds divert attention from their real nesting site beneath by entering this false chamber.

GOLDEN-BREASTED WAXBILL
Amandava subflava

Distribution: Western Africa

Of the three members of the genus *Amandava*, only the Golden-breasted, or Zebra, Waxbill originates in Africa. They are colourful birds, which can be sexed easily and will usually breed readily. Pairs should be kept separate, but can be safely associated with other unrelated species of a similar size.

RED-EARED WAXBILL
Estrilda troglodytes

Distribution: Northern Africa, from Senegal to Ethiopia

One of the most commonly imported waxbills, these attractive birds usually look immaculate. It is possible to sex them during the breeding season when cocks have brighter underparts. They are sometimes confused with *E. astrild*, but can be distinguished by their black rumps.

95

BREEDING

Most pairs prefer to use nesting baskets, but nesting boxes can also be taken over. On a few occasions, the birds may even build their own nest without artificial support, in a suitable bush in the aviary. Many estrildids construct relatively bulky nests, with a separate, conspicuous "cock" nesting chamber on the top. This is built as a decoy for potential predators, and remains empty throughout the breeding period. The cock bird frequently uses nesting material to attract a potential mate. Once the nest is completed, a clutch of about five eggs is then incubated by both adult birds for approximately 12 days. The resulting chicks should fledge by three weeks of age.

Where it is impossible to sex a species by sight, several birds of the same species should be purchased. Many estrildids can be kept in mixed groups, but not in the company of larger finches, even of the same family. When the adult birds nest again, it is often more satisfactory to remove the earlier youngsters from the aviary.

GENUS NIGRITA

The Negro Finches are a very rare genus in aviculture, probably because they spend much of their time high in the forest canopy, rarely descending to ground level. These estrildids are found in central West Africa and are usually associated with areas where oil palm trees grow. They have been observed feeding on the palm tree fruits. A few pairs of these rather dull birds have reached Europe over the past few years, but very little is known about their breeding behaviour.

LAVENDER WAXBILL
Estrilda caerulescens

Distribution: Tropical West Africa

This waxbill is a very lively bird, which can be fully appreciated in an aviary. Keep them warm when newly acquired. They often take nectar readily and insects should feature prominently in their diet. There are two related species: the Black-tailed (*E. perreini*) and the Red-flanked (*E. thomensis*) Lavender Finches.

RED-CHEEKED CORDON BLEU
Uraeginthus bengalus

Distribution: Tropical Africa, as far south as Zambia

There are three predominantly blue species of waxbill usually advertised as "Cordon Bleus". If fostering is necessary, the chances of success will be higher if other species of Cordon Bleu, such as the distinctive Blue-headed (*U. cyanocephala*), are used, rather than *Estrilda* waxbills. A rare orange-cheeked form is sometimes seen.

COMMON GRENADIER WAXBILL
Uraeginthus granatina

Distribution: Africa, from Angola southwards

The Common or Violet-eared Grenadier and the Purple Grenadier used to be grouped in a separate classification, but are now grouped within the Cordon Bleus. They have striking violet coloration and rank among the most expensive waxbills. They are also more aggressive and pairs should be housed on their own.

GENUS URAEGINTHUS

All five species in this genus occur in Africa and rank among the most striking of the waxbills. They feed primarily on the ground, rather than by clinging on to grass heads and removing the seeds. They also take a relatively high proportion of insect matter in their diet throughout the year, and in winter must be kept in a temperature above 7°C (45°F), once acclimatized. Cordon Bleus will breed quite readily. They prefer white feathers for lining the nest cavity and, in true waxbill style, both parents incubate the eggs and assist in rearing the chicks. The youngsters are usually independent about 14 days after fledging. The Blue-breasted Waxbill (*U. angolensis*) is similar in appearance to the Red-cheeked Cordon Bleus, but lacks their cheek patches. Where their distribution in the wild overlaps with the Red-cheeks they do not seem to hybridize.

GENUS NESOCHARIS

The members of this genus have a fairly localized distribution. The exception is the Grey-headed Olive-back (*N. capistrata*) which occurs across a wide belt of west and central Africa. Olive-backs are extremely rare in aviculture and little is known about their habits. One report suggests that they may take over the disused nests of weavers, which they then adapt and line for their own eggs. Olive-backs were seen in Belgium during 1985, and a few of these birds were later sold at a high price in Britain, possibly being the first living specimens seen in the country. If at all possible, obtain a group, rather than just a pair.

PURPLE GRENADIER WAXBILL
Uraeginthus ianthinogaster

Distribution: East Africa, from Somalia to Tanzania

Particular care must be taken when acclimatizing Grenadiers and livefood should be freely available. These birds typically occur in relatively arid country, feeding on termites, which may provide an additional means of obtaining water.

RED-BILLED FIREFINCH
Lagonosticta senegala

Distribution: Africa, south of the Sahara

The popular name of these finches is derived from the fiery red coloration of their plumage. About ten species are recognized. All are delicate, needing to be transferred to heated quarters before the temperature falls below 7°C (45°F). Established pairs can prove prolific breeders under suitable conditions, producing four or five clutches in succession. They build a typical estrildid nest, and at this time may resent the close attention of other members of the genus.

GENUS SPERMOPHAGA

Bluebills have become more widely available during recent years, but even now are not common. They naturally occur in forested areas, and should be provided with adequate seclusion (plants or shading) in aviaries. In the past, bluebills have proved difficult to establish, but one British importer experienced success when he mixed their seed with natural yoghurt. This contains *Lactobacillus*, which will populate the intestinal tract and help to guard against digestive disturbances. Bluebills will often take other soft food readily and their natural diet includes a high proportion of insects. They have been bred successfully, lining their nest with soft feathers. In cold climates, heat and additional light will be necessary during the winter.

GENUS PYRENESTES

These species are named seedcrackers because of their relatively large bills. Some individual birds have larger beaks than others which may be related to differences in their feeding habits. The three species are almost identical in appearance. They appear to have similar habits to bluebills and do well when kept under similar conditions. Their claws may need to be cut back regularly as they can become overgrown.

GENUS CRYPTOSPIZA

These four species of Crimson-wings are scarce avicultural subjects, and are believed to be related to both the Twin-spots and Bluebills, needing similar care. The Red-faced Crimson-wing (*C. reichenovii*) has been bred successfully. The nest is built rapidly, mainly by the cock bird. Spiders seem to be a favoured rearing food, but other livefood is usually taken and should be provided regularly.

GENUS ORTYGOSPIZA

The Quail Finches are highly specialized waxbills. They spend most of their time on the aviary floor, frequenting grassy areas in the wild and only flying up when danger is near at hand. These finches should not be kept alongside other ground-dwelling birds such as Chinese Painted Quails, if breeding is to be encouraged. Pairs are best housed individually. They will nest on the floor if adequate seclusion is available. Their calls are louder than those of other waxbills, and may help to keep the birds in touch when they are hidden in grass.

GENUS AMANDAVA

Of the three members of this genus, only the Golden-breasted Waxbill (*Amandava subflava*) originates in Africa. The Green Avadavat (*A. formosa*) and the Red Avadavat or Tiger Finch (*A. amandava*) are both Asiatic. Another unusual characteristic of the Red Avadavat is its high frequency of acquired melanism, with many birds developing blackish plumage, although their bills remain red. This could be linked to a deficiency of Vitamin D_3, tending to predominate in birds kept inside and fed largely on seed, with little insect matter or greenfood in their diet. Under more favourable conditions,

SCHLEGEL'S TWINSPOT
Mandingoa nitidula schlegeli

Distribution: Mainly Southern Africa

Pairs will breed quite readily, building a relatively large nest for this purpose. They will live together as a group even when breeding, without serious signs of aggression. However, as a general rule, they are not hardy birds. The classification of twinspots is confused, with only six species divided between the four genera *Hypargos*, *Clytospiza*, *Mandingoa*, and *Euschistospiza*. Their common name stems from the spots on the sides of their bodies. The only one of these species available with any regularity is Peter's Twinspot (*H. niveoguttatus*). The nominate race of Schlegel's Twinspot is usually known as the Green Twinspot. Indeed, because of the relatively large number of isolated populations which have arisen, as many as five sub-species are recognized by taxonomists.

normal coloration will re-emerge at the next moult.

The Green Avadavat is similar in habits to its red cousin, but less frequently available. Golden-breasted Waxbills are colourful birds, which can be sexed easily and will usually breed readily. Pairs should be kept separate, but can be safely associated with other unrelated species of a similar size.

GENUS PYTILIA

Five species are included in this genus, and all can be sexed visually. The best-known is probably the Melba Finch (*P. melba*), but the Pytilias generally are really birds for the specialist. They are usually aggressive, and pairs are best accommodated individually. Although apparently not as dependent on livefood as some other estrildids, the likelihood of breeding them successfully will be increased if a supply of insects is provided. In the case of birds that are reluctant to take soft food or an insectile mixture, place livefood in the feeding pot where the birds may be persuaded to take the loose food as well as the insects.

GENUS PARMOPTILA

The two species of Ant-pecker are unusual members of this family, at first sight being more reminiscent of warblers than waxbills. Their bills are relatively thin, while their tongue is brush-like, suggesting that they feed on nectar, but in reality, as far as is known, they are insectivorous in their feeding habits. They have been very occasionally available to aviculturists, and their management requires a daily supply of insects.

MELBA FINCH
Pytilia melba

Distribution: Much of Southern Africa, excluding rain forest

There are five species in the Pytilia genus, and all can be sexed visually. The best known is probably the Melba, or Green-winged Finch. They are usually aggressive and pairs are best kept in separate accommodation.

RED AVADAVAT
Amandava amandava

Distribution: India and South-east Asia

The Red Avadavat, or Tiger Finch, is unique among the estrildids, the males moulting into nuptial plumage at the onset of the breeding season. The Red Avadavat has another unusual characteristic – a high frequency of acquired melanism (see text above).

GREEN AVADAVAT
Amandava formosa

Distribution: Central India

The Green Avadavat is similar in habits to its red cousin, but it is less frequently available. Livefood is vital for the successful rearing of chicks, and if possible, the adult birds should be accustomed to suitable foods, such as whiteworm, before the onset of the breeding season.

MANNIKINS and MUNIAS

Family: Estrildidae

This large and popular group of estrildids are frequently housed in colonies, where successful breeding results are more likely as the birds' natural flocking instincts will be satisfied. In addition, it increases the chances of pairs being acquired, since it is often impossible to sex these birds by visual means. Follow the recommendations given previously for colony breeding (*see page 65*). The only drawback is that sometimes only the dominant pair of birds will go to nest, and little can be done to overcome this problem.

Mannikins and munias have a wide distribution, extending from Africa eastwards to Australasia. Mannikins should not be confused with the totally unrelated group of softbills known as manakins, which occur in Central and South America.

A number of colour mutations are now established in the case of the Java Sparrow and, perhaps surprisingly, may prove more free-breeding than the normal grey form. White javas have been known for a long time, being first bred in the Orient. They tend to be slightly smaller than the grey. Many are not pure white, showing traces of grey in their plumage. Strains of pied Java Sparrows have been evolved, and in some instances, the markings are effectively standardized, giving rise to the saddleback. One of the most attractive mutations is the Fawn, which has been developed in Australia since the 1960s.

There is no difference in plumage between the sexes, but as in other similar species, cock birds can be recognized by their song. Java Sparrows

CUT-THROAT
Amadina fasciata

Distribution: Northern and East Africa

Cut-throats can be kept in groups, or in the company of other reasonably large finches. Hens are highly prone to egg-binding. If this occurs repeatedly, there is a risk of prolapse, in which part of the rectum will protrude from the vent as a fleshy mess.

JAVA SPARROW
Padda oryzivora

Distribution: Java and Bali

Known under various common names, including "Rice Bird" in the United States. This refers to its habit of plundering ripening crops in its native lands. Keeping these birds is illegal in some parts of the United States, as escaped birds could become a threat to agriculture.

AFRICAN SILVERBILL
Lonchura malabarica cantans

Distribution: North Africa, from Senegal to Sudan

Two sub-species of this Silverbill are recognized, with the Indian race being the nominate form. These birds are easy to feed and generally prove ready nesters. They can be kept with *Estrilda* waxbills. Chicks can be reared, successfully without livefood. Useful as foster-parents.

are relatively hardy once acclimatized and can be kept safely out of doors throughout the year. They prefer a nesting-basket for breeding, and build a nest (typical of its group) in which the hen will deposit up to eight eggs.

GENUS LONCHURA

This genus comprises nearly 30 species. Although many of these are popular aviary birds, others – notably those confined to islands in and close to the Celebes Sea – are virtually unstudied. These birds frequently develop over-grown claws, a natural adaptation that helps them to grip on to the stems of grass when feeding on a seed head. However, it can prove dangerous in aviary surroundings. If these birds are kept in mixed groups, hybridization may occur.

Other species often available are: **Spice Bird** (*L. punctulata*): Like other members of this genus, Spice Birds are less dependent on livefood for the successful rearing of chicks compared with other estrildids. They normally use fresh material for nest construction, and generally prefer to nest and roost in thick vegetation. **Chestnut Munia** (*L. malacca*): Also known as Tri-coloured Nun, this bird is easy to maintain once acclimatized. A group should be housed together for the best chance of success. **White-backed Mannikin** (*L. striata*): This species is thought to be the original ancestor of the Bengalese Finch, and certainly has been kept in aviaries for centuries. **Magpie Mannikin** (*L. fringilloides*): These black and white mannikins possess sturdy beaks and can prove quite aggressive.

CHESTNUT-BREASTED MANNIKIN
Lonchura castaneothorax

Distribution: Coastal zone of eastern and northern Australia up to New Guinea

This is one of the less-commonly available munias, but is equally easy to keep. Various sub-species are recognized; thus plumage differences may not indicate sexual dimorphism. Occasionally feed on insects, although seeds form the basis of their diet.

BRONZE-WINGED MANNIKIN
Lonchura cucullata

Distribution: Africa, excluding the south-west

The African mannikins were formerly a separate genus, *Spermestes*, but have now been combined with the Asiatic species. They tend to be more aggressive and should not be mixed with smaller birds. A variety of nesting sites will attract them and they breed readily.

WHITE-HEADED MUNIA
Lonchura maja

Distribution: Malay Peninsula and neighbouring islands

Known under a variety of common names, including "White-headed Nun" and "Pale-headed Mannikin", these birds present no special difficulties. It is not unusual for them to construct a nest in suitable vegetation, ignoring any artificial nesting sites provided.

WHYDAHS, WEAVERS and SPARROWS

Family: Ploceidae

This group of birds offers considerable scope for the specialist, but is relatively neglected in this respect at present, compared with waxbills. Many whydahs and weavers in particular are extremely colourful, and can be kept together in groups. They are also relatively hardy in most cases once acclimatized, and will often attempt to nest under aviary conditions.

The cock whydahs in the sub-family Viduinae undergo a dramatic change in appearance at the onset of the breeding season, growing long black tail plumes which gave rise to their alternative name of "widow birds". At this stage, they are advertised as CIC, meaning cocks in colour, and are correspondingly more expensive. They are parasitic in their breeding habits, the hens laying in the nests of specific waxbills, which then hatch and rear the whydahs' chicks alongside their own. In most cases it is impossible to distinguish visually between the sexes when the birds are out of colour (OOC), as cocks resemble their dull coloured partners.

FEEDING

Whydahs are easily fed on a diet of the smaller cereal seeds, augmented with greenfood, grit and cuttlefish.

GENERAL CARE

These birds cannot be accommodated satisfactorily in cages, and their magnificent tail plumes will only show to good effect in a spacious aviary. Perches should be positioned so that the tail will not be damaged by the aviary mesh when the bird alights and turns around on a perch. As whydahs frequently descend to the ground in search of food, a clear area on the floor is also recommended.

BREEDING

Although in some respects these whydahs are undemanding avicultural subjects, breeding successes are few because of their highly specialized reproductive needs. Each species shows a preference for waxbills that occur in their native range. Therefore, a large, well-planted aviary housing three pairs of the appropriate species is to be recommended. A cock and several hen whydahs should be introduced prior to the start of the breeding season, so as not to disturb the waxbills later. If at all possible, once whydahs commence breeding they should be accommodated alongside the waxbill species which normally rears its chicks, but success with other waxbills has been reported. In Australia, where imports have not taken place for many years, viable aviary populations of certain whydahs still exist, which shows what can be achieved by dedicated breeders.

Other species include: **Paradise Whydah** (*Vidua paradisaea*): Whereas the Pin-tailed cock in colour has relatively slender tail plumes, those of the Paradise Whydah are very broad. *Pytilia* species are the usual hosts, particularly the Melba Finch (*P. melba*), but firefinches have also reared Paradise Whydah chicks. Cocks in eclipse plumage may be recognized by their darker body coloration. *V. orientalis*, a broad-tailed

PIN-TAILED WHYDAH
Vidua macroura

Distribution: Most of Africa, from Senegal southwards

This is the only species that does not have a closely defined relationship with a particular waxbill during the breeding period. Possibly as many as 19 species have been host to its eggs. Red-eared Waxbills (*E. troglodytes*) are often used as hosts in aviaries.

FISCHER'S WHYDAH
Vidua fischeri

Distribution: East Africa, from Somalia to Tanzania

This uncommon, but striking species uses an equally colourful host – the Purple Grenadier (*Uraeginthus ianthinogaster*). The cock mimics the call of these waxbills to perfection. Its alternative common name is "Straw-tailed Whydah". They may remain in colour for six months or more.

form of the Paradise Whydah with shorter and more elaborate tail plumes is also available occasionally. **Queen Whydah** (*Vidua regia*): Resembles the Pin-tailed when out of colour, but has red rather than brownish legs. The Violet-eared Waxbill is the usual host species, but cordon bleus have also been accepted. **Senegal Combassou** (*Vidua chalybeata*): Relatively dull in their breeding finery in comparison with males of previous species, Combassous are also described as "Indigo Birds", due to the plumage coloration of cocks

in colour. Up to seven species are recognized, according to some taxonomists, with firefinches normally acting as the unwitting hosts. In a few cases however, Combassous have been known to hatch and rear their own chicks, showing a possible affinity with the *Euplectes* whydahs in the sub-family Ploceinae, which are not parasitic in their breeding habits.

SUB-FAMILY PLOCEINAE

Like the preceding group, some members of this sub-family of weavers and non-parasitic whydahs also undergo

striking colour changes at the onset of the breeding season. The weavers are so named because of their ability to construct elaborate nests, often hanging from tree-branches, out of reach of predators.

FEEDING AND GENERAL CARE

As for the sub-family Viduinae.

BREEDING

Many species in this group are colony nesters and should be housed accordingly, although breeding successes are

YELLOW-MANTLED WHYDAH
Euplectes macrourus

Distribution: Africa, from Senegal to Tanzania and south to Angola

The *Euplectes* whydahs, unlike the *Vidua* species, are not parasitic in their breeding habits, but cocks moult into nuptial plumage in a similar manner. When breeding, cocks are polygamous and should be kept in the company of several hens.

RED-COLLARED WHYDAH
Euplectes ardens

Distribution: Much of Africa, from Senegal southwards

These whydahs have a very wide distribution and sub-species are recognized throughout their range. The cock bird shown here is from East Africa. The red throat markings are absent in individuals of the western race, *E. a. concolor*, which are sometimes known as "Black Whydahs".

FAN-TAILED WHYDAH
Euplectes axillaris

Distribution: Much of Africa, from the Sahara southwards

Also known as the "Red-shouldered Whydah", this tends to be a relatively docile bird in aviary surroundings. They usually nest in long grass and have been bred successfully in planted flights. The male retains its red shoulder markings outside the breeding period.

103

not common. Weavers tend to be destructive in a planted flight, seeking fresh nesting material. Small trees or branches arranged like miniature trees make ideal breeding sites. Raffia, available from garden centres and similar outlets, is used readily to form the distinctive pendulous nests. In some instances, these may be woven in such a manner that they are attached to the aviary roof. The average clutch comprises three or four eggs and the incubation period is likely to be about two weeks. Chicks fledge when little over a fortnight old, and are usually independent by the age of one month.

GENUS EUPLECTES

All mature cock members of this genus of bishops and whydahs undergo a nuptial moult. *Euplectes* whydahs are less commonly available than certain *Vidua* species, although both Yellow-shouldered (*E. macrourus*) and White-winged (*E. albonotatus*) have recently been imported into Britain. Unless Orange Weavers (*Euplectes orix*) are colour-fed, their striking fiery orange coloration tends to fade over the course of successive moults. These birds are polygamous, and should be kept in groups, with one cock alongside several hens. The cock bird starts to prepare the nest, and in the latter stages is assisted by a hen. When fledged, the youngsters should be watched to ensure they are not persecuted by the cock. Unfortunately, *Euplectes* weavers often breed during the latter part of the year in northern climates, which can lead to disappointments. It may be possible to overcome this if the birds are in an indoor flight.

GRENADIER WEAVER
Euplectes orix orix

Distribution: Africa, south of the Sahara

There is often confusion over the common names of these weavers, since five distinct sub-species are recognized. The Grenadier is generally accepted as the nominate race. Individuals can be aggressive, especially when kept as part of a mixed collection.

NAPOLEON WEAVER
Euplectes afer

Distribution: Much of Africa, south of the Sahara

Also known as the "Golden Bishop", this is one of the species where cocks have predominantly yellow plumage during the nuptial period. At other times, cocks often have darker backs than hens. They nest in reed beds and will need similar cover to breed in an aviary.

RED-HEADED QUELEA
Quelea erythrops

Distribution: Africa, south of the Sahara

Members of this genus, like certain other weavers, are serious pests in parts of their range. All quelea will thrive if kept in a flock in aviary surroundings. When breeding they nest communally and the young are reared on livefood. The Red-billed Weaver (*Q. quelea*) is monogamous.

GENUS PLOCEUS

This is a large genus, and it can be difficult to identify the various species correctly without reference to a detailed field guide. Even then, some *Ploceus* weavers are scarce in aviculture and little is known about their habits. The Village Weaver (*P. cucullatus*) is a typical member of the genus: robust and often aggressive towards other species. Cocks are thought to be polygamous when breeding, and moult into their bright olive-yellow plumage as the breeding season approaches.

SUB-FAMILY PASSERINAE

Sparrows and their immediate relatives are not widely kept by aviculturists, although they are undemanding and settle well under aviary conditions. Their lack of popularity may stem from their usually rather dull coloration. An exception is the cock Golden Song Sparrow (*Passer luteus*).

Two species of weaver belonging to the genus *Sporopipes* are occasionally seen: the Scaly-crowned Weaver (*S. squamifrons*) and the Speckle-fronted Weaver (*S. frontalis*). Both species may prove difficult to acclimatize successfully. Neither is brightly coloured and the sexes are similar in appearance. If chicks are hatched successfully, large quantities of livefood will be required to rear them successfully.

As with the whydahs, weavers offer considerable potential for the specialist. Apart from their striking coloration in many instances, they are robust birds once established, and easy to maintain as aviary occupants, while their breeding habits are fascinating to observe.

MADAGASCAR WEAVER
Foudia madagascariensis

Distribution: Madagascar

Also known as the "Madagascar Fody", this bird breeds quite readily under aviary conditions and is well-established in avian collections. Other fodies from neighbouring islands remain virtually unknown in aviculture.

BAYA WEAVER
Ploceus philippinus

Distribution: Indian sub-continent to South-east Asia

A common weaver that can be kept on its own in a mixed flight of similarly-sized companions, but shows to best effect when kept in a group. Cocks will readily weave their nests, which are entered by means of a tunnel extending below the globular-shaped nesting chamber.

SUDAN GOLDEN SPARROW
Auripasser luteus

Distribution: Across Africa, from Nigeria to Arabia

In spite of their name, song sparrows are not talented songsters. They are best kept in groups on their own, although they can be housed with waxbills. Adequate cover must be present in their aviary for breeding purposes, since they are shy birds. Hens are predominantly brown, lacking this bright yellow coloration.

BUNTINGS

Family: Emberizidae

Members of this family show considerable diversity in their feeding habits, with the tanagers and related species comprising the subfamily Thraupidae being grouped in the softbill section. Although the species below feed on seeds, they also tend to be highly insectivorous, especially when breeding. Pairs are generally ready to nest and this group offers considerable scope for the enthusiastic specialist. Many species remain unknown to aviculturists however, and only a few are regularly available.

FEEDING

A wide variety of seeds, and an insectile mixture plus livefood should be offered. Care must be taken when feeding hemp however, because of its addictive qualities.

GENERAL CARE

The members of this family have a wide distribution and many species are hardy once acclimatized properly. They need to be kept in flights or planted aviaries, where they can forage for livefood. The cocks of some species are talented songsters, but will not thrive if housed in the close confines of a cage. They are reasonably compatible with their own kind, and other birds of similar size, but difficulties may arise during the breeding season.

BREEDING

In most instances, these birds will construct an open, cup-shaped nest, although this is sometimes covered, notably in the case of New World species. The task is usually undertaken by the hen, and the location chosen may be

GOLDEN-BREASTED BUNTING
Emberiza flaviventris

Distribution: Southern Africa

These buntings can be confused with the Eurasian Yellow-breasted Bunting (*E. aureola*). However, they can be easily distinguished by their head markings, with cocks of the African species having white head stripes. As a general rule, the Eurasian species are hardier, and possibly less insectivorous.

JACARINI FINCH
Volatinia jacarina

Distribution: Central and South America

Sometimes described as the Blue-black Grassquit, this species is a typical member of the group, which also includes the Olive (*Tiaris olivacea*) and the Cuban Finch (*T. canora*). Grassquits can rear their chicks without livefood. Cocks tend to be aggressive when breeding. Nests are close to the ground.

WHITE-THROATED SEEDEATER
Sporophila albogularis

Distribution: North-east Brazil

Although not common as a group in avicultural circles, some species of *Sporophila* are occasionally available. This particular species has been bred in the past, but wild stock is now no longer available. Try to obtain a small group as this gives a greater likelihood of establishing breeding stock. Hens, in particular, may be scarce.

quite close to the ground. Ideally, for breeding purposes, pairs should be housed in individual, well-planted aviaries. Up to six eggs may be laid, and these normally hatch within two weeks. The chicks leave the nest about two or three weeks later. To rear them successfully, livefood will be vital.

SUB-FAMILY CARDINALINAE

The members of this group do not differ significantly in their habits from other species, although they are relatively scarce in aviculture. The Saltators (*Saltator* spp) tend to require a larger proportion of fruit in their diet however, and are especially fond of berries. Certain cardinals are included in this sub-family, notably the Virginian Cardinal (*Cardinalis cardinalis*), which will require colour-feeding to prevent its red plumage from fading over successive moults.

The grosbeaks are not common avicultural subjects, although the Yellow Grosbeak (*Pheucticus chrysopeplus*) has become more available in Britain during recent years. These birds have powerful beaks, and can easily cope with sunflower seeds. If they cannot be kept on their own, they are probably best accommodated with birds of similar size.

The colourful New World buntings are also included in this sub-family. Unfortunately, there is a preponderance of males normally available, since they are more brightly coloured. The scarcity of hens can handicap attempts to obtain breeding pairs. Their diet should consist of the smaller seeds, with livefood again being particularly important during the breeding season.

PARROT-BILLED SEEDEATER
Sporophila peruviana

Distribution: Ecuador and Peru

A member of a large genus, comprised of approximately 31 species, these birds are characterized by their short, stout bills. They are easy to maintain on a diet of millets, soaked seed and greenfood, with some insects. Pairs prove keen to nest, although they are best housed individually.

RED-COWLED CARDINAL
Paroaria dominicana

Distribution: Brazil

These birds can be kept almost exclusively on seed. However, they should be given a much wider range of foods, including softbill food and greenstuff. They are not usually aggressive, and can be kept in an outside aviary with a suitable shelter once acclimatized. The Red-crested Cardinal (*P. coronata*), found over a wider area of South America, needs similar care.

CINNAMON WARBLING FINCH
Poospiza ornata

Distribution: Argentina

There are about 16 species in this genus, which is relatively unknown in avicultural circles. They have a fairly dainty appearance, compared with the *Sporophila* seedeaters, yet eat a fairly similar diet, including insects. Livefood, such as spiders, appears to be vital for breeding success. Cocks tend to be aggressive at this time.

TANAGERS

Family: Emberizidae

Softbills are grouped together in aviculture on the basis of their feeding habits, rather than as part of a strict zoological classification. They are popularly regarded as being more demanding than seedeaters, but the majority of species featured in this section are quite straightforward to look after. Pairs will breed successfully when kept in suitable conditions, some even proving prolific.

The more insectivorous species, such as flycatchers, can prove difficult to adapt to artificial diets, and livefood must always be available to them. Some softbills are hardy once acclimatized, but during the colder months of the year in temperate regions, most will benefit from the provision of artifical heat and lighting.

Tanagers initially became known in Europe during the 16th century, though the first living examples were not actually seen until the latter years of the 19th century. They occur exclusively in the New World, extending northwards from Argentina as far as Canada. Over 200 species are now recognized, and through their wide range, these birds are found in varying habitats. Some species are found at relatively high altitudes, and prove reasonably hardy once acclimatized. Others, occurring in tropical forests, can only be kept safely in outdoor aviaries during the warmer months of the year.

Some members of this group are extremely colourful, others are duller. These variations are usually reflected in the prices quoted for individual species. None are talented songsters; their calls consisting largely of metallic sounding cheeps and harsher notes. They range in size from the small Euphonias, which are little bigger than 10 cm (4 in), to the larger species like the Magpie Tanager (*Cissopis leveriana*), which is approximately 23 cm (9 in) in length. As a general rule, the larger species are hardier than their smaller counterparts.

Many species remain totally unknown in aviculture. Indeed, it can prove difficult to identify some tanagers cor-rectly, since over 600 sub-species are recognized by taxonomists. Birds showing slight variations in markings therefore may not be of the opposite sex, but simply different sub-species. Once established, tanagers can live for a decade or longer and, especially when housed in a planted flight, a true pair are likely to attempt to breed. If conditions are favourable, they can be quite prolific, nesting three or four times in succession.

Tanagers are active birds, and should never be housed in cages. They are also essentially omnivorous, consuming both fruit and insects, though the actual proportions vary according to the species concerned. The following groupings cover those which are most commonly available, on the basis of the individual genera.

GENUS TANGARA

Approximately a quarter of all known species are grouped in this genus, which is the most significant in avicultural terms. Even so, many of these tanagers are not often available. Two possible

BLUE-NECKED TANAGER
Tangara cyanicollis

Distribution: South America from Colombia to Brazil, between tropical and sub-tropical zones

Seven sub-species are claimed to exist. One, *T. c. albotibialis*, is known only from a single specimen. As its name suggests, this bird had white legs. Blue-necked tanagers have been bred successfully in Britain in 1966, constructing a nest of moss and leaves in a hollow tree trunk.

EMERALD-SPOTTED TANAGER
Tangara guttata

Distribution: South America from Costa Rica to north Brazil

As with many other *Tangara* tanagers, a significant number of sub-species has been identified. In the wild, the northern race is said to prefer dark nesting material. On fledging, the young are duller than their parents, moulting into adult plumage by the age of nine months.

species are only represented in museum collections, being known solely from their skins. *Tangara* tanagers are largely confined to northern South America. They are essentially forest-dwellers and often found in small groups.

These tanagers tend to be more frugivorous in their feeding habits than members of some related genera. Their food should consist of a variety of chopped fruit, augmented with mynah pellets. If these pellets are not available, a good quality insectile mixture can be sprinkled over the fruit instead. Tan-agers are capable of nibbling chunks out of large slices of apple for example, but when feeding, they can become territorial, and may chase off other birds. Diced food offers less opportunity for an individual to monopolize the available food in this way. A small quantity of livefood should also be offered, especially soft-bodied invertebrates such as spiders or redworms. Mealworms can prove indigestible to these smaller birds.

When first acquired, *Tangara* tanagers also benefit from a supply of a nectar solution. Provide this in a tubular drinker however, because these tanagers are inveterate bathers, and will immerse themselves in an open pot of nectar, with catastrophic results. Apart from drinking water therefore, a daily supply of fresh water for bathing purposes should be available. This will help to keep the bird's feet clean and ensure that its plumage remains in top condition.

Cleanliness is vital in keeping tanagers in good health. Like many other softbills, they tend to be susceptible to pseudotuberculosis. Affected birds may simply appear slightly off-colour at first,

OPAL TANAGER
Tangara velia

Distribution: Northern South America, east of the Andes

These tanagers have been represented in European collections since the 1890s. Females can be recognized by the greenish-blue side of their heads; this area is distinctly purplish in cock birds.

SILVER-THROATED TANAGER
Tangara icterocephala

Distribution: South America, from Costa Rica to Ecuador

These birds have been bred on various occasions. Hens tend to be greener and duller in coloration than cock birds. They show less tendency to flock than related species, often being encountered in individual pairs. The female is probably responsible for nest construction, with moss being a favoured material for the purpose.

GOLDEN TANAGER
Tangara arthus

Distribution: Northern and eastern South America

This species, also known as the "Black-eared Golden", is relatively common in aviculture and has been bred successfully on several occasions. Indeed, pairs may have as many as three clutches in succession under favourable conditions in a planted flight. They will probably have to winter indoors.

with weight loss becoming evident later. Any sick birds must be removed from the aviary immediately, since this disease is spread via the droppings.

These tanagers can prove rather delicate until established in their quarters, and should be overwintered in an indoor flight. Although usually they will live in harmony with other softbills, certain individuals can prove aggressive, even to birds considerably larger than themselves. Such behaviour is particularly evident when the tanagers are in breeding condition, and at this time, they may persecute other birds in their aviary, in order to obtain feathers to line their nest.

Some *Tangara* species can be sexed visually, as the hens are often duller than cocks. For a serious breeding programme, it will be necessary to purchase at least four birds of the same species. With just a pair, if one member is lost several years later, it is likely to prove very difficult to obtain another, particularly of the same sub-species.

Housing pairs individually will probably offer the greatest chance of breeding success. *Tangara* tanagers build a cup-shaped nest, either in a nestbox or a dense bush in the aviary. Dried fine strands of grass are a popular nesting material. Two or three brown speckled eggs form the usual clutch, and the hen incubates them alone. The chicks should hatch after about a fortnight and will fledge around the age of 16 days, with increasing amounts of livefood being taken during the rearing period. They will be independent three weeks or so later, and their parents may start breeding again, particularly if these

SEVEN-COLOURED TANAGER
Tangara fastuosa

Distribution: Eastern Brazil

A forest-dwelling species, the Seven-coloured, or Superb, Tanager is perhaps the most striking member of a very colourful genus. Although it has bred in aviaries in the past, it is now exceptionally rare in avicultural circles.

PALM TANAGER
Thraupis palmarum

Distribution: Central America, and South America east of the Andes

The Palm Tanager is often readily available, although it is not one of the most striking species. The birds are easy to cater for, and are relatively hardy.

BLUE-CAPPED TANAGER
Thraupis cyanocephala

Distribution: North-western South America to Peru

Several distinct races of this tanager are recognized. It is often found in forests and thus prefers a densely planted area when in aviary conditions. Hens lay clutches of two eggs, which are pale green, with darker brown spots.

youngsters are removed to separate quarters.

The dietary needs of these birds do vary, in terms of their precise requirements, and this is not entirely a matter of size. Indeed, the large Magpie Tanager, which occurs over a large area of South America, has proved a highly insectivorous species, skilled at catching certain insects in flight, and able to devour mealworms whole without difficulty. The most unusual member of this group of birds is the Swallow Tanager (*Tersina viridis*), which nests in natural cavities. This, too, is highly insectivorous.

EUPHONIAS

These small birds belonging to the genus *Euphonia* range from Central America as far south as Argentina. They and the related Chlorophonias (*Chlorophonia* spp) should be treated like *Tangara* tanagers, with a significant level of mixed fruit included in their diet daily. Twenty-four species of euphonia are recognized. Although cocks are colourful, hens are drab by comparison, and it can be difficult to distinguish between females of different species.

GENERA RAMPHOCELUS, THRAUPIS AND ANISOGNATHUS

Members of these genera rank among the easiest to cater for, and are relatively hardy. The Palm Tanager (*T. palmarum*) is often available, although it is not the most striking species, by comparison with the various Scarlet Tanagers (*Ramphocelus* spp), and the Mountain Tanagers (*Anisognathus* spp). It may be necessary to use a colour food.

SILVER-BEAKED TANAGER
Ramphocelus carbo

Distribution: South America, east of the Andes

One of the most striking tanagers, these birds are unfortunately no longer seen in many collections, although they are easily cared for. Insects, fruit, mynah pellets and colour food should be part of their diet. All larger tanagers tend to be aggressive and pairs are best kept separately.

PURPLE HONEYCREEPER
Cyanerpes caeruleus

Distribution: Most of South America

Closely related to the tanagers, the birds belonging to the genera *Dacnis*, *Chlorophanes* and *Cyanerpes* are often described as "honeycreepers". Although they are omnivorous, nectar should always be available. Soaked mynah pellets and finely diced fruit suit them well. Livefood is important during the nesting period. Pairs will breed with relatively little difficulty.

RED-LEGGED HONEYCREEPER
Cyanerpes cyaneus

Distribution: Northern and eastern South America

Also known as the "Yellow-winged Sunbird", the male undergoes a striking change in coloration at the onset of the breeding season, but for the remainder of the year its brighter red legs serve to distinguish it from the female. Sugarbirds are among the easiest nectivores to keep, but require winter heating.

BARBETS and HORNBILLS

Families: Capitonidae and Bucerotidae

Barbets are found throughout the tropical regions of the world, and are characterized by the bristles surrounding their stout beaks. These birds are found in a variety of environments, from tropical forest to open, arid scrubland. These differences are reflected in their needs as aviary occupants. All species can be destructive to woodwork however, and should not be mixed with other birds. Barbets can even prove very aggressive towards each other. Larger species, such as the Giant Barbet (*Megalaima virens*), are particularly savage. If they become too aggressive the pairs will have to be kept separated.

The South American species, including the striking Flame-headed Barbet (*Eubucco bourcierii*) and the Toucan Barbet (*Semnornis ramphastinus*) are rarely seen, but when available, need a diet of fruit, mynah pellets and some livefood. They are very sensitive to the cold, and should be kept indoors during the winter months. Conversely, they do not thrive in very high temperatures, and will breathe with their beaks open when suffering from heat stress.

The Fire-tufted (*Psilopogon pyrolophus*) is a colourful Asiatic species that needs similar care to its New World counterparts. It is not known whether differences in iris coloration are a sign of sexual dimorphism.

HORNBILLS

The members of this family, ranging from Africa across Asia are too large in most cases to be accommodated satisfactorily by most aviculturists. But the smaller species make fascinating aviary occupants. Most notable among these is

BLACK-COLLARED BARBET
Lybius torquatus

Distribution: East and South Africa

This species tends to prefer scrubland, rather than dense forest, and is seen in flocks in the wild, although pairs are best kept on their own. This applies to all barbets, in view of their powerful beaks. They are not difficult birds to maintain however, and make lively aviary occupants. They will require warm winter surroundings: indeed their plumage is relatively thin.

LEVAILLANT'S BARBET
Trachyphonus vaillantii

Distribution: Southern Africa

Like the preceding species, these barbets inhabit bush, and need a relatively high ration of livefood in their diet, especially when rearing chicks. A closely-related species known as D'arnaud's Barbet (*T. darnaudii*) may tunnel into the aviary floor, rather than nesting in a tree-hole. Chicks have been lost in this way during bad weather.

CRIMSON-BREASTED BARBET
Megalaima haemacephala

Distribution: India and South-east Asia to the Philippines

These barbets are often described as Coppersmith Barbets, because of the sounds of their calls. They rank among the smallest species, and cannot be considered hardy. Like other Asiatic species, they show a distinct preference for fruit. Another popular member of this genus is the Blue-throated (*M. asiatica*).

the Red-billed Hornbill (*Tockus erythro-rhynchus*) and the less common Yellow-billed Hornbill (*T. flavirostris*). A diet of mynah pellets and insects, plus some meat or pinkies (*see p.42*) and diced fruit will keep these birds healthy. They drink relatively little, but water should always be available in an open container.

These species have been bred quite frequently. When nesting, a suitable hollow is chosen and there the hen is sealed in by her mate. He then feeds her through a narrow slit, until after the chicks have hatched. It is not unusual for the hen to break out towards the end of the nesting period, the hole being repaired by the youngsters. This enables both parents to search for the increasing quantities of food, especially insects, demanded by their growing brood.

Apart from a nestbox or hollow log, a mixture of damp clay and mud should be provided. Experiment until you achieve a suitable mixture as it is important to ensure that the combination does not set too hard, thus preventing the birds from breaking out. These dwarf hornbills may lay two or three times in succession, and their chicks may need to be removed if the adult birds show signs of aggression after they have fledged. A clutch may have as many as five eggs, the incubation period being about one month. The chicks should emerge when between eight and nine weeks old.

Provide a variety of livefood for the adults, in particular during the breeding period. Young birds reared largely on mealworms may show signs of calcium deficiency. Unlike their larger relatives, these small birds cannot take day-old poultry chicks whole, but relish pinkies.

SOWERBY'S BARBET
Buccanodon whytii

Distribution: East Africa

This is one of the less colourful of the African barbets. For a serious breeding programme, it is best to obtain a small group. Reports from the wild suggest that these barbets may roost together in groups in suitable tree-holes. Although little is known about their breeding habits, the average clutch appears to be comprised of about five eggs.

PIED HORNBILL
Anthracoceros albirostris

Distribution: India, South-east Asia and China

Young birds can become quite tame and are particularly adept at catching food thrown to them. Particular care must be taken when introducing two birds for the first time. If one individual becomes overtly aggressive, then it is safest to separate them to adjoining flights, until it is clear that they are more amenable to each other. These bigger hornbills are long-lived birds, with a life-expectancy measured in decades. Although hardy, all hornbills require adequate protection during cold weather, since they tend to be very susceptible to frost-bite. A heating element, in the form of a strip fitted to the sides of the perch and emitting gentle heat, may be necessary. They should also be protected from cold winds by screening their aviary with clear plastic sheeting.

113

TOUCANS and BULBULS

Families: Ramphastidae and Pycnonotidae

The toucan family is comprised of approximately 40 species, confined exclusively to Central and South America. The Toco Toucan (*Ramphastos toco*) is a popular sight at zoos and bird gardens, but the smaller toucanets are possibly more suitable for the average aviculturist. The Crimson-rumped Toucanet (*Aulacorhynchus haematopygus*) is a typical example. Unfortunately these birds often remain nervous, whereas the slightly larger Aracaris, such as the Black-necked (*Pteroglossus aracari*) tend to become more tame, revealing their playful natures. Their calls are also less strident than those of the *Ramphastos* and Mountain Toucans (*Andigena* spp).

Although young toucans are sometimes available, they should only be kept in flights, and never in cages. They may damage their large beaks in such a confined area, and cannot express their lively, active natures. Toucans are unable to mimic the human voice, and their thin feathering means that they may need to be kept in warmer surroundings during the winter.

As a group, these birds require a mixed diet of fruit and soaked mynah pellets. A complete dog food is probably more suitable for the larger species. Toucans will not receive sufficient sustenance from fruit alone, and yet are incapable of eating loose insectile mix.

Considerable breeding successes with members of this family have occurred in the United States during recent years. The incubation period is around 17 days, and the average clutch numbers about three eggs. Toucans prefer a fairly deep nesting site, and will frequently

SPOT-BILLED TOUCANET
Selenidera maculirostris

Distribution: Amazonian Brazil to north Argentina

The small toucanets bear some resemblance to barbets, but they are easier to accommodate and less vocal. The Spot-billed is not as common as the various green toucanets, but is similar in its requirements. However, it is possibly less hardy. *Selenidera* toucanets can be sexed easily, in contrast to other genera in the family.

CUVIER'S TOUCAN
Ramphastos cuvieri

Distribution: Northern South America

There is some dispute over the status of this species. Closely-related forms include the Red-billed (*R. tucanus*) and Inca Toucan (*R. inca*), and it may be that they are simply sub-species. The distinctive beaks of these birds may look very heavy, but in reality, they are extremely light, being honeycombed inside. The *Ramphastos* toucans are characterized by having the broadest beaks of all toucans, and these are often highly coloured. They toss their food into the air before swallowing it, and they feed naturally on whole items such as fruits, berries and small animals, which they are adept at catching. A low-fat diet is of particular significance since toucans tend to be at risk from atherosclerosis, with a build-up of fat occurring on the walls of their arteries.

hammer away at the entrance and surrounds prior to egg-laying. Pairs need to be kept separate, and aggression may break out even between members of a pair if the hen rejects her mate's advances.

BULBULS

The bulbuls form a large family of about 120 species, with a wide distribution through Africa and Asia. The African bulbuls are less often seen than those occurring in Asia. They rank among the easiest softbills to maintain. They breed in aviary surroundings, and are generally amenable to other birds. Unfortunately, it is impossible to sex bulbuls visually, but several can be housed together, and will pair off themselves.

They are relatively hardy, and can be kept in an outside flight throughout the year in mild areas without artificial heat. A mixture of fruit, softbill food or mynah pellets and some livefood should keep these birds in good health.

Red-eared Bulbul (*Pycnonotus jocosus*): One of the crested species, these birds will thrive in a planted flight. They often prefer to construct their own nest in a bush, rather than use a nestbox. The average egg clutch is four, which should hatch after being incubated for about 12 days. The young are reared on livefood for the first few days.

The two species of Finchbill are also members of the bulbul family. The Crested form (*Spizixos canifrons*) is seen less often than the Collared (*S. semitorques*), but both are similar in appearance. They are characterized by their relatively thick beaks, and will take seed readily, as well as a softbill diet.

WHITE-EARED BULBUL
Pycnonotus aurigaster

Distribution: South-east Asia

Also known as the "Yellow-vented Bulbul", this species has an attractive call, and generally becomes quite tame in an aviary. They cause considerable damage to fruit crops in the wild and are persecuted as a result. When breeding, like other bulbuls, they tend to build their nest in a thick bush, and do best therefore when housed in a densely planted flight.

RED-VENTED BULBUL
Pycnonotus cafer

Distribution: India and South-east Asia

A somewhat duller species, but similar in its habit to the Red-eared Bulbul. These birds also have quite an attractive song, apart from their harsh warning call. The red markings under the tail are used during the display by the cock, while the hen should respond by lowering her crest, and dropping her wings.

CHINESE BULBUL
Pycnonotus sinensis

Distribution: Vietnam, Taiwan and south China

These bulbuls are easy to keep, and will also breed under suitable conditions. They construct a typical cup-shaped nest, using leaves and moss, along with other suitable material. Like other species, they are ideal for the novice softbill-keeper, being easy to cater for, and although not especially colourful, are nevertheless attractive.

LEAFBIRDS, BABBLERS and THRUSHES

Families: Irenidae, Turdidae & Timaliidae

Some softbills are excellent songsters, and these include the leafbirds and the shamas pictured below. The definition between softbills and seedeaters is not entirely clear-cut however, as shown by the parrotbills. Although closely related to the babblers, they are usually classified in a separate family, Paradoxornithidae. As with the Pekin Robin, parrotbills will take some seed as part of their diet.

Two main genera of the Irenidae family are of significance to aviculturists. The fruitsuckers or leafbirds are regularly available, but tend to be aggressive towards each other. A cock will also often persecute his intended mate relentlessly so that she has to be removed from the aviary. As the genus *Chloropsis* are birds of wooded areas, such difficulties can be partially overcome by introducing a pair together to a densely planted flight, and providing a number of feeding points.

Fairy Bluebirds (*Irena* species) are similar to fruitsuckers in their requirements, with cocks ranking among the most colourful of the softbills normally available. However, they will readily develop foot infections if kept under unhygienic conditions. Two or three eggs will be laid in the open cup-shaped nest, and should hatch within a fortnight. Livefood is then required in increasing quantities, with the young birds fledging when only about 12 days old, although they will not be independent until several weeks later.

FAMILY TURDIDAE

This is a very large family, and only a relatively small proportion of the species

GOLDEN-FRONTED LEAFBIRD
Chloropsis aurifrons

Distribution: India to South-east Asia

These fruitsuckers tame readily, and cock birds have an attractive song. Their diet should consist of fruit, nectar and an insectile mixture, as well as livefood. Fruitsuckers dislike cold, damp weather and should be transferred inside prior to the onset of such conditions. They have been bred occasionally, laying up to three eggs in a clutch.

WHITE-RUMPED SHAMA
Copsychus malabaricus

Distribution: India and South-east Asia

These long-tailed birds are very talented songsters, and lively, if somewhat aggressive, aviary occupants (particularly towards related species). Shamas are bred in aviaries in small numbers each year. They become almost exclusively insectivorous when breeding, and adequate supplies of livefood are essential if the chicks are to be reared.

GREY-HEADED PARROTBILL
Paradoxornis gularis

Distribution: From the Himalayas to South-east Asia and China

Parrotbills are named after the shape of their bills, with 20 species being recognized. They tend to be shy and little is known about their habits. They will feed on both seed and softfood, as well as fruit and insects. They can be kept in a group. A densely-planted flight is recommended.

included therein are known in avicultural circles. A varied diet, including livefood and berries when available suits them well, in conjunction with an insectile mixture and soaked mynah pellets. Some species, such as the Orange-headed Ground Thrush (*Zoothera citrina*) spend much of their time foraging close to the ground in thick forests, while others prefer more open country.

FAMILY TIMALIIDAE

Approximately 280 species of babbler are recognized, their distribution being confined to Europe and Australasia. They vary considerably in appearance and size, and revisions of classification in this group could prove advantageous.

The jay thrushes of the genus *Garrulax* comprise 44 species in the Babbler family, and although some are of subdued coloration, their active natures compensate in aviary surroundings. They are aggressive however, and should not be housed with smaller birds, which may otherwise be killed. Pairs of jay thrushes housed on their own usually attempt to breed, constructing an open nest in a suitable bush. Their diet should include pinkies (*see p.42*) if possible, as well as plenty of insects.

The White-crested (*G. leucolophus*) species is perhaps the most often represented in collections, but is not so highly rated as a songbird as the Hoami or Chinese Nightingale (*G. canorus*), also known as the Melodious Jay Thrush. Normally, these thrushes can live out of doors throughout the winter months in all but the most severe weather. It is dangerous, however, to introduce a new individual to an established group.

BLACK-HEADED SIBIA
Heterophasia capistrata

Distribution: India

One of the less common babblers in aviculture, this species should not be confused with the smaller Sivas (*Minla cyanouroptera*). The Sibia is a relatively easy species to cater for, accepting a wide variety of softbill foods and fruit without any difficulties. They tend to be somewhat shy and retiring, but the larger species can also prove rather aggressive.

PEKIN ROBIN
Leiothrix lutea

Distribution: From India to China

These lively birds have an attractive song, and can be kept safely in a mixed collection of seedeaters, although in some cases they have a deserved reputation for plundering nests. They may be persuaded to use an open-sided nestbox as a basis for their nest and often develop a liking for egg-food during the rearing period. It is safer to winter them indoors.

WHITE EYES, SUNBIRDS and HUMMINGBIRDS

Families: Nectariniidae, Zosteropidae, & Trochilidae

The birds listed on these two pages are diverse in terms of their classificatory positions, but in practical terms, their management needs are similar. They all depend on nectar to form at least part of their diet. With the exception of the Zosterops, which make an ideal introduction to the keeping of nectivores, as these birds are collectively known, the remainder are essentially birds for the specialist, but they can be bred successfully under the correct conditions. Indeed, aviculturists in Germany have been extremely success-ful in breeding hummingbirds during recent years. In one collection alone, over 40 have been reared successfully in a single season. The breeding habits of many species still remain a mystery, but hens appear to be responsible for nest construction, using fine materials such as cobwebs, and even hair.

WHITE-EYES

The Zosterops, or White-eyes, have a very wide distribution, but it is perhaps surprising that no less than 85 species have been recognized by taxonomists. Zosterops are similar in appearance, although those from Africa tend to be more yellow than their Asiatic relatives.

Although nectar should feature in their diet, their maintenance is straight-forward, and they will take fruit and mynah pellets. Zosterops can generally be housed safely with finches, as well as the smaller species of softbill. Members of a group in a planted flight will start to nest, and males can be recognized during the breeding season by their song. After the nest is built, the task of incubation is shared. The chicks should

BLACK-CHINNED YUHINA
Yuhina nigramenta

Distribution: Himalayas and China

These small babblers should be housed in individual pairs, although they can be kept safely alongside finches. They require nectar and small livefood such as greenfly, as well as fruit and a fine insectile mixture. Nine species of Yuhina or Flowerpecker are recognized, their breeding habits being similar to those of the Pekin Robin.

AFRICAN WHITE-EYE
Zosterops senegalensis

Distribution: Africa, south of the Sahara to Angola

White-eyes are a fairly uniform group, although this is perhaps one of the more colourful species. Indeed, it can be difficult to separate the species with ease. This species is sometimes known also as the Kikuyu Zosterops (*Z. kikuyuensis*). They are social birds, and can be kept safely as a colony without any fear of serious outbreaks of fighting.

CHESTNUT-FLANKED WHITE-EYE
Zosterops erythropleura

Distribution: Asia

This is one of the most distinctive species of Zosterops, characterized by its chestnut-brown flank markings. The characteristic white eye-ring is still apparent however, and it does not differ significantly in its habits from related species.

hatch after about 12 days, and become fully independent five weeks later.

SUNBIRDS

The sunbirds form a huge family of about 106 species, characterized by their long, slender beaks. They feed on nectar and small insects, although they will also take fruit chopped into very small pieces and chopped mynah pellets.

Scarlet-chested Sunbird (*Nectarinia senegalensis*): This is one of the more robust species, and has been bred successfully. The woven nest can be sus-

pended, or may be built in a nestbox using fine material, including moss. The incubation period is about 13 days, and if the chicks are to be reared successfully, the adults must be given large quantities of small insects such as spiders or hatchling crickets. Two eggs appear to form the usual clutch. The young sunbirds are independent when just over three weeks old, and may live for 15 years or more under captive conditions. The Scarlet-chested is an African species. Among those from Asia, the genus *Aethopyga* are often considered

most striking, with bright scarlet-red coloration in their plumage.

HUMMINGBIRDS

This family is comprised of over 300 species, many of which are unknown in aviculture. They range in size from about 6 cm (2½ in) up to the Giant Hummingbird (*Patagona gigas*), which is about 20 cm (8 in) overall. Hummingbirds are confined to the New World, and hover when feeding on nectar. They also take small insects, notably fruitflies, under captive conditions.

PURPLE-BANDED SUNBIRD
Nectarinia bifasciata

Distribution: Africa, from Somalia and Gabon to Angola and Mozambique

It can be difficult to identify some African sunbirds correctly. This species, for example, closely resembles the Mariqua Sunbird (*N. mariquensis*), but tends to have a more bluish throat, as well as being smaller. Hens can be especially difficult to distinguish, but reference to a reliable field-guide should help to overcome any confusion.

VAN HASSELT'S SUNBIRD
Nectarinia sperata

Distribution: South-east Asia to the Philippines. Also occurs in Pakistan.

This widely-distributed species is sometimes described as the Purple-throated Sunbird. Hens, as in many other species, are predominantly green. The dazzling irridescence of the cock's plumage can only be appreciated when viewed in a good light. It is possible to keep these birds in a sheltered outdoor aviary when the weather is warm.

BOOTED RACQUET-TAILED
HUMMINGBIRD
Ocreatus underwoodii

Distribution: The Andes, from Venezuela to Bolivia

A spectacular species, yet one which is short-lived and not to be recommended for the novice. The Violet-ears (*Colibri* species) are much more satisfactory in this respect, as are the Emeralds, comprising the genus *Amazilia*. Pairs must be watched closely for signs of aggression however.

MYNAHS and STARLINGS

Family: Sturnidae

The members of this family are very popular aviary occupants, with one species – the Hill Mynah – being better known as a pet bird. They are easy birds to maintain, on a diet of mynah pellets or an insectile mix, with some fruit and livefood included daily. The amount of livefood required depends on the species concerned. The beautiful Royal Starling (*Cosmopsarus regius*) for example, is highly insectivorous.

A nestbox is used for breeding purposes, and pairs will often have several clutches in succession. It is vital to remove the youngsters as soon as possible however, since they may well be attacked and even killed by their parents shortly after fledging. Starlings and mynahs are generally hardy once acclimatized, provided that they have the protection of a shelter.

The various members of this family vary in terms of their behaviour. Glossy Starlings as a general rule will spend little time on the floor of their aviary, preferring instead to move from branch to branch. By way of contrast, Asiatic mynahs will feed readily on the ground, foraging quite naturally for insects and other items. The grackles, a term which should be used to describe members of the genus *Gracula* only, will avoid descending to ground level if this can be avoided.

Perhaps the most unusual member of the family is the Coleto Mynah (or 'myna' as it is still occasionally spelt), known scientifically as *Sarcops calvus*. These birds have a virtually bald head, which varies in colour depending on the bird's mood and the prevailing weather

COMMON MYNAH
Acridotheres tristis

Distribution: Afghanistan eastwards to India and Sri Lanka, also South-east Asia

This is a highly adaptable and opportunistic species, which has established itself in many areas, including parts of Africa as well as Australia. As might be expected therefore, it is not a difficult species to cater for, although hardly very colourful.

HILL MYNAH
Gracula religiosa

Distribution: India, extending across South-east Asia

These highly talented mimics also make attractive aviary birds, although if kept within sound of parrots, it will not take long for the mynahs to be calling in a virtually indistinguishable fashion. They are quite hardy, but dislike damp, cold weather, when they are probably more at risk from respiratory diseases.

CHINESE JUNGLE MYNAH
Acridotheres cristatellus

Distribution: Eastern Asia, Indo-China extending into China

A relatively dull species, known under a wide variety of common names, including the Crested Mynah. An easy bird to cater for, but best kept on its own, especially for breeding purposes. Related species sometimes available include the more colourful Bank Mynah (*A. giginianus*), which has pinkish underparts.

conditions. When excited, or during hot weather, the bird's head becomes bright pink as bloodflow to the skin increases. Conversely, it can be very pale, and this may be indicative of illness, although clearly not in every case. Coleto mynahs are confined to the Philippine islands where they live in forests. Like other species, these mynahs are aggressive, and should not be kept alongside smaller birds. They will build a loose nest within their nestbox, choosing a wide variety of material for this purpose, and may even strip leaves from any aviary plants.

Among other members of this group seen in avicultural circles is the Pied Mynah (*Sturnus contra*), which is essentially black and white in colour, with a long and quite narrow beak. This Asiatic species is easy to cater for, and delights in bathing, as do other members of this family. Once acclimatized, they can be kept outdoors, when provided with a suitable shelter, for most of the year, except in extreme weather.

The Black-collared Starling (*Sturnus nigricollis*) is also predominantly black and white in colour, but can be distinguished from the Pied by virtue of its size and head coloration. It is significantly larger, being nearly 30 cm (1 ft) overall, with a totally white head. It also has a black bill, whereas that of the Pied Starling is whitish, becoming red towards its base.

The distinctive white Bali Mynah (*Leucospar rothschildi*) is also known as Rothschild's Grackle. Found only on the Indonesian island of Bali, where it is scarce, the species has bred freely in aviary surroundings.

PURPLE GLOSSY STARLING
Lamprotornis purpureus

Distribution: Northern Africa, south of the Sahara, from Senegal to Sudan

Extremely attractive birds with purplish body coloration, these starlings show to best effect in an outside flight where sunlight enhances the gloss of their plumage. A similar long-tailed form, *L. caudatus*, is also seen occasionally and makes a spectacular aviary occupant.

GREEN GLOSSY STARLING
Lamprotornis chalybaeus

Distribution: Equatorial Africa and areas of southern Africa

This species, also known as the Blue-eared Glossy Starling, is identical in its requirements to the previous species. A distinct smaller form is referred to as the Lesser (*L. chloropterus*). Again, the iridescence in their plumage is most marked when these birds are kept in an outside aviary.

SPREO STARLING
Spreo superbus

Distribution: Parts of East Africa

This highly attractive species is also known as the "Superb Starling". They are often fairly tolerant in a mixed aviary containing birds of a similar size, although the most likely chance of breeding success will result if a pair are housed on their own. As with other members of the family, nesting material will be used to construct a loose nest within the box.

121

CROWS and TOURACOS

Families: Corvidae and Musophagidae

While crows are not popular avicultural subjects, other more colourful corvids are kept in relatively spacious aviaries. As a group, these birds are hardy and will thrive on a basic diet of soaked mynah pellets or a dog food, augmented with pinkies or larger mice, livefood and fruit. Pairs need to be housed on their own; they will eat small birds, and so should never be included in a mixed collection, unless their accommodation is large and their companions are suitably robust. These birds live out of doors once established, but must always have adequate protection available, to minimize the threat of frost-bite. The average clutch may consist of four eggs. These should hatch after approximately 18 days, the youngsters fledging around three weeks later.

Apart from the jays and magpies, other members of the family include the treepies (*Dendrocitta* species) from Asia, which tend to be rather subdued in terms of their coloration, and the striking cissas (*Cissa* species), which are also Asiatic. The spectacular Hunting Cissa (*C. chinensis*) is pale green, with maroon wings and a narrow black stripe extending from the beak either side of the face to the back of the neck. These birds are also sometimes described as green magpies. In this case, as with most corvids, the sexes are similar in appearance.

MUSOPHAGIDAE FAMILY
The 18 species in this family occur exclusively in Africa. They are medium-sized, active birds, with unusually-shaped head crests in many instances. Touracos are essentially frugivorous,

BLACK-CRESTED JAY
Cyanocorax affinis

Distribution: Southern Central America, to northern South America

These striking jays make attractive and hardy aviary occupants once they are acclimatized. Yet they are aggressive, and are best housed on their own, and never in the company of smaller birds. They may even disagree among themselves, so that once a pair have been identified they should be kept separate. Like other related species, these jays are lively and have naturally inquisitive natures. Closely related to the Plush-crested Jay (*C. chrysops*), found in southern parts of South America, this species is not especially noisy and soon becomes quite tame, although they are not suitable as pets.

RED-BILLED BLUE PIE
Urocissa erythrorhyncha

Distribution: Much of South-east Asia into China

Also known as the Occipital Blue Pie, this species is frequently seen in zoological collections. It is not difficult to cater for, but requires a large flight area, to display its active nature. A related form known as the Yellow-billed Blue Pie (*U. flavirostris*) is occasionally available.

but also readily partake of greenstuff in many cases.

Spinach beet, for example, should be cut and shredded into small pieces, whereas chickweed can be given whole. Soaked mynah pellets, or an insectile mixture liberally sprinkled over their food should also be provided. Touracos may also take some livefood, although mealworms are not always popular. Clean earthworms, or redworms are often taken in preference. It is important for them to take some animal protein, especially when they are breeding.

OTHER SPECIES

The **Grey Go-away Bird** (*Crinifer concolor*) and the other related species certainly comprise the dullest genus of the family, also known as 'plantaineaters'. Indeed, these birds often do take banana readily. In contrast, the **Violaceous Plantain-eaters** (*Musophaga violacea*) rank among the most striking touracos, with an iridescent purplish sheen on their plumage. The subspecies known as Lady Ross's Touraco (*M. v. rossae*) is also seen occasionally.

As in the case of pigeons and doves, the plumage of these birds is relatively loose, and will be shed readily if they are handled clumsily. Although hardy, touracos living out-of-doors are at risk from frost-bite during the winter, and will need protection. Ideally, their enclosure should be adequately planted with hardy, dense shrubs, and a pair may even attempt to breed in these surroundings. At the onset of the breeding period, pairs need to be watched closely, since some cock birds can be extremely aggressive towards their mates, and may even have to be temporarily separated.

WHITE-CHEEKED TOURACO
Tauraco leucotis

Distribution: Ethiopia and Eritrea

An aviary for these birds needs to be quite spacious, and should enable the birds to run along the perches in their characteristically lively fashion. Like other members of the family, they are best housed in individual pairs, but can be kept alongside other non-aggressive softbills. The close proximity of other birds may deter breeding activity in the case of the touracos however. The White-cheeked is normally quite prolific under aviary conditions, and may nest successfully twice in a season.

HARTLAUB'S TOURACO
Tauraco hartlaubi

Distribution: East Africa

Members of this genus are essentially green in coloration, with significant differences in head markings and crest shapes. Since the advent of surgical sexing, touracos generally have been bred in increasing numbers, and this species tends to be among those most commonly available. The birds will build a loose nest of twigs on a supporting platform.

PIGEONS and DOVES

Family: Columbidae

Pigeons and doves are among the most versatile members of the avian kingdom. Their high reproductive rate and generally undemanding feeding habits enable them to thrive successfully both in cities and countryside throughout the world. There is no strict means of separating pigeons and doves, although the latter description is usually applied to smaller species.

FEEDING

Smaller doves require a mixture of canary and millet seeds, often preferring to feed off the floor if given the opportunity. Correspondingly large seeds can be given to the bigger species, and seed mixtures marketed as domestic pigeon food will suffice for birds of equivalent size. A basic maintenance diet should be used until the breeding period, when the level of protein should be increased. Grit of a suitable size, plus cuttlefish bone should always be available, and many pigeons and doves will take greenfood, particularly young leafy plants such as chickweed. When breeding however, they may prefer to use leafy greenfood as nesting material. To avoid this, greenfood should be cut into small pieces.

Most species do not consume insects, although terrestrial pigeons and doves may take invertebrates whole. These birds also consume seeds without dehusking them, ingesting them directly. They drink water by active sucking rather than passive swallowing. Fruit pigeons and doves should be fed a diet of soaked mynah pellets and diced fruit.

GENERAL CARE

The pigeons and doves mentioned here

BARBARY DOVE

This bird is unknown in the wild, but has been evolved from the African Collared Dove (*Streptopelia roseogrisea*). Barbary Doves are very tame, and will often perch freely on the hand. They are also extremely free-breeding, and may even nest on the floor in the corner of a cage. It can be difficult to distinguish pairs; cocks generally are of a paler coloration than hens, but the degree of paleness is variable. Barbary Doves make ideal parents, but breeding with closely-related stock will produce offspring of poor quality. Various modifications to the basic plumage are known, including a pied form and a pure white variety, sometimes described as the Java Dove.

DIAMOND DOVE
Geopelia cuneata

Distribution: Australia

These small doves are widely kept in aviaries. They are not aggressive to smaller birds. Several broods will be reared during the year, two eggs forming the normal clutch. Apart from the Silver form, other mutations of South African origin have been introduced, in which the basic grey plumage is tinged with red, orange or yellow.

are most suitable as aviary rather than cage birds. Larger species in particular often prove very nervous if kept in confined surroundings, and may injure themselves.

These birds cannot walk up wire mesh like parrots, but if frightened, especially after dark, they will fly around wildly. They may also cling on to the aviary mesh, ferociously flapping their wings against it. When they are caught, loose plumage is shed easily. The resulting feather loss can be minimized by gentle handling.

Few aviculturists specialize in pigeons and doves, although many are both colourful and ready nesters. It must also be said that, although these are not noisy birds, their repeated calls can prove monotonous at close quarters. The majority are housed in mixed collections. Smaller species like the Diamond Dove are ideal for accommodating with finches, while the larger species make better companions for either cockatiels or the less aggressive, bigger softbills.

While most pigeons will not interfere directly if they are housed with smaller passerines, they are likely to create a disturbance in the aviary, which may discourage other birds from breeding successfully. Also, in spite of their popular image as a symbol of peace, doves and pigeons tend to be aggressive towards each other, and pairs generally need to be housed in separate aviaries unless their quarters are very spacious.

Once acclimatized properly, pigeons and doves are quite hardy and can be kept outside throughout the year without the need for artifical heating.

ZEBRA DOVE
Geopelia striata

Distribution: South-east Asia to Australia

This versatile, adaptable species has been introduced successfully to a number of countries outside its native range and is a popular aviary bird. Although it can be difficult to recognize pairs, Zebra Doves are usually reliable breeders.

TAMBOURINE DOVE
Turtur tympanistria

Distribution: Forested areas of Africa

The Tambourine Dove is terrestrial by nature, and requires livefood such as mealworms when housed in aviary surroundings. They are fast on the wing and fly rapidly when frightened. Related species in this genus are described collectively as Wood Doves and require similar care, thriving under planted aviary conditions.

YELLOW-BILLED GROUND DOVE
Columbina cruziana

Distribution: Ecuador, south to Chile

This is one of a group of small South American terrestrial doves, known as "pygmy doves". They are suitable companions for finches. Hens may lay clutches of three eggs, which should hatch after an incubation period of a fortnight. They are prolific breeders and may have four clutches in a season.

On very cold nights they will be at risk from frost-bite however, if they are permitted to roost in the open. Pigeons are long-lived, and individuals may survive well into their 20s.

BREEDING

Pairs will normally nest readily, and are capable of rearing several rounds of chicks in rapid succession. They must be given suitable supports for their sloppy nests. Either nestpans or wooden shelves will suffice. Larger species will use some sticks, whereas canary nesting material is frequently utilized by smaller birds.

Courtship can be a rough process, with a cock bird driving a hen ferociously, barely giving her an opportunity to feed without harassment. The back of the neck is the usual site of a physical assault, where blood can be drawn in severe cases. Since cock birds are usually ready to breed prior to hens, it is particularly dangerous to introduce an unfamiliar bird to a cock at the start of the breeding season.

Both partners take turns at incubating the eggs, and then raise the chicks. The unique feeding system evolved by this group of birds means that their breeding cycle is not dependent on a supply of suitable livefood, as in the case of waxbills for example. The adult birds produce a secretion popularly known as crop milk, which is high in protein, and has virtually no carbohydrate present. This is fed exclusively for the first few days of life. Then, gradually, seed is introduced to the chicks' diet. While still in the nest, the young birds are described as "squabs", and then

GREEN-WINGED DOVE
Chalcophaps indica

Distribution: India, South-east Asia to Australia

These birds have certain similarities with wood doves. They are often found in forested areas and do best in aviaries that afford seclusion and enable them to walk unmolested on the floor. Without sufficient cover, they can prove very nervous birds. There can be considerable differences in coloration between individuals.

CAPE DOVE
Oena capensis

Distribution: Most of Africa, south of the Sahara

"Masked Dove", "Namaqua Dove", "Black-throated Dove" and "Long-tailed Dove" are all descriptions applied to this species. Their nest is frequently positioned close to the ground and two eggs form the usual clutch. Cape Doves may take two years before attempting to nest. Keeping pairs together may help, but watch for serious aggression.

SENEGAL DOVE
Streptopelia senegalensis

Distribution: From Africa to Asia, including India

These birds feed on seeds and will also take insects, especially during the breeding season. Their alternative name of "Laughing Dove" stems from their cheerful call. Chicks will be independent by four weeks of age and should be removed as soon as they are feeding themselves.

"squeakers", because of their plaintive calls for food.

The majority of pairs only lay one or two eggs in a clutch, and the chicks frequently fledge before they are fully able to fly. Once they are independent, the young birds should be removed as soon as possible, since cocks frequently start to attack their earlier offspring if the hen is about to lay again.

Some pigeons and doves are particularly nervous when breeding, and may refuse to incubate their eggs. The nesting site may be too exposed, in which case it should be moved accordingly. If this fails, foster the eggs under Barbary or Diamond Doves, depending upon the size of the bird concerned. If possible, the foster parents should have laid about the same time, so that when the chicks hatch, crop milk will be available for them. At present, it is extremely difficult to hand-rear pigeons and doves successfully for the first few days of life. The absence of carbohydrate from the natural milk is a vital consideration when attempting to devise a suitable replacement diet. Additionally, very young pigeons require large amounts of fluid to hydrate their tissues.

Individual pairs will vary in their ability to rear chicks successfully. If two eggs hatch, it is not unusual for one chick to fall behind its sibling, and it will be necessary to supplement its food intake if it is not to be lost. This is relatively straightforward however, as by this time the birds are no longer dependent on crop milk, and a mixture of soft food and seeds can be given, taking care not to damage the relatively soft beak of the young bird concerned.

WHITE-WINGED DOVE
Zenaida asiatica

Distribution: From Central America and the Caribbean, south to Chile

These doves, characterized by their distinctive wing markings, require identical care to the Eared Dove. Since they can be found wild in the United States, there may be restrictions there on keeping them, as with other native species. They frequent areas of scrub and mangrove.

EARED DOVE
Zenaida auriculata

Distribution: Much of South America

A relatively dull species, closely allied to the Mourning Dove (*Z. macroura*) of North and Central America. They are easy birds to keep, but can prove nervous. Therefore, their housing should incorporate an adequate retreat. They feed essentially on seed and are quite hardy in most climates. Pairs nest freely.

QUAILS

Family: Phasianidae

Quails are short, chubby birds, which naturally divide into two broad groups, known as the American Perching Quails and the Ground Quails. These categories reflect a difference in their habits which can be very significant in the aviary environment, particularly when being kept in the company of small finches. They are often included in mixed collections alongside seedeaters, doves, pigeons and softbills, and will spend time foraging on the floor of the flight, feeding on spilt seed.

The American Perching Quails will perch readily, and can create a considerable disturbance in view of their nervous natures, coupled with their relatively large size. Birds in this group are therefore best kept in big aviaries, with cover to which they can retreat. If threatened in the open, they tend to fly vertically with considerable force, and are liable to injure themselves fatally if they collide with the roof of the aviary.

FEEDING

Quails are essentially omnivorous in their feeding habits, taking seeds, in-sects and greenstuff as part of their regular diet. Poultry foods are perhaps the best means of ensuring that these birds receive a balanced intake of essential nutrients. The provision of grit and cuttlefish bone is also important, especially for those on a seed diet.

GENERAL CARE

The aviary should give the quails easy access to and from the shelter, which may necessitate cutting and hinging a small door for them on the side of the main connecting door. This will be safer

CALIFORNIAN QUAIL
Lophortyx californica

Distribution: United States, from Oregon to California

One of the larger species of crested quail, the Californian is well established in aviculture. They tend to perch readily, and this can be a deterrent to keeping them in a mixed aviary. These birds will not thrive in damp, muddy surroundings, particularly while breeding. If they refuse to sit, bantams have been used to incubate their eggs.

BOB-WHITE QUAIL
Colinus virginianus

Distribution: United States, Central America, and the Caribbean

This species is the most readily available of the larger quails, but it can prove nervous in an aviary and tends to roost on the highest perches. Cocks should be kept apart, as they show a tendency to fight, and this will also disturb the other occupants of the aviary. These quails can live for a decade or longer, but need a dry shelter where they can retreat when the weather is unfavourable. It is possible for bantams to hatch their eggs successfully, but hatchability is likely to be better if the eggs are transferred to an incubator.

than a flap, which could be dislodged accidentally, creating a disturbance even if it does not actually harm the birds directly. If breeding is to be successful it is essential that quails have adequate cover and protection against the elements, and are not kept in the company of larger, omnivorous softbills. These larger birds may otherwise steal the eggs or chicks.

BREEDING

While quails are essentially monogamous, it may be preferable with the smaller species to keep one cock in the company of two or three hens.

They lay their eggs on the ground, concealed by clumps of grass or other vegetation. Clutches may consist of eight eggs which, in the smaller birds, should hatch after about 18 days. Unfortunately, in aviary surroundings, eggs may simply be scattered around the floor, and the hen makes no attempt to incubate them. In such instances the only option will be to transfer the eggs to an incubator. Unfortunately, studies suggest that birds reared in this way over numerous generations lose their brooding instincts, compounding the difficulty in the future. Wild-caught quails are much more reliable in this respect.

Unlike all the other birds featured in this book, young quails are independent from hatching, and can start pecking around immediately for suitably small particles of food. Canary rearing foods and a fine grade insectile mix provide suitable nourishment for hatchlings. Provide only shallow water pots or, preferably, closed drinkers. This will safeguard against accidental drowning.

JAPANESE QUAIL
Coturnix coturnix

Distribution: South-east Asia

Japanese Quail are bred commercially for consumption. Although larger than the Chinese Painted, which may detract from their inclusion alongside certain aviary birds, this species is ground-dwelling, easy to cater for and lays readily. Since being domesticated, these birds can start breeding at only six weeks.

CHINESE PAINTED QUAIL
Excalfactoria chinensis

Distribution: Asia extending to Australia

Now bred in huge numbers around the world, this terrestrial species is most suitable for a mixed aviary, where it will not usually disturb the other occupants. Provide adequate cover to ensure that hens are not persecuted by their prospective partners. Even so, they may still be plucked around the head. It can be difficult to obtain hens in sufficient numbers to allow for keeping several with each cock in separate accommodation, yet this will help to prevent outbreaks of aggression from a cock towards a hen. The resulting eggs can be hatched in an incubator if necessary. As with other species of quail, the Chinese Painted will appreciate a tray of sand in an aviary. This enables the birds to have a dust bath and clean their feathers, removing excess oil from the plumage. A silver colour form has now been developed and is quite widely available.

BUDGERIGARS

Family: Psittacidae

The Budgerigar is a native of Australia, and the first living examples of these parakeets were seen in Europe during 1840. It is said that the famous ornithologist, John Gould, passed the pair in question to his brother-in-law, Charles Coxen. They soon nested, and the popularity of the Budgerigar began to spread throughout Europe.

FEEDING

Part of the reason for the growth in interest in budgerigars during the last century stemmed from their undemanding feeding habits. These parakeets will live and breed on a mixture of plain canary seed and millets. They are particularly fond of millet sprays, which can be soaked prior to feeding. They should be given greenfood on a regular basis. Oats are offered by some breeders during the breeding season, along with a high protein rearing food. Budgerigars have a specific need for iodine, and nibbles should always be available to them, along with cuttlefish bone and grit.

GENERAL CARE

Budgerigars are naturally gregarious, and normally housed on a colony basis, although not usually kept in the company of other birds, since they tend to be aggressive. Budgerigars can make suitable companions for cockatiels, and certain large finches, such as weavers and java sparrows, but outbreaks of fighting may occur.

.In the case of exhibition stock, it is not usual for the sexes to be kept segregated outside the breeding season. However this management system, said to im-

BUDGERIGAR
Melopsittacus undulatus

The domesticated Budgerigar of today has evolved into a much larger bird than its wild relative. It is also bred in a wide variety of colours, not to mention feather variants. The exhibition of budgerigars is a popular pastime in many countries, with prescribed standards being laid down for type and the different colours. Millions are also highly valued as pet birds, or aviary occupants. On average, budgerigars will live about eight years, although individuals having a much longer lifespan, into their early 20s, have been known. The birds shown here are the pet bird type, which tend to be smaller than exhibition budgerigars.

BUDGERIGAR: NORMAL COBALT

Cobalt: The dark factor in blue series birds gives rise to the Cobalt, which corresponds to the Dark Green, and the Mauve with two dark factors.
Violet: The visual Violet is perhaps one of the most sought after colours. It appeared in Britain, Australia and Denmark in about 1936 and is dominant in its mode of inheritance. The visual form results only from a combination of the violet factor with cobalt budgerigars.

prove fertility, is not recommended by all breeders.

BREEDING

Budgerigars can be sexed in a unique way, the cere above the beak acting as the distinguishing feature. In mature cock birds, this is blue, with the notable exception of lutinos, albinos and recessive pieds whose ceres are purplish in colour. Hen birds invariably have brown ceres, which are paler when they are not in breeding condition. Young hens also have paler, flatter ceres than cock birds when they fledge, but it is not always straightforward to sex budgerigars just after they have left the nest.

Exhibition budgerigars are usually bred in cages, but it is quite feasible to breed these parakeets in a group, providing the nestboxes are all positioned at the same height. Some hens can still prove belligerent however, and may squabble over a nesting site, leading to a loss of eggs and possibly chicks. The hen is responsible for incubating the white eggs, which are characteristic of psittacines. They should hatch after 18 days.

The average clutch is about four eggs, but can exceed eight on occasions.

The young birds will be independent by about five weeks of age, when they should be moved, so that they will not soil or damage the second round of eggs. Hens should be restricted to two rounds in a season. Do this by removing the nestboxes all at once from a colony aviary, or transferring them to a flight from the breeding cage. Budgerigars are normally not permitted to breed until they are a year old, but they will be mature before this time.

BUDGERIGAR: CINNAMON DARK GREEN NORMAL

The **Cinnamon** mutation has been combined with several other colours. It has proved to be sex-linked in its mode of inheritance, and dark black areas of plumage are diluted to brown. The **Dark Green** mutation has been recorded in the wild, but first emerged in captive stock in France in 1915. The dark factor responsible has since yielded olive greens and has been introduced to blue series birds.

BUDGERIGAR: OPALINE DARK GREEN

Opaline is a mutation which alters the patterning on the head, back and wings rather than the overall coloration. It is a sex-linked characteristic, which appeared in the 1930s in Europe and Australia, and has been introduced into both green and blue series birds. Some birds are heavily marked however, and those showing flecking on the forehead are penalized in exhibition circles.

BUDGERIGAR: OPALINE LIGHT GREEN

The description **Light Green** is given to the original colour of the budgerigar. Ironically, pure, good quality exhibition birds of this colour have become increasingly scarce during recent years, being highly valued for the development of other colours.

PLUMAGE VARIANTS

The only recognized plumage variant is the Crested Budgerigar, which can occur in one of three forms: the full-circular crest extends over the head; the half-circular crest is confined to the forehead, extending down towards the cere; the tufted variety is characterized by a vertical crest. The crested mutation first appeared in Australia, in 1935, and subsequently emerged elsewhere. It can be combined with any single colour or several colours.

For a period of time, budgerigars known as "Long-flights" were popular. In this instance, the flight feathers actually crossed, but this practice has now been outlawed. One unwelcome plumage variant is the so-called "Feather Duster". Such birds develop rapidly in the nest, but their plumage does not stop growing as would normally happen. Plumage over the eyes will have to be cut back to enable these budgerigars to find food. The disorder could result from a thyroid malfunction, but in any event, such birds are relatively short-lived.

COLOUR MUTATIONS

In addition to the mutations pictured, the following colours are equally well-known:

Albino: Birds of white coloration with red eyes are described as "albinos". The first references to this variety date back to 1932, when albino budgerigars appeared in both Germany and Britain.

Clearflights: Birds of this mutation resemble normals, but their flight and tail feathers are clear. Both white- and yellow-flights occur, with this characteristic being dominant.

BUDGERIGAR: CINNAMON OPALINE GREY GREEN

The depth of coloration of the **grey green** can vary, since light, dark and medium forms can be distinguished. This variety has grey cheek patches, whereas those of the normal **light green** are violet. This particular bird also shows the characteristics of opaline and cinnamon markings. One of the appealing features of the budgerigar is the many colour combinations which can now be bred.

BUDGERIGAR: CINNAMON OPALINE GREY

The dominant form of the **grey** is now widely distributed, and has been combined with other colours, including the yellow-faced mutation. It originated in Australia, although a recessive form is known to have occurred in England, also during the 1930s. The latter mutation is now extinct, but may re-emerge at some point in the future.

BUDGERIGAR: CINNAMON OPALINE BLUE

It may be that the **skyblue** mutation was known in the Netherlands during the 1890s, but the first specimens exhibited in Britain did not appear until 1910. They were immediately sought after, but remained scarce for another decade or more. Skyblues are the blue series equivalent of the light green and are recessive to this colour.

Clearwings: This is the collective description applied to white- and yellow-winged budgerigars, associated with blue and green coloration respectively. Clearwings are of Belgian origin, dating back to the early 1940s.

Dark-eyed clears: When mature, these budgerigars lack the usual white circular irides around the black pupils of the eyes. They resemble white and yellow birds over all but are of purer coloration.

Fallow: Various fallow mutations have been reported, and in the German mutation are characterized by their red eyes. The depth of body coloration can be quite clear.

Greywings: These birds were known during the 1920s, but were not especially popular, being viewed by some as poorly marked yellows. Today they are quite scarce.

Half-siders: A distinct rarity, but such birds always attract attention, as their body coloration is divided into two exactly symmetrical halves.

Lacewings: A sex-linked mutation, which has now been combined with green, blue and yellow-faced characters.

Light Yellow: Birds of this colour were the first mutants to be recorded, during the 1870s in Holland. Various shades of yellow are now recognized, with dark factor birds, for example, being known as "Dark" and "Olive" yellows.

Slates: The overlaying effect of this mutation darkens the body coloration. It is sex-linked. Slates have never become very popular and are uncommon.

White: This form can be distinguished from the Albino on the basis of their dark eye coloration. First bred in 1920, they have faded in popularity.

BUDGERIGAR: YELLOW-FACED OPALINE BLUE

The **yellow-faced** mutation appeared first in England in 1935, creating considerable comment at a time when it was believed there was a clear division between yellow and blue coloration in the budgerigar. It emerged that several yellow-faced mutations existed, the deeper-coloured varieties being known as the "golden-faced". The yellow-faced character can be combined with all blue series budgerigars.

BUDGERIGAR: LIGHT GREEN OPALINE PIED

Birds of the **dominant pied** form were known in Australia, but were not seen in Britain until the mid-1930s. In some cases the pied markings create a distinctive band across the lower belly, hence the description "banded pied". The **recessive pied** was developed in Denmark during the early 1930s. Apart from being smaller than their dominant counterparts, recessive pieds have no white irides, so they have dark eyes.

BUDGERIGAR: SPANGLED LIGHT GREEN

The most recent mutation is **spangled**. It is of Australian origin and was introduced to Europe during the early 1980s. Dominant in its mode of inheritance, the perimeters of the feathers are darkened, creating a spangled effect. Exhibition birds of this mutation are relatively small in size at present, with most effort being expended on the development of markings rather than the type.

LOVEBIRDS

Family: Psittacidae

Lovebirds have become one of the most popular groups of small psittacines, and the free-breeding habits of some species have given rise to numerous mutations over the past decade or so. Nine species are recognized, but the Swindern's Black-collared Lovebird (*Agapornis swinderniana*) has still not been seen alive outside Africa.

FEEDING

Canary seed and millets, augmented with groats, sunflower seed and small pine nuts will serve as a suitable basic diet. Greenfood is often taken readily, but lovebirds are less keen on items such as sweet apple and carrot.

GENERAL CARE

Pairs are usually housed on their own, especially in the case of mutant birds, where it will be vital to know the parentage of the offspring. Lovebirds tend to prove spiteful, both towards each other and members of other species, and will fight with neighbours. Flights must therefore be effectively double-wired, with both faces covered in mesh and leaving a clear gap of about 5 cm (2 in) between them, so the birds cannot reach their neighbour's feet. Lovebirds can be bred successfully in relatively small covered flights, about 1.8 x 0.9 m (6 x 3 ft), or even cages in some cases.

Australian breeders do keep lovebirds successfully on a colony basis, and this is probably because over the years, aggressive traits have been bred out of the stock. In addition, the colonies are generally established groups, with all birds being introduced at once, and no new individuals being released at a later date.

FISCHER'S LOVEBIRD
Agapornis fischeri

Distribution: Tanzania

First seen alive outside Africa during the mid-1920s, Fischer's are popular aviary birds. Mutations are largely unknown, although they have been reported. In 1979, a blue form was bred for the first time in California. This differed from the greyish South African Blue Fischer's recorded two decades previously.

MASKED LOVEBIRD
Agapornis personata

Distribution: Tanzania

The normal form of this species has become quite scarce in aviculture, yet the Blue Masked form (*right*), derived from wild-caught mutants in the 1920s, is being bred on a regular basis. A yellow strain is also known, but less commonly available and from these mutants, a whitish colour form has been developed. The species on this page are grouped as the white eye-ring species.

MASKED LOVEBIRD: BLUE

A mutation of the Masked Lovebird, this form is often bred successfully. The related species completing the white eye-ring group, the Nyassa and Black-cheeked Lovebirds (*A. lilianae* and *A. nigrigensis*) gained a reputation for free-breeding in the 1920s, but have become scarce subsequently. Weak stock may be partially responsible. The autosomal recessive Lutino form of the Nyassa Lovebird is also rare.

The majority of lovebirds are hardy once established, but they should be provided with a suitable nestbox for roosting purposes. This can be transferred to the interior of the shelter during the colder months, from the outside flight. Keep newly-imported lovebirds of any species indoors for their first winter, releasing them into the aviary only when the weather is warm.

BREEDING

Sexing is straightforward in three species, yet these have proved the most difficult to establish, compared with the Peach-faced and the members of the so-called White eye-ring group, where no visual sexual differences exist. Careful observation may be of value however, since hens in breeding condition will often flare their tails close to a nestbox.

Lovebirds must have fresh-cut branches as nesting material. The nest varies in size, depending upon the species. At one extreme Abyssinians simply prepare a small pad, often using feathers from their own breasts, whereas the Masked Lovebird and related species construct a bulky, domed structure within the nestbox, which can make inspection difficult. The number of eggs laid normally varies from between three and eight; four or five being the average. Hens sit alone for 23 days before the eggs hatch, although cocks may roost alongside their mates for periods each day.

A large number of colours of the Peach-faced are now being bred, and many are freely available, especially in North America and Europe. The most common mutations are Pastel Blue, Dark Factor, Lutino, Pied and Yellow.

PEACH-FACED LOVEBIRD
Agapornis roseicollis

Distribution: South-west Africa

Peach-faced Lovebirds can be prolific breeders, but should be restrained from breeding during the cold months by moving the nestbox and withholding nesting materials. The chicks emerge covered in reddish down. They fledge at about six weeks old. Soaked millet sprays and soft food will be taken by pairs with chicks in the nest.

PEACH-FACED LOVEBIRD:
PASTEL BLUE

One of the older Peach-faced mutations, Pastel Blues first appeared in Holland in 1963. Since some carotenoid pigment remains, their body has a greenish tinge, while their heads tend to be a very pale shade of pink. This coloration is variable, with certain bluer birds being described as "White-faced Blues". It has been combined with other mutations, yielding offspring of composite colours.

BLACK-WINGED LOVEBIRD
Agapornis taranta

Distribution: Ethiopia

Also known as the "Abyssinian Lovebird", this species used to be regularly imported, but has become scarce in recent years. Pairs can produce two rounds of chicks in a season. Another sexually-dimorphic species, the Madagascar Lovebird (*A. cana*) should be housed inside for the duration of the winter.

COCKATIELS and PARAKEETS

Family: Psittacidae

Cockatiels are unusual within the parrot family in that both sexes take turns at incubating the eggs, as well as brooding the chicks. When in the nestbox, they will attempt to prevent intrusions by fluffing themselves up, rocking back and forth, hissing and lunging if they feel threatened. After an incubation period of 19 days, the chicks should hatch covered in yellow down.

In some instances, cockatiels do not prove good parents, and losses of chicks can be quite high in the early stages. Excessive interference at this time may be responsible in some cases, but American studies suggest that candidiasis (*see p.55*) is a major cause of mortality in newly-hatched cockatiels. As a precaution against this, it is worth supplementing the diet of the adults with Vitamin A, administered in the drinking water, prior to hatching of the eggs.

Once the chicks are older, especially if they are lutino cockatiels, the adults may start to pluck their offspring. This is often a sign that they are keen to nest again. Eggs may be laid before the earlier chicks have left the nest, normally when they are about 30 days old.

Cockatiels are prolific breeders, and will lay throughout the year if the opportunity presents itself, so nestboxes should only be provided from the spring until the autumn. Unfortunately, when cockatiels are kept in groups, one nestbox alone may be favoured. Consequently, a large number of eggs will be laid within. These are then likely to become chilled, as the birds will not be able to cover them adequately; the average clutch is about five eggs.

GENERAL CARE
Their needs are very straightforward. They make undemanding aviary occupants, and can be kept outside safely throughout the year. Cockatiels are relatively long-lived birds, and are likely to survive into their 20s.

PARAKEETS
There is no real distinction between parakeets and parrots, as all belong to the same family, but "parakeet" is often used for birds with long tails. With New World species, parakeets formerly included in the genus *Conurus* are frequently known as "conures". Terminology does vary according to the country: in Australia, psittacines are often described as "parrots", whereas in the United States, parakeets are often referred to collectively as "hookbills".

AUSTRALIAN PARAKEETS
These birds rank among the most popular aviary subjects. They are colourful, easy to maintain in most instances and usually keen to nest. Australian species are far less destructive than other parakeets, and their calls are more mellow.

FEEDING
A diet of seed, including some sunflower but based largely on cereals, is ideal. Their undemanding feeding habits have occasioned their rise to popularity, dating back to a time when psittacines as a group received little more than seed and water. Greenfood, soaked seed and fruit will also be taken readily, along

COCKATIEL
Nymphicus hollandicus

Distribution: Australia

These attractive birds make ideal aviary birds because, unlike many parrots, they are neither noisy nor destructive. In addition, they can be kept in breeding groups, and are not aggressive even to much smaller birds, such as waxbills. Cockatiels kept as pets will also learn to say a few words and become very tame. Various mutations have occurred in cockatiels over the past 30 years.

CINNAMON PEARL PIED

This is one of the composite colour forms now being bred in increasing numbers. The Cinnamon and the more common Lutino mutations are both sex-linked recessive mutations. In the case of the popular Lutino, the coloration can be quite variable. Those which are more yellowish than white are described as "buttercup". It is possible to produce such birds by selectively pairing the best coloured breeding stock.

with bread and milk, especially when there are chicks in the nest.

GENERAL CARE

Pairs need to be housed individually, and are quite hardy as a general rule, although they dislike damp, cold conditions. Australian parakeets tend to feed on the ground, and are thus most at risk from parasitic worm infections passed via the droppings. It is usually worth deworming newly-acquired birds as a precaution against spreading parasites to healthy stock.

BREEDING

Pairs will invariably nest during the spring and summer months, but some cocks, especially of the larger species, can turn aggressive, and may harass their mates relentlessly. Fatalities can occur in such instances. It may therefore be prudent to clip one of the cock's wings, to handicap his flight, if the hen is being badly persecuted.

Australian parakeets will only use a nestbox during the breeding period, and do not roost for the remainder of the year. Their average clutch is about four or five eggs. The incubation period is around 19 days, but varies, depending on the species. All young birds should be removed as soon as possible after fledging however, because they are likely to be attacked by the cock. This applies particularly to male offspring. Unlike other species, Australian parakeets rapidly feed themselves after fledging, and this presumably is a natural dispersal mechanism. It enables the adults to nest again in rapid succession under favourable conditions, without having to cater for their previous brood.

TURQUOISINE PARAKEET
Neophema pulchella

Distribution: Australia

Like other members of the genus, this species is thought to have declined in the wild, but has been domesticated in aviaries for a number of years. Known collectively as Grass Parakeets, these colourful birds are ideal for the small garden aviary where space is limited and neighbours preclude keeping the larger, noisier parrots. An orange-bellied form has become increasingly common.

RED-RUMPED PARAKEET
Psephotus haematonotus

Distribution: Australia

These parakeets are bred in large numbers every year, and have an attractive musical call. Some cocks will persecute their mates and offspring severely and pairs must always be housed on their own. A dull yellowish mutation that first appeared in Australia is widely-known in Europe and is sex-linked in its mode of inheritance. A scarce blue form has also been recorded.

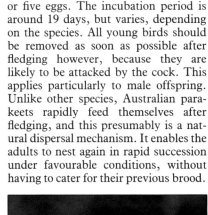

EASTERN ROSELLA
Platycerus eximius

Distribution: Australia

The larger Rosellas require more space than the Grass Parakeets and should have a minimum flight length of 2.7 m (12 ft). They are hardy, but rather aggressive birds. The Eastern, or Golden-mantled Rosella is perhaps the most widely-kept, being relatively inexpensive and easy to keep. Others include the Pennant's (*P. elegans*) and the Stanley Parakeet (*P. icterotis*).

AFRO-ASIAN PARAKEETS

The single genus, *Psittacula*, is comprised of 13 species, some of which are not represented in avicultural collections. These parakeets tend to be colourful, and the larger species are correspondingly more vocal and destructive.

FEEDING

A parrot mixture will suffice for most psittaculid parakeets, but the smaller members of the genus also require canary seed and spray millet. Pine nuts are favoured by the majority of these birds. Fruit and greenfood must be provided daily. Other items, such as bread and milk, may be taken when there are chicks in the nest.

GENERAL CARE

While certain species such as the Derbyan Parakeet (*P. derbiana*) occur in cold climates, all members of the genus are prone to the effects of frost-bite. Therefore, they should always be encouraged to roost in a nestbox rather than on a perch in the open. In all but the most extreme climatic conditions, once acclimatized, they can be kept safely out of doors without heat.

BREEDING

These parakeets often start to breed earlier in the year, particularly in a mild spring, but a sudden cold snap may cause a fatal chilling of eggs or chicks. The incubation period can vary from between 24 and 28 days, after which the young are fledging from about seven weeks onwards. Unless an early round is lost, the adults are unlikely to nest more than once in a season. Psittaculids are

ALEXANDRINE PARAKEET
Psittacula eupatria

Distribution: South-east Asia and India

Similar to the Ring-necked, but bigger and with a more powerful beak and strident voice, these parakeets make spectacular aviary occupants. Pairs nest regularly, but not all hens prove adept at rearing their chicks. Young cocks should not be paired with older hens. Alexandrines can live for at least 20 years.

RING-NECKED PARAKEET
Psittacula krameri

Distribution: Africa and Asia

Ring-necks can be kept and bred in a group, but in the case of mutations, pairs need to be housed individually. The Lutino form is currently most widespread, although the Blue is becoming increasingly common. Other colours have also been recorded, including a yellow-headed variant and albinos, bred from a combination of blue and yellow stock.

PLUM-HEADED PARAKEET
Psittacula cyanocephala

Distribution: South-east Asia

An attractive and relatively quiet aviary bird, the Plum-headed will also breed successfully, provided a true pair can be obtained. This is not easy, as cocks resemble hens and there is often a shortage of mature females. Nestboxes should be well-sheltered as chicks can be lost in cold weather. They usually lay just once a year even if no chicks are reared.

likely to be mature by their third year, when the cocks gain their collars.

CENTRAL AND SOUTH AMERICAN PARAKEETS

The *Aratinga* conures predominate in this category, and have been increasingly appreciated during recent years, in spite of their often powerful calls. By way of contrast, the *Pyrrhura* conures are rarely available, with the one notable exception of the Red-billed Conure. They require similar management to that outlined in the previous section, although the Quaker Parakeet (*Myiopsitta monachus*) builds a bulky nest of twigs, rather than using a nestbox for breeding and roosting purposes.

Some concern has arisen, particularly in the United States, with the realization that conures can be symptomless carriers of the herpes virus infection, Pacheco's Parrot Disease. This can cause severe mortality in other species, but is not common in Britain. It is most likely to emerge when conures are quarantined with other psittacines, and can be diagnozed by means of blood tests.

OTHER SPECIES

Red-headed Conure (*Aratinga erythrogenys*): This is the most distinctive of the predominantly green *Aratingas*, with its red head. These birds have powerful voices and are destructive to woodwork.

Brown-throated Conure (*Aratinga pertinax*): Approximately 13 races of this conure are recognized, so their appearance can be quite variable.

Patagonian Conure (*Cyanoliseus patagonus*): The largest of the conures, this species nest in burrows in the wild, but will accept a nestbox quite readily.

SUN CONURE
Aratinga solstitialis

Distribution: North-east Brazil and Guyana

One of the most beautifully coloured of all psittacines, these conures are now being bred freely in numerous collections. Other similarly coloured species are the Golden-capped (*A. auricapilla*) and Jendaya (*A. jandaya*), but neither is as vividly coloured.

RED-BELLIED CONURE
Pyrrhura frontalis

Distribution: South-western South America

A member of the so-called "Scaly-breasted" group, this species, like other *Pyrrhuras*, is prolific. They may lay six eggs in a clutch. These birds, also known as Maroon-bellied Conures, tame readily, and are not noisy unless frightened suddenly. Their greenish plumage shows to best effect in sunlight.

ORANGE-FLANKED PARAKEET
Brotogeris pyrrhopterus

Distribution: Peru and Ecuador

One of a group of seven species, these lively parakeets are exceptionally destructive for their size and can be quite noisy. They are gregarious and do best when kept in small groups. However, the introduction of a new bird will be strongly resented. Also known as Grey-cheeked Parakeets, young birds can become very tame.

PARROTS and COCKATOOS

Family: Psittacidae

The difficulties of housing many of the bigger birds covered in the following section, as well as the initial cost of purchasing pairs, will be a deterrent to keeping them, but breeding the larger psittacines is a truly satisfying experience. Their chicks have considerable presence and character, especially when they are hand-reared.

FEEDING

The majority of species will do well on a basic diet of parrot food, with a selection of other items such as sprouted mung beans, fruit, greenstuff and pellets or dog chow being offered daily. A good variety is essential to encourage reproductive activity. The lories and lorikeets, as well as the hanging parrots must have a fresh supply of nectar and fruit on a daily basis. They should also be offered seed in small quantities, and sponge cake soaked in nectar is usually popular.

GENERAL CARE

The larger psittacines are hardy when properly acclimatized, but should receive adequate protection from cold winds and the worst of the winter weather. The harsh calls of these birds make it impossible to keep them out-of-doors in built-up areas and, having due consideration for their very powerful beaks, constructing a suitable aviary is a costly undertaking. Breeding in inside flights is possible however, and is becoming increasingly popular.

The value of such stock has led to the emergence of insurance schemes, and aviculturists are fitting alarm systems to their aviaries as an adjunct, which can

WHITE-WINGED PARAKEET
Brotogeris versicolor

Distribution: Much of South America

These attractive parakeets are very similar to the preceding species in their habits. Two distinctive forms occur, with the more southerly Canary-winged Parakeet, which is the sub-species, being lighter in overall coloration than the form shown here. They live well in established groups, and breeding results tend to be better if the birds are kept on a colony system.

BLUE AND YELLOW MACAW
Ara ararauna

Distribution: Parts of Central and much of northern South America

In spite of their huge and powerful beaks, macaws can be extremely gentle. This species is one of the biggest and most striking members of the group. They are easy to cater for, but they have destructive ways and loud calls. Surgical sexing means these birds are being bred on a much wider scale than ever before. They can have six chicks in a season if their first round of chicks are removed early for hand-rearing. The 14 species of macaw in the genus *Ara* vary considerably in size. While the Red and Green (Greenwinged) Macaw (*A. chloroptera*) is of similar size, the Hahn's Red-shouldered Macaw (*A. nobilis*) is more reminiscent of the Aratinga conures in size and appearance, often breeding on a colony system. The smaller species, known as dwarf macaws, are predominantly green.

also reduce the cost of these policies. Up-to-date advice on the best systems can be obtained from crime prevention officers, or from commercial firms specializing in this type of equipment.

BREEDING

The larger parrots may well become aggressive towards their owners at this time. In view of the relatively long incubation and fledging periods, most pairs will only have one clutch of chicks if kept out of doors, unless the first round of eggs is infertile, or removed for artificial incubation. In the case of lories and lorikeets, which may breed twice or more in a year, it is not unusual for their chicks to be plucked while still in the nest. Such chicks should be given adequate protection once they fledge, until their plumage has regrown, which is likely to take several weeks.

OTHER SPECIES

The neo-tropical genus *Amazona* is comprised of 27 species of Amazon parrots, certain members of which are well-known in aviculture, and as popular pets. Unfortunately, their loud calls, often uttered at first light, detract from the possibility of keeping them in outdoor flights. Young birds can be recognized by their darker irides.

Orange-winged Amazon (*Amazona amazonica*): One of the commonly available species, considered a pest in certain parts of its range, the Orange-winged was possibly only bred for the first time in Britain in 1980. However, it had been reared successfully in the United States prior to this time. The numbers of amazons being bred is increasing rapidly, as

BLUE-HEADED PARROT
Pionus menstruus

Distribution: Much of South America

These parrots make attractive occupants of an outdoor aviary, where the subtle shades of their plumage can be fully appreciated. Youngsters can become very tame, although they will be duller in appearance than adult birds. Pionus parrots may not mature until their third year, and some pairs can be nervous when breeding. Their calls are relatively inoffensive.

LESSER SULPHUR-CRESTED COCKATOO
Cacatua sulphurea

Distribution: Indonesia and Celebes

The scattered distribution of this species over numerous islands has given rise to distinctive sub-species, of which the most obvious is the Citron-crested (*C. s. citroncristata*), with its bright orange crest and ear coverts, found on the island of Sumba. Variations in size are also apparent, with the Timor (*C. s. parvula*) being the smallest race.

ECLECTUS PARROT
Eclectus roratus

Distribution: New Guinea, Indonesia and northern Australia

When first discovered, cock and hen Eclectus were thought to be two different species, because of the radical difference in their appearance, with hens being bright green. These birds can prove prolific, laying repeated clutches of two eggs, especially when housed indoors. They need relatively large amounts of greenfood and fruit.

141

a result of surgical sexing. Before this technique was available, birds would be housed together for years in the belief that they behaved as a pair, but never bred, simply because they were of the same sex.

Yellow-fronted Amazon (*Amazona ochrocephala*): Seven sub-species of this amazon are recognized, typically varying in the amount of yellow plumage on their heads. The Double Yellow-headed Amazon is comprised of three sub-species and yellow predominates, covering the head and neck. These are partic-

ularly noisy birds, rivalling the Mealy Amazon (*A. farinosa*) in this respect.

Blue-fronted Amazon (*Amazona aestiva*): Reliable reports suggest this species can live for nearly a century under captive conditions. It has long been valued as a pet, being one of the commonly available "Green Parrots". Blue-fronts were bred for the first time during the 19th century. The incubation period is approximately 28 days, and the usual brood of three chicks will fledge when about nine weeks old.

Goffin's Cockatoo (*Cacatua goffini*):

This species was virtually unknown in aviculture until the early 1970s, when there was wholesale deforestation of the birds' native islands. They are rather shy by nature, and extremely destructive. However, breeding successes have occurred repeatedly in some cases, the clutch consisting of the usual two eggs. Incubation of the chicks is shared by both adults, as with other cockatoos.

Moluccan Cockatoo (*Cacatua moluccensis*): Although certain Moluccan Cockatoos are of very pale coloration, they can always be distinguished from

SENEGAL PARROT
Poicephalus senegalus

Distribution: Western Africa, from Senegal to Mali

An attractive species that is not fully appreciated. Its calls are comprised of various rasping whistles, which, although unmusical, are not offensive. *Poicephalus* parrots, which include the Meyer's (*P. meyeri*), can be nervous, and prefer a nestbox in a dark position. They take peanuts readily, but may be slow to sample fruit.

GREY PARROT
Psittacus erithacus

Distribution: Across equatorial Africa

The Grey Parrot is the traditional pet parrot, but it has also been appreciated increasingly as an aviary bird during recent years. Various colour forms can be seen. Silver Greys are not a mutant form, but tend to originate in Zaire and surrounding countries, whereas the darker individuals come from Ghana. The dullest form of the Grey is the Timneh sub-species, which can be immediately distinguished by its dark maroon, rather than red, tail. It tends to be significantly cheaper as a result. The only colour variants known in the Grey Parrot are whites, which retain their red tails, and birds with reddish areas of body plumage. This latter condition may be a sign of age, or a nutritional shortcoming, and may prove to be a transitory characteristic variable, disappearing at a subsequent moult. Greys are often poor parents, and chicks may have to be hand-reared.

the similar Umbrella Cockatoo (*C. alba*) by their pink crests. Both species are relatively large, and have exceptionally loud calls.

Black-headed Caique (*Pionites melanocephala*): This is the more common species, compared with the White-bellied Caique (*P. leucogaster*) found to the south of the River Amazon. Caiques are very playful birds, but are liable to prove noisy. Best breeding results have been obtained by positioning their nest-box in a dark locality.

Celestial Parrotlet (*Forpus coelestis*):

These small psittacines are often prolific once they start breeding. However, it is not unknown for them to turn viciously on newly-hatched chicks, particularly when nesting in the close confines of a cage. Up to six eggs can form the clutch, and should hatch after 18 days. Parrotlets can live into their 20s, and have a long reproductive life. During recent years, the Yellow-faced species (*P. xanthops*) has been available occasionally, and again, has nested successfully.

Vernal Hanging Parrot (*Loriculus vernalis*): One of the few groups of psitta-

cines that can be kept safely in a planted flight, in the company of other birds if desired. The hanging parrots are so-named for their unusual habit of hanging upside down to roost, in a similar manner to bats. They construct a nest in a suitable box, with the chicks fledging when about one month old. Soft food will often be taken during the rearing period, and hanging parrots may consume mealworms as well. Although now relatively scarce, these birds make fascinating aviary occupants. A bath should always be available to them.

CHATTERING LORY
Lorius garrulus

Distribution: Indonesian islands

These lories, and especially the sub-species known as the Yellow-backed, shown here, are particularly colourful. Unlike finches and other birds, parrots do not need to be colour-fed to retain their bright red plumage over successive moults. Although tame and lively in most instances, the Chattering Lory has a loud call, and can be vocal after dark. They are hardy once acclimatized.

RED LORY
Eos bornea

Distribution: Indonesian islands

The tongues of these parrots show the typical features associated with nectar-feeding psittacines. As with most lories and lorikeets, pairs tend to nest readily, and may take increasing amounts of soaked seed as a rearing food when they have chicks in the nest. This particular species is believed to range through the Moluccas from island to island seeking flowering shrubs and trees.

RAINBOW LORIKEET
Trichoglossus haematodus

Distribution: New Guinea, neighbouring islands, and Australia

Lorikeets have longer tails than lories, as a general rule. This species has a wide range, with as many as 18 distinctive races being recognized. This is Mitchell's Lorikeet (*T. h. mitchellii*) from the Indonesian islands of Lombok and Bali. The Green-naped is the nominate race, and the best known form outside Australia.

SPECIES
SUMMARY

These quick-reference tables condense the information given in **The Breeds and Species**. The birds are arranged in the same sequence. Their Latin names and alternative common names can be found in the index. The tables should not be interpreted too literally, since various factors may influence clutch size, hatching and fledging time.

NAME	SIZE/HEIGHT	DESCRIPTION	IMMATURES	EGGS	INCUBATION	FLEDGING
Wild Canary	11.25cm (4½in)	Hens duller; notably less yellow on the side of the head	Even duller, with little yellow	3-4	14 days	14 days
Domestic Canary	10.6-20cm (4¼-8in)	Sexes alike, apart from cock's song	Resemble adults; may have paler flight feathers	4	14 days	14 days
Black-hooded Red Siskin	11.25cm (4½in)	Hens have grey heads	Duller than the hen, showing slight streaking	4	13 days	14 days
Himalayan Greenfinch	13cm (5in)	Hens duller; reduced areas of yellow on wings	Duller than hen; may show streaking	4	14 days	14 days
Bullfinch/Canary Mule	Influenced by canary	Infertile hybrid				
Masked Hawfinch	24cm (9½in)	Hens duller, notably on the wings	White streaking on body; lack black head of adult	3-4	14 days	14 days
Grey Singing Finch	11.25cm (4½in)	Sexes alike, except for cock's song	More streaking than adults	3-4	14 days	14 days
Yellow-rumped Seedeater	15cm (6in)	Sexes similar; hens have more yellowish-olive rump	Similar to adult hen; may show more definite streaking	4	14 days	14 days
House Finch	14cm (5½in)	Hens have greyish-brown, rather than red breast	Similar to hens, but more heavily streaked over breast	4-6	14 days	15 days
Zebra Finch	10cm (4in)	Hens have paler red beaks in all cases, and lack the characteristic barring on the chest of cocks	Dark beaks	4-6	12 days	18-19 days
Gouldian Finch	13cm (5in)	Hens have paler breasts	Mainly greenish at first	4-5	14 days	21 days
Diamond Firetail Finch	11.25cm (4½in)	Hens tend to have narrower breast band and reduced extent of orbital skin	More olive in appearance	5-6	14 days	24 days
Bicheno's Finch	10cm (4in)	Sexes alike	Duller; barring less distinct	4-5	14 days	22 days
Star Finch	10cm (4in)	Hens have reduced area of red on face	Significantly greyer overall	4-6	13 days	21 days
Pin-tailed Parrot Finch	14cm (5½in)	Hens lack red on abdomen; blue areas on head reduced	Greyish upperparts, with greenish tint on back	4-5	14 days	23 days
Bengalese	11.25cm (4½in)	Sexes similar, but cocks can be distinguished by their song	Duller, with paler underparts	5-6	15 days	24 days
Orange-cheeked Waxbill	10cm (4in)	Sexes alike; hens may be paler	Greyish-brown at top of head; paler than adults overall	4-6	12 days	20 days
Black-cheeked Waxbill	10cm (4in)	Sexes similar; hens tend to have paler red flanks	Greyer throat and breast; duller overall	3-6	12 days	22 days
Common Waxbill	10cm (4in)	Hens duller, with reduced areas of red and black below	Black beaks and narrower stripes to the eyes	4-6	12 days	21 days
Golden-breasted Waxbill	10cm (4in)	Hens lack eye stripes; paler overall	Relatively dull, lacking eye stripes and red rump; blackish bills	4-6	12 days	21 days
Red-eared Waxbill	10cm (4in)	Hens tend to have paler bellies	A dark bill; no eye stripes	4-5	12 days	21 days
Lavender Waxbill	10cm (4in)	Hens tend to be slightly smaller and greyer	Paler, lacking white markings on flanks	3-5	12 days	19 days

NAME	SIZE/HEIGHT	DESCRIPTION	IMMATURES	EGGS	INCUBATION	FLEDGING
Red-cheeked Cordon Bleu	11.25cm (4½in)	Hens lack red cheek patches	Resemble adult hens; blue areas paler and reduced in size; legs brownish for a period after fledging	3-6	11 days	19 days
Common Grenadier	13cm (5in)	Hens significantly paler, notably on the abdomen	Notably duller, lacking much of the purple colour of the adults	3-5	12 days	16 days
Purple Grenadier	13cm (5in)	Hens have more brownish upperparts, and are paler overall, occasionally with white feathers around the head	Dark blackish bills; resemble adult hens, but are paler overall	4	12 days	20 days
Red-billed Firefinch	10cm (4in)	Hens noticeably duller, with greyish-brown upperparts	Similar to adult hen, but have black beaks and no red on the face	3-5	12 days	19 days
Schlegel's Twinspot	12.5cm (5in)	Hens paler, with orange noticeable on the head, especially around the eyes	Greyish-olive, lacking spots on the flanks	4	12 days	21 days
Melba Finch	12.5cm (5in)	Hens have grey heads, with no red apparent	Areas on rump and tail that are red in adults, coloured rusty-orange	4	12 days	20 days
Red Avadavat	8.75cm (3½in)	Hens brownish-grey; can be distinguished from cocks in eclipse plumage by paler yellow abdomens and lack of any black feathering there	Greyish-brown, with two distinctive buff wing bars	5	12 days	21 days
Green Avadavat	10cm (4in)	Sexes similar; hens tend to be paler and duller, with less well-defined markings on flanks	Tend to be greyish, with black beaks initially; yellowish individuals may be cocks	5	12 days	21 days
Cut-throat	12.5cm (5in)	Hens lack characteristic red throat marking	Paler; throat band of young cocks also paler	4	12 days	21 days
Java Sparrow	12.5cm (5in)	Sexes alike, but beak of hens may be paler; only cocks sing	Streaking on breast plumage; dark beaks	4-6	13 days	26-28 days
African Silverbill	10cm (4in)	Sexes similar; hens may be smaller, with a more reddish-brown tail	Resemble adults	6	12 days	21 days
Chestnut-breasted Mannikin	11.25cm (4½in)	Sexes similar; hens may be duller and paler overall	Buff overall, with indeterminate dark barring on throat plumage	5	12 days	21 days
Bronze-winged Mannikin	10cm (4in)	Sexes alike	Black bills; greyish-brown facial plumage	4-6	12 days	20 days
White-headed Munia	11.25cm (4½in)	Sexes similar	Greyish-brown facial plumage; a warmer shade of brown overall	4-5	12 days	20 days
Pin-tailed Whydah	Cocks in colour – 37.5cm (15in); 11.25cm (4½in) when out of colour	Hens show less prominent streaking, and bills are pinkish	Resemble adult hen, but have even less streaking; bills black	3	As for host species of Waxbill	As for Waxbill
Fischer's Whydah	Cocks in colour – 32.5cm (13in); 11.25cm (4½in) when out of colour	Hen similar to cock in eclipse plumage	Brown below, with white belly; black bill	3	See Purple Grenadier	See Purple Grenadier

NAME	SIZE/HEIGHT	DESCRIPTION	IMMATURES	EGGS	INCUBATION	FLEDGING
Yellow-mantled Whydah	Cocks in colour – 22.5cm (9in); hens about ⅓ smaller		Resemble adult hen; pale bills	3	14 days	15 days
Red-collared Whydah	Cocks in colour – 37.5cm (15in) overall; only 15cm (6in) when out of colour. Hens	slightly smaller, 13.75cm (5½in) and show less streaking than cocks out of colour	Similar to hens, but streaking finer	2-4	14 days	16 days
Fan-tailed Whydah	Cocks in colour – 17.5cm (7in) overall	Hens can be distinguished from cocks out of colour by black shoulder-patches	Black shoulder-patches, edged with buff, rather than red plumage	2-4	14 days	15 days
Grenadier Weaver	12.5cm (5in)	Hens similar to cocks out of colour, but have no black traces in plumage	May be paler	3	14 days	15 days
Napoleon Weaver	12.5cm (5in)	Hens tend to be similar to cocks out of colour, but heavier streaking	More narrow streaking; tend to be browner on upperparts	2-4	14 days	15 days
Red-headed Quelea	11.25cm (4½in)	Hens resemble cocks in eclipse plumage, but lack any red feathering on their foreheads	Horn-coloured bills	2-3	12 days	13 days
Madagascar Weaver	12.5cm (5in)	Hens resemble males in eclipse plumage	Similar	2-5	13 days	14 days
Baya Weaver	15cm (6in)	Hens closely resemble cocks out of colour	Difficult to distinguish from adult hens and cocks in eclipse plumage	2-5	14 days	15 days
Sudan Golden Sparrow	12.5cm (5in)	Hens have brownish coloration, lacking the bright yellow markings of cocks	Similar to hens, but tend to have paler lowerparts	3-4	12 days	14 days
Golden-breasted Bunting	16.25cm (6½in)	Hens noticeably duller, with brownish-white heads	Resemble adult hens	4	13 days	14 days
Jacarini Finch	10cm (4in)	Hens mainly brown	Resemble hens, but cocks can be recognized by their song	3-4	11 days	10 days
White-throated Seedeater	10cm (4in)	Hens much duller than cocks, being greyish-brown overall	Similar to adult hens	3	12 days	14 days
Parrot-billed Seedeater	10cm (4in)	Hens have greyish-buff, rather than black bib	Resemble adult hen	3	12 days	14 days
Red-cowled Cardinal	17.5cm (7in)	Sexes similar, but cocks can be slightly bigger	Brown heads; duller overall	3-4	14 days	14 days
Cinnamon Warbling Finch	12.5cm (5in)	Hens noticeably paler than cocks	Tend to be streaked on breast; greyish overall; similar to the adult hen	3	13 days	12 days
Blue-necked Tanager	12.5cm (5in)	Hens may be greener	Duller than adults	2	14 days	20 days
Emerald-spotted Tanager	12.5cm (5in)	Hens tend to be smaller, with duller coloration	Less spots than adults	2	13 days	15 days
Opal Tanager	12.5cm (5in)	Hens have the sides of their heads, including ear coverts, glossy blue	Black underparts; duller and paler overall	2	13 days	15 days

NAME	SIZE/HEIGHT	DESCRIPTION	IMMATURES	EGGS	INCUBATION	FLEDGING
Silver-throated Tanager	12.5cm (5in)	Hens resemble cocks, but are greener overall	Duller	2	14 days	14 days
Golden Tanager	12.5cm (5in)	Sexes alike	Duller	2	14 days	14 days
Seven Coloured Tanager	13.75cm (5½in)	Hens duller; plumage on upper part of tail and rump have more orange	Dull blue; green spots on wings	2	14 days	14 days
Palm Tanager	17.5cm (7in)	Sexes alike	Tend to be pale olive	2	13 days	14 days
Blue-capped Tanager	17.5cm (7in)	Sexes alike	Duller	2	14 days	14 days
Silver-beaked Tanager	17.5cm (7in)	Hens less colourful, with reduced areas of red plumage	Duller	2	12 days	12 days
Purple Honeycreeper	8cm (3¼in)	Hens significantly paler than cocks, lacking their violet-blue coloration	Resemble adult hens	2	12 days	14 days
Red-legged Honeycreeper	10cm (4in)	Hens resemble cocks out of colour, but have paler legs	Resemble hens	2	12 days	19 days
Black-collared Barbet	17.5cm (7in)	Sexes alike	Lack red on forehead	3	14 days	33 days
Levaillant's Barbet	20cm (8in)	Hens slightly smaller and duller than cocks	Duller, with browner upperparts	3-5	14 days	23 days
Crimson-breasted Barbet	15cm (6in)	Sexes alike	Duller	2-4	15 days	25 days
Sowerby's Barbet	17.5cm (7in)	Sexes alike	Black, rather than brown forecrown; base of lower bill horn-coloured	4	15 days	26 days
Pied Hornbill	75cm (30in)	Sexes similar; hens have smaller beaks	Smaller and duller	2-3	120 days	
Spot-billed Toucanet	33cm (13in)	Hens have brown rather than black heads	Duller	2-4	16 days	40 days
Cuvier's Toucan	45cm (18in)	Hens may have smaller beaks	Duller	2-4	19 days	49 days
White-eared Bulbul	17.5cm (7in)	Sexes alike	Resemble adults	2-4	13 days	12 days
Red-vented Bulbul	22.5cm (9in)	Sexes alike	Resemble adults	2-3	13 days	13 days
Chinese Bulbul	20cm (8in)	Sexes alike	Resemble adults	3-5	13 days	12 days
Golden-fronted Leafbird	25cm (10in)	Hens have a green forehead and less black plumage	Duller overall	2-3	13 days	14 days
White-rumped Shama	cocks – 27.5cm (11in)	Hens duller, with grey replacing black plumage, and smaller	Similar to hens, with relatively short tails	3-5	13 days	17 days
Grey-headed Parrotbill	17.5cm (7in)	Sexes alike	Duller	3-4	12 days	12 days
Black-headed Sibia	22.5cm (9in)	Sexes alike	Similar	4	14 days	13 days
Pekin Robin	15cm (6in)	Sexes alike; hens can be paler, with greyer lores	Duller	4	14 days	14 days
Black-chinned Yuhina	10cm (4in)	Sexes similar; hens may have smaller crests, and do not sing like cocks	Duller	3-4	13 days	15 days
African White-eye	10cm (4in)	Sexes similar	Paler bills on fledging	2-4	12 days	12 days
Chestnut-flanked White Eye	10cm (4in)	Sexes similar	Similar to adults	2-4	12 days	12 days
Purple-banded Sunbird	10cm (4in)	Hens olive-grey on upperparts, yellowish-white below, with some darker streaking apparent	Similar to adult hen, but with black throats	1-3	13 days	17 days

NAME	SIZE/HEIGHT	DESCRIPTION	IMMATURES	EGGS	INCUBATION	FLEDGING
Van Hasselt's Sunbird	10cm (4in)	Hens duller, being predominantly yellowish-green	Resemble adult hen	1-3	13 days	17 days
Booted Raquet-tailed Hummingbird	Cock with tail plumes – 12.5cm (5in); hens 7.5cm (3in)	Hens lack the magnificent tail plumes of the cock	Resemble hen, but immature cocks can be distinguished by upright stance	Not known – 2?	16 days	21 days
Common Mynah	22.5cm (9in)	Sexes alike	Paler head coloration	4-6	17 days	22 days
Hill Mynah	30cm (12in)	Sexes alike	Less well-developed wattles on sides of head	2-3	15 days	28 days
Chinese Jungle Mynah	25cm (10in)	Sexes similar; hens may have smaller crests	Resemble adults	4-5	18 days	23 days
Purple Glossy Starling	22.5cm (9in)	Sexes alike	Resemble adults, but duller overall	2-3	16 days	20 days
Green Glossy Starling	22.5cm (9in)	Sexes alike, but hens may be smaller	Darker and less glossy	3-5	14 days	21 days
Spreo Starling	20cm (8in)	Sexes alike; hens may be smaller	Duller, with dark eyes	4	16 days	20 days
Black-crested Jay	30cm (12in)	Sexes alike	Duller	3-4	16 days	20 days
Red-billed Blue Pie	60cm (24in)	Sexes alike	Duller, with shorter tails	3-6	17 days	21 days
White-cheeked Touraco	37.5cm (15in)	Sexes alike	Dark beaks	2	20 days	28 days
Hartlaub's Touraco	40cm (16in)	Sexes alike	Duller, with dark beaks	2	20 days	28 days
Barbary Dove	25cm (10in)	Hens darker in colour	Lack collar	2	14 days	17 days
Diamond Dove	17.5cm (7in)	Hens fewer white spots on wings; less prominent red skin around eyes	Predominantly brown, with grey skin around eyes	2	13 days	12 days
Zebra Dove	20cm (8in)	Sexes similar; hens tend to be smaller	Pinkish tint on breast; barred underparts	2	13 days	12 days
Tambourine Dove	22.5cm (9in)	Hens more greyish-white upperparts	Barred feathers	2	13 days	13 days
Yellow-billed Ground Dove	15cm (6in)	Hens tend to be browner overall	Similar to adult hen, but paler overall	3	14 days	11 days
Green-winged Dove	25cm (10in)	Hens lack white markings on head and shoulders	Duller, with blackish bars on reddish-brown underparts	2	14 days	13 days
Cape Dove	22.5cm (9in)	Hens lack black markings on face and throat of cocks	Speckled	2	14 days	13 days
Senegal Dove	25cm (10in)	Sexes similar, but hens may be duller	Lack black neck collar	2	13 days	12 days
White-winged Dove	25cm (10in)	Sexes similar; hens tend to be paler	Duller overall	2	13 days	15 days
Eared Dove	25cm (10in)	Hen duller	Duller and brown overall	2	14 days	14 days
Californian Quail	25cm (10in)	Hens have much shorter crests; duller, with no white on head	Downy feathering	12-20	23 days	Chicks move on their own after hatching
Bob-white Quail	22.5cm (9in)	Hens have buff rather than white throat plumage	Downy feathering	12-20	23 days	Chicks move on their own from hatching

NAME	SIZE/HEIGHT	DESCRIPTION	IMMATURES	EGGS	INCUBATION	FLEDGING
Chinese Painted Quail	12.5cm (5in)	Hens are brown with darker streaks	Downy feathering	7-10	18 days	Chicks move on their own from hatching
Japanese Quail	15cm (6in)	Sexes similar; hens have paler breasts	Downy feathering	10-12	18 days	Chicks move on their own from hatching
Budgerigar	20cm (8in)	Hens have brown ceres	Pinkish ceres; no rings around irises; possibly barring extending down to cere, depending on colour variety	4-6	18 days	35 days
Fischer's Lovebird	13.75cm (5½in)	Sexes alike	Duller, with black markings on beaks	5	23 days	40 days
Masked Lovebird	13.75cm (5½in)	Sexes alike	Duller	5	23 days	40 days
Peach-faced Lovebird	15cm (6in)	Sexes alike	Duller	5	23 days	42 days
Black-winged Lovebird	16.25cm (6½in)	Hens do not have red forehead, or black on the wings	Similar to adult hen, but have a yellowish, rather than red bill	3-4	23 days	45 days
Cockatiel	30cm (12in)	Hens have darker heads, and barring on tail which is even apparent in the lutino mutation	Resemble adult hen, but have pinkish ceres on fledging	5-6	19 days	35 days
Turquoisine Grass Parakeet	20cm (8in)	Hens duller; lack red on wings of cock birds	Resemble adult hen	5-6	19 days	32 days
Red-rumped Parakeet	25cm (10in)	Hens duller; essentially olive-green in colour, lacking characteristic red rump	Similar to adults, but duller	4-6	21 days	30 days
Eastern Rosella	30cm (12in)	Hens duller, with a wing-stripe	Resemble adult hen, but have green at back of the head, extending to nape	5-7	21 days	35 days
Alexandrine Parakeet	50cm (20in)	Hens lack characteristic neck collar and black facial coloration	Similar to adult hen, but have shorter tails and a dark beak on fledging	3-5	29 days	60 days
Ring-necked Parakeet	40cm (16in)	Hens lack collar and black facial stripes of adult cocks	Resemble adult hens	4-5	26 days	52 days
Plum-headed Parakeet	32.5cm (13in)	Hens have greyish head coloration	Resemble hens, although in young cocks, traces of purplish feathering may be seen on top of head at first	5-6	25 days	49 days
Sun Conure	30cm (12in)	Sexes alike	Tend to be greener than adults	3-4	26 days	56 days
Red-bellied Conure	25cm (10in)	Sexes alike	Duller, with shorter tails	5-8	25 days	52 days
Orange-flanked Parakeet	20cm (8in)	Sexes alike	Tend to have pure green crown, lacking any trace of bluish suffusion	4-5	27 days	45 days
White-winged Parakeet	22.5cm (9in)	Sexes alike	Show less colour on wings; greener overall	4	26 days	50 days
Blue and Yellow Macaw	82.5cm (33in)	Sexes alike	Dark irides, whereas eyes of adults appear yellow	2-3	28 days	90 days
Blue-headed Parrot	27.5cm (11in)	Sexes alike	Duller, with reduced areas of blue on head	3-5	26 days	70 days

NAME	SIZE/HEIGHT	DESCRIPTION	IMMATURES	EGGS	INCUBATION	FLEDGING
Lesser Sulphur-crested Cockatoo	30cm (12in)	Hens can usually be distinguished by reddish-brown eye coloration	Resemble adults, but have grey eyes, with a whitish tinge to beak	2	28 days	75 days
Eclectus Parrot	35cm (14in)	Hens have reddish coloration	Assume adult coloration in nest, but eyes remain dark for a considerable period after leaving nest	2	30 days	77 days
Senegal Parrot	25cm (10in)	Sexes alike	Characterized by dark eyes, which gradually turn yellow	3-4	28 days	84 days
Grey Parrot	32.5cm (13in)	Sexes similar, although hens tend to be lighter	Resemble adults, but have dark eyes	3-4	29 days	90 days
Chattering Lory	30cm (12in)	Sexes alike	Darker irides and browner, rather than red beaks	2	28 days	77 days
Red Lory	27.5cm (11in)	Sexes alike	Tend to be darker, having blue edging to their plumage, dark eyes and blackish beak	2	24 days	63 days
Rainbow Lorikeet	22.5cm (9in)	Sexes alike	Duller, with dark beaks	2	25 days	72 days

PLANTS FOR THE GARDEN AVIARY

Clearly, your choice will be influenced by the prevailing soil and weather conditions, as well as the size of the aviary, but the following is a representative sample of suitable plants:

BUSHES

Pyracantha (*Pyracantha coccinea*)
Best trained against the sides of the aviary. Red berries will be eaten by the birds in the autumn.

Elderberry (*Sambucus nigra*)
Easy to grow, but can smell rather unpleasant, and provides little cover for nesting purposes.

Holly (*Ilex aquifolium*)
Can be slow to develop, but will give suitable nesting sites for birds which build their own nests. Berries may not be produced.

Snowberry (*Symphoricarpus albus*)
An attractive and versatile plant under aviary conditions.

Blackberry (*Rubus fruticosus*)
Provides good cover and attracts insects. The fruits will be taken by the birds. One of the newer thornless varieties is probably best.

Rhododendron (*Rhododendron* species)
Attractive, especially in large aviaries where flowers can be appreciated. Not suitable for soils which have a high lime content, although it can be grown in containers if necessary.

Silver Fir (*Abies alba*)
A variety of conifer bushes can be grown under aviary conditions. Opt for one of the slow-growing bushes.

CLIMBERS

Honeysuckle (*Lonicera henryii*)
A vigorous climber under favourable conditions, gives good cover and produces attractive flowers.

Clematis (*Clematis* species)
A wide range of species and hybrids are available. Plant in the autumn. Attractive flowers and good cover. Can prove a profuse grower under favourable conditions.

Jasmine (*Jasminum officinale*)
Flowers in the summer. There is also an attractive winter-flowering variety (*J. nudiflorum*).

Morning Glory (*Ipomoea tricolor*)
An annual plant, easily grown from seed, which bears attractive bluish, bell-shaped flowers. Can be trained to partially conceal nesting shelves positioned around the sides of the aviary.

Russian Vine (*Polygonum baldschuanicum*)
Extremely vigorous, can grow 3m (10ft) per year, and will probably have to be curtailed in most aviaries. Attractive flowers.

Flame Creeper (*Tropaeolum speciosum*)
A plant that prefers damp, acid growing conditions. It dies back in winter, but is a perennial, which needs support like other climbers.

Nasturtium (*Tropaeolum majus*)
An annual, that thrives in poor soil. Often attracts blackfly, so is a useful source of livefood in an aviary. Can be used as a climber, or for trailing on the ground if required.

SOME OTHER PLANTS

Bamboo (*Sinarudinaria* species)
Clumps produce good ground cover for birds such as quails, but tend to grow rather tall for the average aviary. Periodically, clumps will die back.

Michaelmas Daisy (*Aster novae*)
Attractive, easily grown plants that flower towards the autumn. Planted in clumps, these asters provide good cover through the breeding season.

Golden Rod (*Solidago* hybrids)
Similar in habit to the Michaelmas Daisy, but has frothy yellow flowers. Can be grown without difficulty, and makes an attractive display when planted in clumps.

There are a wide variety of plants suitable for inclusion in an aviary, and only a few examples of the major groups are mentioned here. Reference to one of the many gardening titles available will provide many other ideas. Some plants should not be included, because they, or their derivatives, could prove poisonous. These include: laburnums (*Laburnum* species), bulbs such as snowdrops (*Galanthus nivalis*), foxgloves (*Digitalis purpurea*) and lupins (*Lupinus*).

GLOSSARY

Addled An egg that was fertilized, but failed to hatch.

Albino A mutation where no colour pigment is present, giving pure white plumage and red eyes.

Autosomal recessive A mutation associated with the autosomes, or chromosomes which have no influence over the sex of the bird. The recessive nature means that the mutation will not be apparent in the first generation if such a bird is paired with a pure normal individual.

Avermectins A new group of drugs which are active against most parasites, both internal and external.

Aviary A combined shelter and flight unit for accommodating birds, usually outside.

Aviculture The keeping and breeding of birds in controlled surroundings – usually birds that are not domesticated in the accepted sense.

Backcross Specific term for inbreeding, entailing the pairing of a young bird back to one of its parents.

Birdroom An enclosed area where birds are kept – usually an adjunct to a flight in a garden.

Buff A description of feather type, most commonly used in canaries. In this instance, birds are paler than in the case of yellows. Buffs should not be paired together if possible.

Cap The whole area of the top of the head. Most significant in the Lizard Canary, which can have various types of cap, from clear through broken to non-capped.

Carotenoid pigments Colouring agents responsible for yellow, orange and red plumage in many birds, and of particular significance in canaries.

Cere The largely unfeathered area at the top of the beak, Most significant in parrots, especially the Budgerigar, where the cere indicates the bird's gender.

Chromosomes The thread-like structures in the nucleus where the genes are located. Usually occur in pairs.

Clear eggs Infertile.

Cloaca Terminal portion of the intestinal tract where the reproductive organs and kidneys also gain access to the exterior of the body.

Clutch size The number of eggs laid by a hen in succession over a short period of time.

Cobby Thick-set appearance – especially refers to certain breeds of canary.

Colour-food Artificial means of improving the colour of certain birds by using a special food containing colouring agents.

Crestbred Bred from a crested parent, but shows no crest itself.

Crop The storage organ for food, prior to its entry to the proventriculus and gizzard.

Dead-in-shell Chicks which fail to hatch.

Dilute A paler form than normal.

Dominant Visually apparent genetic characteristic.

Double-buffing Pairing of two buff-coloured birds together.

Down Fluffy plumage, which provides insulation for the body.

Egg-binding The inability of a hen to expel a formed egg from her body.

Fancy The selective breeding of livestock for particular traits.

Fledgling A bird that has left the nest, but is still being fed by its parents.

Flight An area enclosed in wire-mesh, usually an adjunct to an aviary outside.

French Moult A feather disease, typically encountered in young budgerigars.

Frugivore A bird which feeds largely on fruit of various types.

Genes The basic elements which control the individual's appearance.

Gizzard The part of the digestive tract where seeds and other foodstuffs are ground up into smaller particles.

Going light Weight loss, noticeable each side of the breastbone. There are various causes.

Hand-raising (rearing) The rearing of chicks by human attendants.

Hybridization Breeding between two species.

Hygrometer An instrument used for measuring relative humidity.

Inbreeding The pairing of very closely-related birds together, e.g. mother to son.

Insectivorous food A prepared diet suitable for softbills.

Irides (plural) The iris is visible around the outside of the pupil in the eye. Vital in calculating the age of parrots.

Juvenile moult The first moult of a young bird.

Melanistic Abnormal areas of black plumage.

Moult The replacement of feathers.

Monomorphic Identical appearance.

Mule A hybrid resulting from the mating of a canary and (usually British) finch.

Mutation A sudden change in appearance from one generation to the next, normally of colour.

Nectivore A bird which depends on nectar as part of its diet.

Nominate race The type specimen, being the original form first discovered before other races.

Normal The usual colour.

Nuptial plumage Breeding plumage, as distinct from the significantly duller eclipse plumage.

Phenolic disinfectant A disinfectant based on phenols.

Pied A bird with contrasting light and dark areas of plumage.

Pin feather A (small) body feather yet to emerge from its casing.

Plainhead No crest present.

Preening The grooming process carried out by the bird.

Saddle Area in the middle of the back.

Self Single coloured.

Sex-linked Characteristic linked to the pair of sex chromosomes.

Sexual dimorphism A difference in appearance between the sexes (usually plumage).

Shelter The enclosed part of an aviary.

Softbill A bird which does not feed largely on seeds.

Split Carries a genetic feature which is hidden by a dominant characteristic. Indicated by the symbol "/".

Split rings Bands which are cut, so they can be applied at any age. Used essentially for identification purposes.

Ticked A small mark which contrasts with the remainder of the plumage.

Tours The song passages of roller canaries.

Trinominal system of nomenclature The way in which birds are classified into distinct races.

Type The appearance of a bird, notably domesticated species.

Unflighted A bird still to moult its flight feathers after fledging.

Vent The external area linking with the cloaca.

INDEX

ACKNOWLEDGEMENTS

The Paul Press limited and the author would like to thank the following persons and organizations to whom copyright in the photographs noted belongs:

8 Ardea London Ltd; 13 Mary Evans Picture Library; 35 (b) Southern Aviaries; 54, 56, 57, 59, 60, 61, T.F.H. Publications Inc.; 78 (t) The Mansell Collection; (b) Ronald Sheridan Photo Library.

The author and publisher would also like to thank the following artists and photographers who contributed to the book:

L. Arnall 54, 56, 57, 60, 61; Bill Burnett 22, 36-7, 40-41; I.F. Keymer 59 Anthony Maynard 15, 18-19, 20-21; Kevin Richardson of Garden Studios 9, 10-11, 12, 70-1, 76-7; Alan Suttie 43, 45, 47, 64, 66-7; Malwyn Toothill 16-17, 25, 26-7, 28-9 (b), 30, 32, 53.

The author and photographer would especially like to thank:
Judith K. Nicholas of Databird World Wide Ltd for particular help with the hand-rearing section; Dr Ian Keymer for his assistance with the bird health section; Rita Hemsley and Ken Trestrail-MacKenzie for their invaluable assistance; Sally, Antony and all at The Paul Press for their help; Janet Wakeley, Bob & Pat Mann, Geoff Smith of Attlebridge Pet Farm, Mrs Newman, Bernard and Jean Howlett, Mr Eric Lane, John Cansdale & Len Hopkins, Ken Lawrence, Peter Scott, Mike Attew, Geoff Walker, Arthur Buckberry, Frank Woolham, Kilverstone Wildlife Park, Premier Pets of Norwich and Mr & Mrs Tibbenham for their invaluable help in allowing their birds to be photographed.

Front cover Cut-throat (*Amandina fasciata*)
Back cover Yellow-mantled Whydah (*Euplectes macrourus*); Red Lory (*Eos bornea*)

160